THE EVOLVING CHALLENGES OF
BLACK COLLEGE STUDENTS

THE EVOLVING CHALLENGES OF BLACK COLLEGE STUDENTS

New Insights for Policy, Practice, and Research

Edited by

Terrell L. Strayhorn
and Melvin C. Terrell

Foreword by Lemuel W. Watson

STERLING, VIRGINIA

COPYRIGHT © 2010 BY STYLUS PUBLISHING, LLC.

Published by Stylus Publishing, LLC
22883 Quicksilver Drive
Sterling, Virginia 20166–2102

Library of Congress Cataloging-in-Publication-Data
The evolving challenges of Black college students : new insights for policy, practice and research / edited by Terrell L. Strayhorn and Melvin C. Terrell ; foreword by Lemuel W. Watson.
  p. cm.
Includes index.
ISBN 978-1-57922-245–1 (cloth : alk. paper)
ISBN 978-1-57922-246–8
(pbk. : alk. paper)
 1. African Americans—Education (Higher) 2. African American college—students—Social conditions.
 3. African American college students—Attitudes.
 I. Strayhorn, Terrell L. II. Terrell, Melvin C.
 LC2781.E86 2010
 378.1′982996073—dc22

                                              2010005133

13-digit ISBN: 978-1-57922-245-1 (cloth)
13-digit ISBN: 978-1-57922-246-8 (paper)

Printed in the United States of America

All first editions printed on acid free paper
that meets the American National Standards Institute
Z39–48 Standard.

Bulk Purchases

Quantity discounts are available for use in workshops
and for staff development.
Call 1-800-232-0223

First Edition, 2010

10 9 8 7 6 5 4 3 2 1

$33.95

This book is dedicated to every Black student who has endured challenges and accessed supports to succeed in higher education, as well as every college student educator and parent who enabled these students' success in any way. Particularly, the book is dedicated to my family, which has sustained me throughout life: my two children, Aliyah Brielle and Tionne Lamont Strayhorn; my parents, Wilber and Linda Strayhorn; my brothers, William and Nate Strayhorn; my sister, Kim Strayhorn; and my loving maternal grandmother who has been my lifelong mentor, Creola Evelyn Warner. Thank you all.

CONTENTS

ACKNOWLEDGMENTS

Any scholarly undertaking of this magnitude leaves the editor both excited to write this section of the book as it marks the end of a multi-year journey, but also indebted to a number of individuals without whom none of this would have been possible. Although conventional wisdom holds that one should never attempt to "call names" for risk of forgetting important names in the recesses of the editor's memory or overlooking obvious mentionables, I would like to thank several individuals who have helped me in obvious and less-than-obvious ways as I worked to bring this book to fruition.

First, special thanks to my co-editor and professional mentor, Melvin Cleveland Terrell, who has been a wonderfully supportive colleague ever since I first encountered him at the 2004 annual meeting of the National Association of Student Affairs Professionals (NASAP), which convened at Howard University in Washington, DC. I asked Dr. Terrell to be my mentor and he told me that I would have to work hard as his mentee—he has very high expectations of us all. Since that time, he has held up his end of the deal by maintaining high expectations of me and accepting nothing less than my very best. I only hope that his assessment of my work and productivity, to date, is equally unequivocal.

Second, hearty thanks and appreciation are extended to every colleague-friend who contributed a chapter to this volume: Dafina Stewart, Rachelle Winkle-Wagner, Fred Bonner, Jane Redmond, Belinda McFeeters, Darryl Holloman, Robert Palmer, Estelle Young, and Tonya Saddler. Three of my students also served as co-authors on two of the chapters in this book; special thanks to each of you who brought so much to the writing experience: Amanda Blakewood, James DeVita, and Chutney Walton. Together these talented authors were a joy to work with, and an editor simply couldn't ask for anything more!

Members of my research teams at the University of Tennessee and/or Center for Higher Education Research and Policy (CHERP) also helped to carry out many of the studies that provided data for this volume. Sincere thanks to Fred McCall, Andrew Morse, Colber Prosper, William Roberts-Foster, and Eric Stokes (in alpha order). Without the competent support of my graduate students, this book would not have been possible.

Although it took the hard work and scholarly insights of colleague-friends to start a draft of each chapter in this volume, it was the abiding love and constant support of family and friends that sustained me through the writing, editing, and (re)editing process. My children are my joy and inspiration; much love to Aliyah Brielle (daughter) and Tionne Lamont (son). Special thanks to my immediate family who allowed me time to work on this book: Wilber Strayhorn, Linda Strayhorn, William and Nathan Strayhorn, Kim Strayhorn-Outen, and my maternal grandmother, Creola Evelyn Warner. Several friends deserve special mention for lending a listening ear as I "thought out loud" about the book's content, long after I thought I had written the last line: Evelyn Leathers, Norma Mertz, Ronald Porter, Stephen John Quaye, Gabrielle St. Leger, Lemuel Watson, Mario Williams, and particularly, Joseph Terrell Lockett, who agreed to read previous drafts of my chapters and often engaged in spirited debates about *The Evolving Challenges of Black College Students* over coffee.

Special thanks to John von Knorring and his staff at Stylus Publishing; it has been a pleasure working with all of you. To everyone acknowledged and those who are implied, but not listed, I offer a multitude of "thanks."

Terrell L. Strayhorn, Ph.D.
Associate Professor of Higher Education
Special Assistant to the Provost
Adjunct Professor of Sociology and Africana Studies
Director, Center for Higher Education Research & Policy

FOREWORD

As we exit the first decade of the new millennium, we continue to discuss what it means to be a Black college student. Through much research and many programs and initiatives, it appears that we know more than ever about Black students and their academic and social support needs. However, we continue to be plagued by issues of retention and minority student dropout, especially Black students. The issues look the same as they did years ago when campuses began to consider integration seriously. Yet, the students are not the same, and they come to campus with a multitude of needs that are similar to those of our earlier students, but also vastly different. Black students accept the fact that they are uniquely different as individuals and are not so easily grouped into a neat little category for programming purposes.

The editors of this book have attempted to present the diversity of unique Black students across various types of institutions. Practitioners in higher education, student affairs, and undergraduate studies should find the chapters relevant to understanding today's Black college student. In addition, undergraduate students should also find some comfort in knowing that earlier students had similar experiences. This is a comprehensive text that will enhance understanding of the issues Black students currently face in college.

This volume reminds us that we need to recognize that, although university environments have become more diverse, we should not forget the unique needs of Black students and their role in our society and in their communities. This book discusses how things remain the same across many of our organizations in higher education and educational organizations in general as well as the work needed to educate our K–12 students about their potential if they just choose to prepare themselves for a higher education. Work needs to be done with K–12 teachers, counselors, and administrators so they will operate as a unit to support the pipeline of Black students with the potential to reach postsecondary institutions. Work needs to be done with parents, community leaders, and churches to educate students about their options and how these organizations can support their success. We still have miles to go as higher education scholars, researchers, faculty, practitioners, and administrators to find ways to support our students in their quest to reach their dreams.

The biggest challenge for us as educators, however, is to get Black students to understand their history so they can fulfill their destiny. This book, *The Evolving Challenges of Black College Students: New Insights for Policy, Practice, and Research*, is another reminder of our collective commitment to continue making the world a better place for all of our students, especially for our Black students.

Lemuel W. Watson
2010

THE STATE OF EMPIRICAL RESEARCH ON AFRICAN AMERICAN COLLEGIANS

Terrell L. Strayhorn

C olleges and universities in the United States are more racially, ethnically, and culturally diverse today than ever before in the history of
American higher education, and this trend is likely to continue in
the future. Consider national college enrollment statistics indicating that
approximately 18 million students, a majority of whom are women, are
enrolled at more than 4,200 degree-granting colleges and universities in the
United States. And although more women than men enroll in college today,
and access to higher education has increased significantly among historically
underrepresented students of color—who represented 32% of total undergraduate enrollment in 2006—significant gaps persist across racial/ethnic
groups (U.S. Department of Education, 2006). For instance, while upwards
of 75%–80% of White students enroll in college immediately following high
school graduation, only 35%–68% of African Americans do so (Adelman,
2002; Gándara, 2002), depending on their socioeconomic status (SES). And
even when they do enroll, African Americans tend to be concentrated at two-
year community colleges, less selective four-year institutions, and minority-
serving institutions, such as historically Black colleges and universities
(HBCUs) (Baum & Payea, 2004; Cujet, 2006; Strayhorn & Hirt, 2008;
Thomas & Perna, 2004).

Despite progress in African American students' enrollment in college,
national trends suggest that Black collegians continue to confront arguably
unique obstacles and stressors in educational settings, especially predominantly White institutions (PWIs). The weight of empirical evidence, some

I

of which is my own, documents the myriad challenges that African American students face on predominantly White college and university campuses. Among them are declining enrollments (Harper, 2006); difficult transitions (Hinderlie & Kenny, 2002); lack of supportive relationships (Strayhorn, 2008c); undue psychological pressure to prove themselves academically (Fries-Britt & Griffin, 2007; Strayhorn, 2009); unwelcoming and "chilly" campus environments that offer inadequate social support (Fleming, 1984); social isolation (Clewell & Ficklen, 1986; Solorzano, Ceja, & Yosso, 2000; Willie & McCord, 1972); and racism and discrimination (Jan et al., 2000; Strayhorn, 2008a), to name but a few of these challenges.

Research has shown that HBCUs provide environments that are more welcoming to and supportive of African American collegians than PWIs (e.g., Allen, 1992). Additionally, HBCUs tend to operate on a "family model," where faculty and staff act as surrogate "parents" to nurture and support their students, many whom they perceive as their own "kids" (Hirt, Strayhorn, Amelink, & Bennett, 2006). With a "critical mass" of supportive networks and services, Black students attending HBCUs tend to fare well in higher education, some Black HBCU graduates assume highly prestigious occupations (Strayhorn, 2008a), and other evidence suggests that they graduate at rates higher than their same-race peers at PWIs (Carter & Wilson, 1993). Indeed, campus racial composition affects African American students' academic and social experiences in college (e.g., Flowers, 2002); so, too, do gender and SES.

Data have shown that gender disparities are most pronounced among African Americans. Black women outnumber their same-race male counterparts by a margin of just over two to one (Hawkins, 1996). In addition, two-thirds of all Black men who start college do not graduate within six years of initial enrollment (Mortenson Research Seminar, 2001), the lowest graduation rate among both sexes and all racial/ethnic groups. This may be due, in part, to the fact that Black men face additional challenges in educational contexts, especially in predominantly White classrooms, schools, and colleges. For instance, the media and popular press often describe African American men with words that have negative connotations such as dangerous, endangered, at risk, dysfunctional, uneducable, incorrigible, and lazy (e.g., Ferguson, 2000; Gibbs, 1988; hooks, 2004; Majors & Billson, 1992), which tends to reinforce the negative stereotypes of their White peers and teachers. Unfortunately, some Black men internalize these negative beliefs about themselves, which, in turn, become self-deprecating, self-threatening, and, ultimately, self-fulfilling prophecies (Steele, 1997, 2000).

African American student success rates also vary by family income, a popular measure of one's SES (Strayhorn, 2008b; Walpole, 2003). For instance, while approximately 87% of students from the highest income quartile enroll in some form of postsecondary education directly after high school graduation, only 53% of low-income students do so, representing a 34% "opportunity gap" between the "haves" and the "have-nots" (Hearn, 2001). Rates can be appallingly lower for low-income African American students who face double disadvantages (e.g., being Black and poor), triple quandaries or threats (see Chapter 5 of this volume), often intersecting oppressions, and multiple barriers to college success (Boykin, 1982; Collins, 2000; Crosnoe, 2005; De Jong & Madamba, 2001).

Indeed, African Americans face a number of significant challenges in collegiate settings. Thus, it is increasingly important to identify strategies that can improve educational outcomes of Black students. This is the goal of this book—to understand the challenges Black students face in college using new and existing empirical evidence, thereby identifying ways to support Black students in higher education.

The Book

This book assembles 14 scholars and practitioners in higher education, representing a wide variety of backgrounds: 6 African American women, 5 African American men, and 3 White researchers (a faculty member and 2 doctoral students). They hail from both public and private colleges or universities, including PWIs and HBCUs. Equally diverse is the list of topics they address.

In chapter 1, Dafina Stewart draws on years of research to call attention to recent discussions about the importance of spirituality in student affairs and the role spirituality plays in the lives of African American college students. Rachelle Winkle-Wagner offers a riveting description of the college choice process as a matter of "life or death" for first-generation African American women in chapter 2. Next, drawing on survey data, I present new evidence on economically disadvantaged Black collegians who achieve despite adversity; I call this group "Buoyant Believers" (see chapter 3). Fred Bonner offers keen insights on African American students' academic achievement in chapter 4. He posits that encouraging Black collegians to become involved in campus activities may be one way to improve their academic achievement.

Turning much-needed attention to an "invisible" subpopulation of Black students, whose voices are virtually silent in the higher education literature, Terrell Strayhorn, Amanda Blakewood, and James DeVita identify the challenges and supports of Black gay undergraduate men in chapter 5, drawing on their qualitative study of information-rich participants. In chapter 6, Belinda McFeeters examines the experiences of student leaders using data from the College Student Experiences Questionnaire (CSEQ), specifically offering insights into the experiences of African American student leaders. Acknowledging the historical and present-day significance of Black Cultural Centers in the lives of African American collegians at PWIs (see chapter 7), Terrell Strayhorn, Melvin Terrell, Jane Redmond, and Chutney Walton offer new perspectives on the supportive role of these institutions.

Reflecting the fact that Black men continue to face significant challenges in collegiate settings, chapters 8 and 9 focus exclusively on African American men. Drawing on a qualitative study of Black men enrolled in an academic support program, Robert Palmer and Estelle Young underscore the uniqueness of an HBCU environment in chapter 8. Next, Darryl Holloman and Terrell Strayhorn focus on parental influences in chapter 9. Then Tonya Saddler discusses the importance of mentoring to Black undergraduates' success in chapter 10. Specifically, she presents data from a well-constructed qualitative study to demonstrate the benefits that accrue to Black students who engage in research with faculty mentors. A summary of the book's main points, including new directions for future research, comprises chapter 11.

I developed this book with several audiences in mind. First, educational researchers should benefit from the book's new findings and fresh perspectives on topics that are rarely, or only scantly, addressed in other texts on African American collegians (e.g., spirituality, Black women's college choice, sexuality issues). This may reduce the amount of time one has to spend in the library (or online) hunting for empirical research in these largely uncharted areas. And each chapter includes references that point to other literature and even prior studies conducted by the chapter's author.

Faculty members who teach graduate-level courses on college student populations or developmental theory might also find material in this volume useful. For example, instructors might assign readings from this book to increase students' knowledge of the challenges faced by Black women, low-income students of color, student leaders, or lesbian, gay, bisexual, or transgendered (LGBT) persons of color. Additionally, several chapters (e.g., chapters 1, 3, and 5) include thorough explanations of developmental theories and how they relate to African American college students' experiences; these may be useful readings for theory courses in graduate preparation programs.

There is at least one other group that might benefit from this book, and I owe this "discovery" to my son, Tionne Lamont Strayhorn. While I was busy editing this book over the summer, Tionne asked, "Who is that book for?" Smiling, always happy when my kids express interest in my work, I replied, "Mostly for teachers, researchers, and policymakers." Frozen in what seemed like amazement, he probed, "You mean a book *about* college students isn't *for* college students?" And on further reflection I realized that my little "scholar in residence" had uncovered a third use of this book. That is, college students—especially Black college students—might benefit from the information contained here. In many ways, each chapter may highlight various aspects of their own lived experience, and they may benefit from reading about similar experiences in the pages of this volume. Reading about the experiences of those who share some aspect of their lived experience can be powerfully affirming, and it can help Black students make meaning of unresolved challenges or unsettled conflicts.

Conclusion

Overall, this volume focuses on understanding the challenges Black students face in college and identifies strategies to support their academic success. The authors provide practical recommendations that assist college student educators in fashioning policies that smooth Black students' transitions in and through higher education; creating new or expanding existing programs and services that provide the necessary academic, social, and financial support; and fostering conditions that matter for student success (Kuh, Kinzie, Schuh, Whitt, & Associates, 2005). Indeed, these chapters explore old and new terrain, thereby offering clues to innovative and timeless strategies that seem to hold promise for improving the condition of education for African Americans. Moreover, this text offers fresh insights that should invigorate scholarly discussions and policy debates across the country.

References

Adelman, C. (2002). The relationship between urbanicity and educational outcomes. In W. G. Tierney & L. S. Hagedorn (Eds.), *Increasing access to college: Extending possibilities for all students* (pp. 35–63). Albany: State University of New York Press.

Allen, W. R. (1992). The color of success: African American college students out-comes at predominantly White and historically Black public colleges and univer-sities. *Harvard Educational Review, 62*(1), 26–44.

Baum, S., & Payea, K. (2004). *Education pays 2004.* New York: The College Board.

Boykin, A. W. (1982). Task variability and the performance of Black and White school children: Vervistic explorations. *Journal of Black Studies, 12,* 469–485.

Carter, D. F., & Wilson, R. T. (1993). *Minorities in higher education: 11th annual status report.* Washington, DC: American Council on Education.

Clewell, B. C., & Ficklen, M. S. (1986). *Improving minority retention in higher educa-tion: A search for effective institutional practices.* Princeton, NJ: Educational Test-ing Service.

Collins, P. (2000). *Black feminist thought: Knowledge, consciousness, and the politics of empowerment* (2nd ed.). New York: Routledge.

Crosnoe, R. (2005). Double disadvantage or signs of resilience? The elementary school contexts of children from Mexican immigrant families. *American Educa-tional Research Journal, 42*(2), 269–303.

Cuyjet, M. J. (2006). African American college men: Twenty-first century issues and concerns. In M. J. Cuyjet & Associates (Eds.), *African American men in college* (pp. 3–23). San Francisco: Jossey-Bass.

De Jong, G. F., & Madamba, A. B. (2001). A double disadvantage? Minority group, immigrant status, and underemployment in the United States. *Social Science Quarterly, 82*(1), 117–130.

Ferguson, A. A. (2000). *Bad boys: Public schools in the making of Black male masculin-ity.* Ann Arbor: The University of Michigan Press.

Fleming, J. (1984). *Blacks in college: A comparative study of students' success in Black and White institutions.* San Francisco: Jossey-Bass.

Flowers, L. A. (2002). The impact of college racial composition on African American students' academic and social gains: Additional evidence. *Journal of College Stu-dent Development, 43,* 403–410.

Fries-Britt, S. L., & Griffin, K. A. (2007). The Black box: How high-achieving Blacks resist stereotypes about Black Americans. *Journal of College Student Devel-opment, 48*(5), 509–524.

Gándara, P. (2002). Meeting common goals: Linking K–12 and college interven-tions. In W. G. Tierney & L. S. Hagedorn (Eds.), *Increasing access to college: Extending possibilities for all students* (pp. 81–103). Albany: State University of New York Press.

Gibbs, J. T. (Ed.). (1988). *Young, Black, and male in America: An endangered species.* Dover, MA: Auburn House.

Harper, S. R. (2006, November/December). Reconceptualizing reactive policy responses to Black male college achievement: Implications from a national study. *Focus,* 14–15.

Hawkins, B. D. (1996). Gender gap: Black females outpace Black male counterparts at three degree levels. *Black Issues in Higher Education, 13*(10), 20–22.

Hearn, J. C. (2001). Access to postsecondary education: Financing equity in an evolving context. In M. B. Paulsen & J. C. Smart (Eds.), *The finance of higher education: Theory, research, policy & practice* (pp. 439–460). New York: Agathon Press.

Hinderlie, H. H., & Kenny, M. E. (2002). Attachment, social support, and college adjustment among Black students at predominantly White institutions. *Journal of College Student Development, 43*(3), 327–340.

Hirt, J. B., Strayhorn, T. L., Amelink, C. T., & Bennett, B. R. (2006). The nature of student affairs work at historically Black colleges and universities. *Journal of College Student Development, 47*(6), 661–676.

hooks, b. (2004). *We real cool: Black men and masculinity.* New York: Routledge.

Jan, L. A., Sandra, C., Steven, E. J., Kevin, K., Nance, L., Jaime, W., et al. (2000). Leadership experiences of students of color. *The NASPA Journal, 37*(3).

Kuh, G. D., Kinzie, J., Schuh, J. H., Whitt, E. J., & Associates. (2005). *Student success in college: Creating conditions that matter.* San Francisco: Jossey-Bass.

Majors, R., & Billson, J. (1992). *Cool pose: The dilemmas of Black manhood in America.* New York: Touchstone.

Mortenson Research Seminar on Public Policy Analysis of Opportunity for Postsecondary Education. (2001). College participation by gender, age 18 to 24, 1967 to 2000. *Postsecondary Education Opportunity, 109,* 1–16.

Solorzano, D. G., Ceja, M., & Yosso, T. J. (2000). Critical race theory, racial microaggressions, and campus racial climate: The experiences of African American college students. *The Journal of Negro Education, 69,* 60–73.

Steele, C. M. (1997). A threat in the air: How stereotypes shape intellectual identity and performance. *American Psychologist, 52,* 613–629.

Steele, C. M. (2000, February). "Stereotype threat" and Black college students. *AAHE Bulletin, 52,* 3–6.

Strayhorn, T. L. (2008a). Influences on labor market outcomes of African American college graduates: A national study. *The Journal of Higher Education, 79*(1), 29–57.

Strayhorn, T. L. (2008b). The invisible man: Factors affecting the retention of low-income African American males. *National Association of Student Affairs Professionals Journal, 11*(1), 66–87.

Strayhorn, T. L. (2008c). The role of supportive relationships in facilitating African American males' success in college. *NASPA Journal, 45*(1), 26–48.

Strayhorn, T. L. (2009). The burden of proof: A quantitative study of high-achieving Black collegians. *Journal of African American Studies, 13*(4), 375–387.

Strayhorn, T. L., & Hirt, J. B. (2008). Social justice and student affairs work at minority serving institutions. In M. B. Gasman, B. Baez, & C. S. V. Turner (Eds.), *Understanding minority-serving institutions* (pp. 203–216). Albany: State University of New York Press.

Thomas, S. L., & Perna, L. W. (2004). The opportunity agenda: A reexamination of postsecondary reward and opportunity. In J. C. Smart (Ed.), *Higher education: Handbook of theory and research* (Vol. 19, pp. 43–84). Dordrecht, NL: Kluwer Academic Publishers.

U.S. Department of Education, National Center for Education Statistics. (2006). *The condition of education 2006* (NCES 2006–071). Washington, DC: U.S. Government Printing Office.

Walpole, M. (2003). Socioeconomic status and college: How SES affects college experiences and outcomes. *The Review of Higher Education, 27*(1), 45–73.

Willie, C. V., & McCord, A. S. (1972). *Black students at White colleges*. New York: Praeger.

KNOWING GOD, KNOWING SELF

African American College Students and Spirituality

Dafina Lazarus Stewart

Abstract: In this chapter, the author weaves together findings from multiple studies regarding the role of spirituality in supporting student persistence in higher education, both as cultural resistance and as a factor in student identity development. Implications for developing a holistic understanding of the African American experience with higher education are presented at the end of the chapter, as well as evidence-based recommendations for shaping educational practice.

The role of spirituality in the lives of young adults and its place on college campuses has received considerable attention in recent years (Astin et al., 2004; Chickering, Dalton, & Stamm, 2006; Nash, 2001; Parks, 2000; Rogers & Dantley, 2001; Tisdell, 2003). Even professional preparation programs are considering what role they should play in preparing new professionals to deal with spirituality and students' spiritual searching (Love & Talbot, 1999; Rogers & Love, 2000a, 2007b; Strange, 2001). This literature recounts the importance of spirituality in the lives of young adults as a stabilizing force emphasizing their desire to balance the material and the spiritual (Astin et al., 2004) and providing networks of community (Palmer, 1983; Parks, 2000; Tisdell, 2003). Moreover, spirituality serves as a site for working through questions about purpose and integrity as well as wrestling with values and beliefs (Astin et al., 2004; Parks, 2000).

However, it is important to understand what is meant by "spirituality," especially to distinguish it from "religion." The two words are sometimes used interchangeably, which makes conversations about this topic difficult (Love & Talbot, 1999). "Spirituality" is the engagement of "big questions" (Parks, 2000) about meaning, purpose, belonging, and values that may transcend the organizational and doctrinal dogma of religion (Love & Talbot, 1999; Nash, 2001; Palmer, 1983; Parks, 2000). Moreover, religious institutions (such as churches, synagogues, mosques, and temples) and religious practices (such as liturgical styles, rituals, festivals, and forms of prayer), may serve as locations and spaces to perform cultural norms and traditions beyond engagement in the spiritual concerns noted earlier (Stewart & Lozano, 2009).

Despite the recent attention to spiritual issues in the lives of young adults, a profound and deep sense of spirituality has long been a part of meaning-making and relational systems in African American culture (DuBois, 1903/1994; Myers, 1993; Nobles, 1980). Tracing the existence of a spiritual worldview to the African continent, Bynum (1999) asserts that African Americans have an unconscious connection to the African cultural worldview and perspective, including an acknowledgment and incorporation of spirituality as an essential aspect of one's life. This worldview seeks to balance spiritual and material realities; recognizes the existence of the Divine; and finds meaning and purpose through connection to the past, present, and future generations (Baker-Fletcher, 1998; Bynum, 1999; Myers, 1993; Nobles, 1980). These scholars assert that this spiritual consciousness continues for much of the Black community in the United States.

Writing at the turn of the 20th century, W.E.B. DuBois (1903/1994) acknowledged the dominant role of spirituality in the lives of Black Americans and articulated the role of spirituality as a method for Blacks in the United States to make sense of their duality as both "Negroes" and Americans. Indeed, as Townes (1995) discusses, spirituality in the Black community seeks coherence among myriad identities, responsibilities, and relationships, hoping to "[bridge] artificially and socially constructed dichotomies" (James, 1993, p. 35). Collins (1990) also centers spirituality as a key aspect of Black feminist thought as a means of seeking connection and meaning for Black women. Thus, historically, Black spirituality also has sought to answer the "big questions" common to mainstream discussions of spirituality.

A review of the history of African Americans in the United States shows that spirituality and religion have played significant roles in building leaders and motivating social resistance (Giles, 2003, 2006; Houck & Dixon, 2006). Enslaved and indentured Africans in the United States were denied the right to maintain their own religious traditions and styles (Brooks, 2003; Rucker, 2006). Yet, many of them adopted Christianity's spiritual beliefs and values and, through those, created new, culturally relevant traditions that perpetuated African values of connectedness and the unity of material and spiritual realities (Brooks, 2003; Rucker, 2006). Moreover, these Africans used the language and symbols of sacrifice, salvation, and deliverance to redefine Christianity and reclaim religious traditions and spiritual values that were reminiscent of their cultural traditions (Brooks, 2003; Rucker, 2006). These spiritual symbols and values anchored their cultural resistance to the oppression in U.S. society (Brooks, 2003; Rucker, 2006; Wood, 1990).

During the Civil Rights Era, the role of the Black church and spiritually defined concepts of social justice and redemption formed the basis of Black resistance and the push for social change (Giles, 2003; Houck & Dixon, 2006). Given this historical context, it is imperative to understand that both racial or ethnic cultural identity and religious identity may play salient roles in the lives of the individual, particularly among African Americans (Brooks, 2003; Holmes, Ebbers, Robinson, & Mugenda, 2000; McEwen, Roper, Bryant, & Langa, 1990; Myers, 1993; Tisdell, 2003).

Spirituality in the Lives of Black College Students

Spirituality serves multiple purposes in the lives of Black college students. As a means of support and coping, research has found that Black students use spiritual concepts, such as interconnectedness and transcendence, to adapt, manage, and navigate the college environment (Watson, 2006; Watt, 2003). In a similar vein, Black college students also use spirituality to resist isolation, negative messages, and racial hostility in college (Watson, 2006; Watt, 2003). Spirituality is also incorporated more broadly as an aspect of identity and identity development in Black college students (Stewart, 2002, 2007). Used in this way, spirituality becomes a source of meaning-making reflecting students' centers of value and relationships (Stewart, 2002) as well as meaning-making for students' identities and college experiences (Stewart, 2007). This research, discussed in more detail below, establishes spirituality as a key supportive factor in the lives of Black college students as part of a cultural heritage passed down through generations.

Support and Resistance

Nearly two decades ago, McEwen et al. (1990) asserted that current theoretical conceptions of psychosocial development did not fit the reality and worldview of African American students. Moreover, they recommended that future theoretical models include acknowledgment of the central role of spirituality in the lives, worldviews, and, probably, the development of Black students (McEwen et al., 1990). Other research also has demonstrated the significant role of spirituality as a support mechanism for Black students to aid in retention and persistence (Hughes, 1987; White & Parham, 1990). Studies focusing on Black women during this era also highlighted the need to develop greater empirically based understanding of the role of spirituality in the lives of Black women in college (Goodman, 1990).

Recent research has given more evidence of the role of spirituality as a support mechanism for Black college students. These studies used single-gender samples, recognizing that men and women may understand and incorporate spirituality in their lives in different ways (Baker-Fletcher, 1998). Watt (2003) finds that Black women emphasize the role of spirituality as a coping strategy and a tool of resistance against isolating and racially hostile college environments and as a support for self-esteem and motivation to persist in college. Drawing on work by Robinson and Howard-Hamilton (1994), Watt distinguishes between resistance for survival and resistance for empowerment. The former is characterized by internalization of negative societal messages and leads to withdrawal from the Black community. The latter, rooted in personal meaning-making and transcendence, results in empowerment and the intentional building of cultural support networks. This resistance is essentially a spiritual activity, according to Robinson and Howard-Hamilton, because answering "big questions" about self, meaning, purpose, and coherence are inherent to developing resistance strategies.

In support, Watt found that the African American women in her study had developed ways to resist negative messages through redefining their images of God and sin as well as seeking connection with ancestors, both living and deceased. The acknowledgement of an identity that is informed by spiritual connections with ancestors and those yet unborn is an essential aspect of African spiritual philosophy (Bynum, 1999; Nobles, 1980) that is evidently still a part of the meaning-making and identity formation of African American women today. Maintaining this spiritually grounded perspective has enabled these students to transcend their circumstances and the racial hostility of their college environment.

Watson (2006), writing about African American men's spirituality, also discusses themes of support and resistance. Stewart (as cited in Watson) is credited with distinguishing between these two functions of spirituality as "creative soul force" and "resistant soul force" (p. 114). Creative soul force describes the support function of spirituality, which helps African Americans to adapt and transform their environments through the creative use of Black culture. Resistant soul force, on the other hand, emphasizes the role of spirituality to help Blacks transcend oppressive systems and structures, so they can survive and thrive. Specifically, Watson found that expressing spirituality through religious practices is important to Black men in college and helps them to define their purpose. A sense of spirituality provided motivation to continue to pursue their educational goals in the face of challenges and barriers.

In later work with Black men and women at three different institutions (a predominantly White, public university; a predominantly Black, public university; and a predominantly Black, private college), I found that students were able to access spirituality as a source of support in dealing with the campus racial environment as well as the challenge of persistence and achievement typical for college students. Spiritual frameworks informed their upbringing, and they kept those worldviews with them when they went to college. As Bob said in an interview, "A lot of the nurturing and mentoring that I receive, I receive from the church . . . I was raised in a church." Many of the 13 students in the study echoed this sentiment. For them, religious practices like going to church were difficult to maintain while on campus, but prayer could happen anywhere, and the practice of it, even inconsistently, supported them and helped them to adapt. This is similar to findings in both Watt (2003) and Watson (2006).

For some, maintaining a spiritual perspective and religious practices like prayer also provided spaces to resist the pressures of conformity, fragmentation, and hostility they encountered as Black students on campus. Regina, a student at a PWI, talked about the decision to chemically straighten her hair after wearing it in braids for her first two years on campus and the conflict she felt over that decision:

> I'm not going to say that I regret it, but I think that at this point, I want to do something, I want to be different, so badly that it's like, it's almost like a complex, because in my mind I'm saying, [what] if I'm not going to be able to get a job. Am I going to be able to do this or who's going accept me? [Are] my peers going to accept me? Are African Americans going to

accept me? Am I going to be able to look at myself in the mirror? But . . .
I really do pray on [these] issues, and I think that through time I'll continue to grow, and I think that even as a Christian you go through little, I
guess, trials, I guess you could call them, and when one trial is over, don't
think that there's not another one ahead of you, because there is.

The students in the study who attended the PWI talked about spirituality in this context more than did students in the study who attended
HBCUs. Although students at historically Black colleges did not need to
resist cultural oppression and race-related stress, spirituality was a source of
support for these students as well, including being able to connect with faculty and administrators who used a spiritual orientation to offer support and
encouragement. Angela, a student at a historically Black college, remarked,
"I have administrators [who] are willing to help in anything that I need, and
I know that they're there for me, and they said they're praying for all of us
. . . we're going through so much." Similar to findings from an earlier study
(Stewart, 2002), students in this study across institutions also used spirituality as a way to make sense of their experiences and to help them navigate the
challenges. Again, Angela was quoted as saying, "Recently, a lot of crazy
things have been going on, just in the last year, and it's just acknowledging
the fact that everything happens for a reason and we can't see what the future
has in store for us, but God can. So, just, acting in faith like, okay, this was
meant to happen." Like Angela, these students relied on faith in God and in
God's ability to help them to cope successfully with the academic demands
of college and their search for meaning and purpose.

In the Christian scriptures, faith is defined as the "substance of things
hoped for, the evidence of things not seen" (Hebrews 11:1 [King James Ver-
sion]). This faith, a trust that things "happen for a reason" despite the
absence of rational evidence, was a central aspect in the spirituality of these
students. Moreover, faith is what helped these students to persist in college,
defying social norms and expectations. Practitioners would do well to
remember the importance of spiritual faith when counseling Black students
who are having struggles transitioning and finding their place in the college
environment.

The findings from each of these studies demonstrate the importance of
spirituality in the lives of Black college students. These students persist in
the college environment, cope with different cultural norms and expectations, and resist demeaning and oppressive views and structures through
spiritual frameworks. These spiritual frameworks help Black college students

to redefine reality, access transcendent centers of value and meaning, and locate their source of strength and empowerment in a personal spiritual reality. As Ntozake Shange (1977) wrote, "i found god in myself & I loved her/ I loved her fiercely." (p. 61). In Shange's choreopoem, and in the lives of Black college students, God is symbolic of a transcendent power that unites the disparate fragments of reality and remakes them into a coherent and purposeful whole, without which surviving and thriving would be much more difficult, if not impossible.

Identity and Meaning-Making

These earlier studies focused on spirituality's role as a mechanism for support and resistance for African Americans dealing with the cultural environments of colleges and universities. I used spirituality as a lens to understand how Black students made meaning of their identities and then reflected that meaning-making in how they built networks of association, both informal and formal, though student organization involvement (Stewart, 2002). Investigating identity intersectionality among Black college students, I used a faith-identity typology discussed by Fowler (1981) to understand how Black students' patterns of involvement and sense of identity reflected their centers of meaning and ability to transcend the borders of their identities. This typology, originally developed by Niebuhr (as cited in Fowler, 1981), described individuals' sense of identity, understanding of purpose, and their social involvements as reflecting one of three religio-spiritual orientations.

Polytheists, as the name suggests, exhibited a diffuse sense of personal identity and a mercurial or unknown sense of life purpose. Consequently, such individuals either were unable to commit to any activity for an extended time or maintained involvement at superficial levels across a range of activities, which lacked any unifying value. Those using a henotheistic orientation did exhibit a deep commitment to a center of value and meaning. Such individuals might place an inordinate amount of value on ego, materialism, or status, or even as a member of a particular organization, race, ethnicity, or nationality. However, such a perspective ultimately proved incapable of helping the individual in times of stress, challenge, or combating oppression. In contrast to either the polytheist or the henotheist, the radical monotheist maintained a center of value and meaning anchored in a transcendent, spiritual reality. Involvements were determined by whether they aligned with their values. In times of stress and challenge, this foundation allowed the individual to see beyond his or her present reality and to find meaning and purpose to help him or her persevere (Fowler, 1981; Stewart, 2002).

The five students in the study, both men and women, ranged from polytheistic to more monotheistic centers of value and social involvement patterns (Stewart, 2002). Two students reflected a polytheistic orientation. One of them, Ophelia, constantly shifted back and forth between her identity commitments. She proclaimed ardently that she identified as a "woman who is Black"; however, she was so loosely attached to those centers of meaning that she could pick them up or drop them on a day-by-day or year-by-year basis. As she said in one interview, "Well this whole gender thing . . . last year I was really gung ho knowing about gender and . . . I tended to ignore the whole race factor." In a later interview, Ophelia commented, "You know what, it's not time for me to be Black today. Today I'm a feminist and tomorrow I'll talk about Black stuff and the day after that I'm off, I'm not going to talk about any of that stuff." Ophelia confessed that the "process of synthesizing" was really important but she was "seeing kind of the impossibility of it sometimes." Spirituality was also difficult for Ophelia to articulate and did not serve as a consistent support mechanism or as a source of resistance for her. Moreover, spirituality did not help her to make meaning of the pulls on her identity.

Both of the men in this study (Stewart, 2002) reflected more henotheistic identity commitments and understandings of spirituality. For example, Poke believed strongly in his own ability to educate his peers and to bridge divisions between his disparate groups of friends. When this failed, he was unable to make sense of it and could not articulate a sense of personal identity apart from his role as a "man in the middle." Spiritually, both K.B. and Poke considered themselves to be spiritual but did not identify religiously, and their reliance on spirituality as a means of support or resistance to the racial stress they felt on campus was not evident.

One student had begun to express what Fowler and Niebuhr called a radical monotheistic faith (Stewart, 2002). Sage found meaning and salience in her identity as a Black woman, but transcending that was her foundational faith and commitment to God and her spirituality, which was interwoven with her religious beliefs. Like the other students, Sage also struggled at times with difficult choices related to her competing identity commitments. She often found herself pulled among her "volleyball girls," Christian friends, and sorority friends. Issues of race, gender, and religion segregated the memberships across these groups. As she said in an interview, "I'm straddling all sorts of margins." However, the way she made meaning of that straddling was distinctively rooted in her spirituality. Sage had a profound faith in the purpose of her identity as it was constituted (Black, woman, Christian, working class, college educated). Although she admitted that "people see parts of me [and] pick and choose what they like," Sage fought the temptation to surrender to that for her own understanding of her identity. For Sage, being whole and integrating the facets of her identity helped to make her feel "stronger" and was rooted in an optimism based on her faith in God's providential care. She was striving for an "inner peace" that would enable her to resist the pressure to live a fragmented identity. This inner peace, according to Sage's spiritual philosophy, was strongest when she focused on the Spirit and on recognition of its infinite possibilities, instead of on the finite limitations with which she lived.

These students understood the support that engagement with spirituality could provide them, but most of them were unable to access that support except during times of extreme personal crisis. The daily stresses and fatigue associated with being Black on a predominantly White campus (Smith, Yosso, & Solórzano, 2006; Solórzano, Ceja, & Yosso, 2000), which they acknowledged and articulated very clearly, were not addressed through the spiritual resistance exercised by the Black women in Watt's (2003) study or the Black men in Watson's (2006) work. Yet, the presence or absence of a strongly defined spirituality influenced their ability to integrate the multiple components of their identities and make meaning of who they were and how they should relate to others.

Also emerging in these findings (Stewart, 2002) was that identity development in these students required changes in self-definition from those that are externally supplied to those that are internally supplied. Identifying this as a spiritual process, Watt (2003) references earlier work (Watt, 1997) that found a relationship among self-esteem, race and gender, and faith for African American women. The women in Watt's focus groups reflected spiritual principles of interconnectedness as they used relationships with female family members, fathers (whether present or absent), and younger siblings to make better meaning of their own identities. Moreover, these Black women sought integration and transformation of their identities through intergenerational connections. These intergenerational connections (ancestors, the self, those yet unborn) reflect an African spiritual philosophy (Bynum, 1999; Myers, 1993; Nobles, 1980).

One can also understand these data through another theoretical lens. Optimal theory, an Africentric psychological model (Myers et al., 1991), suggests that the height of identity is an understanding of self as interrelated and interdependent. Indeed, an optimal conceptualization (Myers et al., 1991) holds certain tenets in common with other spiritual development theories. As Fowler (1981) and Parks (2000) posit, the optimal conceptual system marries spiritual and material realities and places primary importance on the spiritual rather the material. Optimal theory also pictures the self as multidimensional and intergenerational, composed of ancestors, the unborn, nature, and community with an intrinsic worth based in the self as an expression of a unique divine or spiritual energy. The material manifestations of identity, such as race, ethnicity, sex, and age, are used as lenses through which the individual can come to a greater degree of self-knowledge. The maturation of identity is reflected in the awareness that the self is not segmented or separate, but rather interconnected; the whole becomes greater than the sum of its parts (Myers et al., 1991). The model of development Myers and her colleagues propose that describes the process of coming to this sense of personal interconnection and integration is known as Optimal Theory Applied to Identity Development (OTAID).

The students I interviewed in 2001 had not reached the ultimate stage of identity maturation the OTAID described (Stewart, 2001). Rather, they were still struggling to find common intrinsic interests on which to form networks and to focus on the material aspects of their identities. The buildup of racially motivated and unfair treatment by Whites and negative experiences within the Black community hindered continued development toward an optimal conceptualization of identity. Some retreated from more expansive networks of community that were multiracial and bound together by intrinsic interests and, instead, focused their energy on others like themselves and withdrawing from the dominant group. Other students were suspended between phases within the OTAID, hovering between two poles of energy: one, exploring aspects of identity previously ignored and fighting to defy negative stereotypes associated with their race and the other, embracing others who were similarly devalued. For these students, the suboptimal environment of their college inhibited growth, and the lack of supportive, mentoring adults (Parks, 2000) exacerbated their struggle to think beyond the boundaries that environment imposed on them.

In recent research, I uncovered evidence that explicitly places spirituality as a lens through which Black college students define and understand identity (Stewart, 2007). I discuss three significant findings from that study related to spirituality. First, there was continued evidence that African American college students perceived their identities as multifaceted, dynamic, and fluid, consistent with previous findings (Stewart, 2002, 2008). Second, these students perceived their identities as coherent and consistent, which reflected a spiritual perspective. Third, spirituality was a lens through which some of the students understood and interpreted their collective identities, giving a rationale for the multiple aspects of self and creating synergy among them.

The students consistently used progressive and dynamic images to describe their identities (Stewart, 2007). Images of water, evolution, and movement typically used by the students, suggested that they recognized the developmental nature of identity and that their identities would become successively complex and be inherently cyclical. Moreover, these students did not talk about a self manifested by sociocultural identity facets (such as race, gender, and class) in a segregated, dissociative fashion. Rather, they embraced the multiple facets of their identities and recognized themselves to be unique expressions of spirit.

These findings mirror Africentric spiritual philosophy that emphasizes the dynamic nature of reality and embraces evolution as a fitting framework for understanding the self and one's experiences (Ani, 1994; Myers et al., 1991). Additionally, these students seemed further along in grasping an optimal conceptualization of identity, recognizing and embracing the interconnectedness of the various aspects of their material identities and unifying them through a spiritual prism (Myers et al., 1991). Repeatedly, the students articulated a relationship between their spirituality and their identity. Spirituality involved making meaning of themselves and their experiences as well as a personal relationship with a divinity. Moreover, this group of students understood their self-identity through a spiritual lens. As a result, they perceived identity facets such as race, gender, sexuality, and age to be outward manifestations of an inward spiritual essence. The students determined that their core identity was best labeled as "spirit" instead of as any single or combined external identity facet. As Regina stated,

> I believe that [God] made me who I am and I am called to a greater purpose. I needed to be in this one little body to do what he had me to do here. Is there a connectedness in all those things? Yes. The starting point is my spirituality. Everything else does connect, highly connects sometimes. You know, in certain situations, my ethnicity may play first and then the gender and then the sexual orientation, then this, then that. Do they all connect? Absolutely. They all connect back to the one thing.

Several other students embraced Regina's understanding, despite differences in religious traditions and spiritual philosophies among the respondents (Stewart, 2007).

Spirituality was the lens through which these students understood and interpreted their collective identity. This clearly reflects the optimal conceptualization of identity Myers and her colleagues called for (1991). This also parallels other findings from Tisdell's (2003) research with a multicultural sample of respondents across the life span. In this study, most of the students identified spirituality as the rationale for the multiple aspects of their identity and the capacity for synergy to exist among them. The findings of this study are related to Parks (2000) and Fowler (1981) as well, who posit the existence of an ineffable, non-unitary core of identity. All of the students in this study believed in the existence of a nonmaterial reality, which they understood as "divine," "spiritual," or "spirit," and this is a direct factor in the language used here of an ineffable core called "spirit." Students at both PWIs and HBCUs shared this ability to discern the spiritual unity of one's multiple identities. What allowed these students to overcome racial hostility and negative stereotypes at the PWI and the challenges of intracommunity relationships at the HBCUs deserves further study. Regardless, it is clear, in company with other research from Watt (2003) and Watson (2006), and upcoming findings from Sharon Holmes (personal communication, June 11, 2008), that African American college students articulate their identities in ways that explicitly incorporate spiritual understandings about the nature of self, purpose, and experience.

Conclusion

Previous research indicates that low self-esteem and struggles with identity are among the *challenges* that contribute to the high attrition rate of Black college students (Holmes et al., 2000). The research discussed in this chapter clearly marks these as spiritual questions, ultimately related to issues of self-valuing, self-worth, and integration. Education is a journey toward self-knowledge, and how educational systems and environments encourage students to embrace self-knowledge and integrate that knowledge is central to *supporting* holistic development in students and their engagement of spiritual questions (Palmer, 1983). For African Americans in college, this journey toward self-knowledge is made more complex by the history of African American education.

In the aftermath of the 1768 Bacon Rebellion, the U.S. government legally forbade Africans in the United States to be educated. Penalties for breaking the federal law were swift and severe; nevertheless, people continued to meet in caves or dense forests by candlelight, determined to teach and to learn (Douglass, 1997). Thus, education became not just a prized possession for personal gain only, as seen by White Americans, an attitude that persists to the present day (Rosovsky, 1990; Rudolph, 1990). Rather, education for African Americans was a symbol and tool of freedom and liberty for the community as a whole, a necessity and the political right of a democratic citizenry (Anderson, 1988; Franklin, 1979). However, gaining an education resulted in what would become known as "double consciousness" (Cooper, 1892; DuBois, 1903/1994), as African Americans struggled to make meaning of their identities and experiences as college-educated Blacks in the different and competing value systems of home and school. Indeed, then, the American college environment presents a fragmenting and invalidating experience for many African American college students (Fleming, 1984; Holmes et al., 2000; Hughes, 1987; McEwen et al., 1990; Parham, 1989).

Consequently, a spirituality that can resist fragmentation and invalidation is necessary and fundamental to the persistence and success of African American college students. As discussed in this chapter, some Black college students have found validation, meaning, and purpose through divine affirmation and have internalized that as a personal resource. Doing so has provided them with much needed *support* to cope with the challenges of higher education and to resist the effects of race-related stress experienced in college. Moreover, maintaining and developing spirituality has also promoted the development of self-knowledge and a sense of meaning and purpose that makes the pursuit of higher education a personally transformative journey (Palmer, 1983).

I encourage practitioners at both predominantly White and predominantly Black colleges to use the research discussed in this chapter to create and augment the development of programs that encourage African American students to engage deeply in the "big questions" that are important in the maturation of young adults (Parks, 2000). In particular, practitioners should prompt Black college students to consider the ways in which the multiple facets of their identities are coherent and interdependent, and to build networks of support that rely on shared common values more than simply on shared race and ethnicity. In this way, African American young adults can begin the process of shifting from suboptimal to optimal conceptualizations of identity (Myers et al., 1991).

Finally, practitioners must not shy away from direct discussions with Black college students about spirituality and religious practices, which they may use to find comfort and support, and to combat negative messages through spiritual resistance. As found in both Watson's (2006) research and in mine, Black college students use prayer and other religious symbols and practices as fundamental elements of building and maintaining a spiritual perspective capable of transcending their immediate circumstances. Moreover, students are seeking adults in the college environment with whom they can have spiritual conversations (Stewart, 2002, 2007). Although faculty and staff should not promote a particular set of religious traditions and beliefs, I encourage them to share various avenues for Black students to explore and practice their faith. This would encourage Black students to keep spiritual perspectives and meaning-makings interrelated with their material realities, consistent with the cultural paradigms in which many African Americans have been raised (Ani, 1994; Holmes et al., 2000; Myers, 1993; Nobles, 1980).

Through such deliberate, focused measures, college and university faculty and staff can support the development of Black students who do not struggle with a double consciousness. Such students would not be torn between the competing pulls of their multiple identities, nor would they be overcome by racial hostility, pressures to conform to a monolithic cultural standard, or negative cultural stereotypes. Instead, such students would be equipped to see beyond these struggles. They would be empowered to transcend their present realities through faith in their creation as unique expressions of the divine, intentionally constituted to reflect divine glory. Black students fully acquainted with the spiritual and engaged in answering "big questions" would not be crippled by the racial stereotypes of the past but would be able to make meaning of those experiences in empowering and transformative ways. These African American students would then be motivated to fulfill the purposes for which they were born and for which their college education was meant to prepare them.

References

Anderson, J. D. (1988). *The education of blacks in the South, 1860–1935.* Chapel Hill, NC: University Press.

Ani, M. (1994). *Yurugu: An African-centered critique of European cultural thought and behavior.* Trenton, NJ: Africa World Press.

Astin, A. W., Astin, H. S., Lindholm, J. A., Bryant, A. N., Calderone, S., & Szelenyi, K. (2004). *The spiritual life of college students: A national study of college students' search for meaning and purpose.* Los Angeles: Higher Education Research Institute.

Baker-Fletcher, K. (1998). *Sisters of dust, sisters of spirit: Womanist wordings on God and creation.* Minneapolis, MN: Fortress Press.

Brooks, J. (2003). *American Lazarus: Religion and the rise of African-American and Native American literatures.* New York: Oxford University Press.

Bynum, E. B. (1999). *The African unconscious: Roots of ancient mysticism and modern psychology.* New York: Teachers College Press.

Chickering, A. W., Dalton, J. C., & Stamm, L. (2006). *Encouraging authenticity and spirituality in higher education.* San Francisco: Jossey-Bass.

Collins, P. H. (1990). *Black feminist thought: Knowledge, consciousness, and the politics of empowerment.* New York: Routledge.

Cooper, A. J. (1892). *A voice from the South: By a Black woman of the South.* New York: Negro Universities Press.

Douglass, F. (1997). *Narrative of the life of Frederick Douglass: An American slave.* New York: Signet.

DuBois, W. E. B. (1994). *The souls of black folk.* New York: Dover.

Fleming, J. (1984). *Blacks in college.* San Francisco: Jossey-Bass. (Original work published 1903).

Fowler, J. (1981). *Stages of faith: The psychology of human development and the quest for meaning.* San Francisco: Harper & Row.

Franklin, V. P. (1979). *The education of black Philadelphia: The social and educational history of a minority community, 1900–1950.* Philadelphia: University of Pennsylvania Press.

Giles, M. S. (2003). *Howard Thurman: A spiritual life in higher education.* Unpublished doctoral dissertation, Indiana University, Bloomington.

Giles, M. S. (2006). Dr. Anna Julia Cooper, 1858–1964: Teacher, scholar, and timeless womanist. *Journal of Negro Education, 75,* 621–634.

Goodman, D. J. (1990). African-American women's voices: Expanding theories of women's development. *SAGE, 7*(2), 3–14.

Holmes, S. L., Ebbers, L. H., Robinson, D. C., & Mugenda, A. (2000). Validating African American students at predominantly White institutions. *Journal of College Student Retention: Research, Theory, & Practice, 2,* 41–58.

Houck, D. W., & Dixon, D. E. (Eds.). (2006). *Rhetoric, religion, and the civil rights movement, 1954–1965.* Waco, TX: Baylor University Press.

Hughes, M. S. (1987). Black students' participation in higher education. *Journal of College Student Personnel, 28,* 532–545.

James, J. (1993). African philosophy, theory, and "living thinkers." In J. James & R. Farmer (Eds.), *Spirit, space, and survival: African-American women in (White) academe* (pp. 31–44). New York: Routledge.

Love, P., & Talbot, D. (1999). Defining spiritual development: A missing consideration for student affairs. *NASPA Journal, 37,* 361–375.

McEwen, M. K., Roper, L. D., Bryant, D. R., & Langa, M. J. (1990). Incorporating the development of African-American students into psychosocial theories of student development. *Journal of College Student Development, 31,* 429–436.

Myers, L. J. (1993). *Understanding an Afrocentric world view: An introduction to optimal psychology.* Dubuque, IA: Kendall/Hunt.

Myers, L. J., Speight, S. L., Highlen, P. S., Cox, C. I., Reynolds, A. L., Adams, E. M., & Hanley, C. P. (1991). Identity development and worldview: Toward an optimal conceptualization. *Journal of Counseling & Development, 70,* 54–63.

Nash, R. J. (2001). *Religious pluralism in the academy: Opening the dialogue.* New York: Peter Lang.

Nobles, W. W. (1980). African philosophy: Foundations for black psychology. In R. L. Jones (Ed.), *Black psychology* (pp. 23–36). New York: Harper & Row.

Palmer, P. J. (1983). *To know as we are known: Education as a spiritual journey.* San Francisco: Harper & Row.

Parham, T. A. (1989). Cycles of psychological Nigrescence. *The Counseling Psychologist, 17,* 187–226.

Parks, S. D. (2000). *Big questions, worthy dreams: Mentoring young adults in their search for meaning, purpose, and faith.* San Francisco: Jossey-Bass.

Robinson, T. L., & Howard-Hamilton, M. (1994). An Afrocentric paradigm: Foundation for a healthy self-image and healthy interpersonal relationships. *Journal of Mental Health Counseling, 16,* 327–340.

Rogers, J. L., & Dantley, M. E. (2001). Invoking the spiritual in campus life and leadership. *Journal of College Student Development, 42,* 589–603.

Rogers, J. L., & Love, P. (2007a). Exploring the role of spirituality in the preparation of student affairs professionals: Faculty constructions. *Journal of College Student Development, 48,* 90–104.

Rogers, J. L., & Love, P. (2007b). Graduate student constructions of spirituality in preparation programs. *Journal of College Student Development, 48,* 689–705.

Rosovsky, H. (1990). *The university: An owner's manual.* New York: W. W. Norton.

Rucker, W. C. (2006). *The river flows on: Black resistance, culture, and identity formation in early America.* Baton Rouge: Louisiana State University Press.

Rudolph, F. (1990). *The American college and university: A history.* Athens, GA: University Press.

Shange, N. (1977). *For colored girls who have considered suicide/when the rainbow is enuf: A choreopoem.* New York: MacMillan.

Smith, W. A., Yosso, T. J., & Solórzano, D. G., (2006). Challenging racial battle fatigue on historically White campuses: A critical race examination of race-related stress. In C. A. Stanley (Ed.), *Faculty of color teaching in predominantly White colleges and universities* (pp. 299–327). Bolton, MA: Anker Publishing.

Solórzano, D. G., Ceja, M., & Yosso, T. J. (2000). Critical race theory, racial microaggressions, and campus racial climate: The experiences of African American college students. *The Journal of Negro Education, 69,* 60–73.

Stewart, D. L. (2001). *Awareness and integration of multiple sociocultural identities among Black students at a predominantly White institution.* Unpublished doctoral dissertation. The Ohio State University, Columbus.

Stewart, D. L. (2002). The role of faith in the development of an integrated identity: A qualitative study of Black students at a White college. *Journal of College Student Development, 43,* 579–596.

Stewart, D. L. (2007). *Perceptions of multiple identities among Black college students.* Manuscript under review.

Stewart, D. L. (2008). Being all of me: Black students negotiating multiple identities. *Journal of Higher Education, 79,* 183–207.

Stewart, D. L., & Lozano, A. (2009). Difficult dialogues at the intersections of race, culture and religion. In S. K. Watt, E. Fairchild, & K. Goodman (Eds.), *Intersections of religious privilege: Difficult dialogues and student affairs* (pp. 23–31). San Francisco: Wiley.

Strange, C. C. (2001). Spiritual dimensions of graduate preparation in student affairs. *New Directions for Student Services, 95,* 57–67.

Tisdell, E. J. (2003). *Exploring spirituality and culture in adult and higher education.* San Francisco: Jossey-Bass.

Townes, E. M. (1995). *In a blaze of glory: Womanist spirituality as social witness.* Nashville, TN: Abingdon Press.

Watson, L. W. (2006). The role of spirituality and religion in the experiences of African American male college students. In M. J. Cuyjet & Associates, *African American men in college* (pp. 112–127). San Francisco: Jossey-Bass.

Watt, S. K. (1997). *Identity and the making of meaning: Psychosocial identity, racial identity, womanist identity, self-esteem, and the faith development of African American college women.* Unpublished doctoral dissertation, North Carolina State University, Raleigh.

Watt, S. K. (2003). Come to the river: Using spirituality to cope, resist, and develop identity. *New Directions for Student Services, 104,* 29–40.

White, J. L., & Parham, T. A. (1990). *The psychology of Blacks: An African American perspective* (2nd ed.). Upper Saddle River, NJ: Prentice Hall.

Wood, F. G. (1990). *The arrogance of faith: Christianity and race in America from the colonial era to the twentieth century.* New York: Knopf.

2

CHOOSING COLLEGE AS A LIFE OR DEATH DECISION

First-Generation African American Women's Reflections on College Choice

Rachelle Winkle-Wagner

Abstract: This ethnographic study focuses on currently enrolled first-generation African American women's reflections on their college choice decision-making processes. The findings indicated that the college choice was a "life or death" decision, rooted in personal challenges, for many of these women. Additionally, financial and academic barriers were linked to the women's choice and transition processes. The findings in this chapter offer a strong rationale for the importance of early-intervention programs that provide academic and financial support to underrepresented students.

There continue to be racial disparities in postsecondary educational access. In particular, African American students continue to face significant barriers to college entry (Carnoy, 1995; Ficklen & Stone, 2002; Myers, 2003; St. John, Chung, Musoba, & Simmons, 2004). Thus, these students are generally less likely to enroll in and graduate from college than are their White counterparts (Pathways to College Network, 2003). Yet, African American *women* have been relatively successful in their college enrollment, compared to African American men. Why do these disparities continue? This chapter offers some insight into this question, exploring first-generation[1] African American[2] women's reflections on their decisions to attend college.

A student's decision to attend college is influenced by many factors, both within and outside of education. For example, a lack of academic preparation can become an obstacle to college enrollment (Myers, 2003). Yet, even if a student is prepared academically, that student may lack the financial resources to pay for college (St. John et al., 2004). Financial and academic factors can also be coupled with background experiences, in both education and one's family, to influence students' college choices (McDonough, 1997; Perna, 2000).

Academic and financial barriers can be particularly constraining to African American students' decisions to attend college (Freeman, 1997). Also, Black students often must contend with additional factors that influence their decision such as racism on campus (Feagin, Vera, & Imani, 1998) or the campus racial climate or environment (Freeman, 1999a; Freeman & Thomas, 2002). In addition, African American students have been shown to be affected by the perceived economic benefits of a college degree (Freeman, 1999b). Yet, even with evidence indicating that different factors may influence African American students' decisions to attend college, relatively few studies focus specifically on the college choice processes of African American students from a qualitative perspective, highlighting their individual stories and experiences.

This chapter provides an alternative approach to the college choice process. In particular, I focus on how college-enrolled (first-year students through seniors), first-generation African American women reflected on their decisions to attend college. As the women reflected on their decision-making processes, their decision to enroll in college emerged in the dramatic terms of life or death—as if going to college both literally and metaphorically facilitated the life or death of their aspirations.

Review of the Literature

I focus on three factors related to postsecondary access: college choice decision-making processes, African American students' college choice processes, and academic and financial obstacles to college access.

College Choice Decision-Making Processes

Many factors influence the process whereby students decide whether to attend college, and if so, which colleges they will attend. This choice process is affected by such factors as students' social networks or social capital[3] (Freeman, 1997; Perna, 2000); students' class-based tastes or cultural capital[4] (Freeman, 1997; McDonough, 1997; Perna, 2000); race and culture (Freeman, 1999a; Freeman & Thomas, 2002); financial capital or financial barriers (Freeman, 1997); high school experiences (Freeman & Thomas, 2002; McDonough, 1997); and the perceived economic outcomes of college degrees (Freeman, 1999b).

One of the predominant models of college choice decision-making processes, the Hossler and Gallagher (1987) model of college choice, specifies three stages in the choice process: the predisposition phase (a student decides whether to attend college); the search phase (a student searches for information about colleges); and a choice phase (the student winnows down to a single choice or top choices). Much of the college choice literature uses econometric models based on Hossler and Gallagher's theoretical model to understand the decision-making processes surrounding choices to participate or not to participate in higher education (Hossler, Braxton, & Coopersmith, 1989). The statistical modeling of econometric models, used to examine college choice, generally maintains that a person makes a decision about attending college by comparing the benefits with the costs for all possible alternatives and then selecting the alternative with the greatest net benefit, given the individual's personal tastes and preferences (Hossler, Braxton, & Coopersmith, 1989).

Providing an example of an alternative to econometric models, McDonough's (1997) qualitative inquiry used Bourdieu's theoretical concepts of cultural capital and habitus[5] to examine the college choice decision-making processes of high school students, finding that those with cultural capital and a peer group habitus associated with the middle class and college going were more likely to choose to attend four-year institutions. McDonough's study indicates the importance of socioeconomic background in shaping students' college-related decisions. But, how might college choice processes differ for African American students in particular?

College Choice and African American Students

One line of inquiry related to African American students' choice process examines students' aspirations or plans to attend college. For example, Perna (2000), expands on traditional econometric models by including social and cultural capital as proxies to interpret expectations, preferences, tastes, and uncertainty in college choice, finding that when one controls for factors related to college enrollment, African American students are 11% more likely than are Whites to enroll in a four-year college or university (p. 136). This study argues that African American students might actually be *more* likely to desire to attend college than might White students if there were no barriers. Hence, there must be other reasons for the disparities in enrollment between Black and White students. For example, St. John and Noell (1989), using the High School and Beyond dataset to consider some of the variables that influence college choice for minority students, analyze the impact of financial aid on college enrollment, finding that financial aid had a positive impact on enrollment decisions.

In her qualitative studies of African American students' college choice decision-making processes, Freeman (1997, 1999a, 1999b, 2005) provides a useful alternative to the econometric models and an example of innovative ways to better understand minority student issues, using the theoretical concept of channeling to guide data analysis, cutting across financial, social, and cultural capital to predict a student's likelihood of choosing to enroll in postsecondary education. A qualitative project regarding the college-related decision-making processes of African American students in seven cities indicated that decision-making processes for African American students were different from what the predominant college choice models would suggest, indicating that researchers and theorists studying college choice should be more aware of the differences in cultural contexts, especially for minority students (Freeman, 1999a). For example, in one of her recent studies, Freeman (2005) suggested that family is an integral part of the decision-making process for African American students.

While econometric models provide aggregate-level data, outlining the general issues, Freeman's (1997, 1999a, 1999b) qualitative analyses offer insight into what is behind the aggregate-level data, shedding light on the microlevel issues that are often ignored in statistical modeling. This line of research suggests that further qualitative studies are needed to elucidate the unique factors that influence African American students' college-related choice processes. This line of work adds to the college choice literature by providing insight into the motivating factors influencing the choice of African American students to participate in higher education, factors such as economic expectations (Freeman, 1999b); race and culture (Freeman, 1999a); family influences (Freeman, 2005); and economic barriers and psychological barriers (Freeman, 1997).

Many of the aforementioned studies consider the college-related decision-making process *while* students were making their decisions (i.e., during their last year of high school). In this chapter, I provide a unique perspective on college choice because currently enrolled African American women were reflecting back on their decision-making process after some time had passed. Thus, the women had been able to consider the impact of their decision-making process on their college choice and, more generally, on their college experience. The findings provide an alternate perspective on the choice process of African American women.

Academic and Financial Obstacles to College

There are both academic and financial obstacles to college access, particularly for students of color and students from lower socioeconomic backgrounds. Academic preparation, or lack thereof, is often pitted against financial need (Sanoff & Powell, 2003). Using a deficiency model, where individual students are blamed for their lack of academic preparation, many studies focus on the need to be "college qualified," or the link between college-preparatory course work (math, science, and English) and college enrollment (Berkner & Chavez, 1997; Horn & Bobbitt, 2000). The statistical models and findings in these studies often suffer from problems such as sample selection bias (e.g., focusing only on students who took the SAT or ACT exams); omitted variable bias (e.g., excluding financial aid as a variable); endogeneity bias (e.g., ignoring the effects of finances on steps toward enrollment); and collinearity (e.g., family income and parental education are collinear, or often have the same effects) (Heller, 2004).

Taking a different approach to the academic preparation debate, using both statistical and qualitative methods, scholars have found that students face academic barriers for reasons such as lacking high school preparatory programs and classes (McDonough, 1997); tracking into curricula that is not college-preparatory (Blau, 2004); differential cultural capital or rewards of cultural capital (McDonough, 1997; Roscigno & Ainsworth-Darnell, 1999); or unequal educational opportunities in primary and secondary schooling (Allen & Jewell, 1996; Blau, 2004; Fries-Britt & Turner, 2002).

Feagin's (1991) qualitative work, drawing on social psychological traditions, interviewing middle-class Blacks regarding anti-Black discrimination in public places, provides another possibility for the lower academic preparation of some minority students. This work revealed that some participants felt it was more difficult to achieve academically because of the anxiety of discrimination. This type of scholarship points out the complex nature of this process, providing a background for further research on the academic disengagement of minority students (Cureton, 2003; Osyerman et al., 2002) and stereotype threat, leading to lower academic achievement (Steele, 1995, 1997).

Recently, the academic preparation literature has investigated an "academic pipeline" for students (Pathways to College Network, 2003), which allows for a seamless educational experience from primary school through college, called the P-16 model (Longanecker & Blanco, 2003; Pathways to College Network, 2003). Each level of the pipeline feeds into the next level, and, finally, higher education is a vital link that feeds into the economy (American Association of State Colleges and Universities, 2002; Longanecker & Blanco, 2003; Myers, 2003). An important aspect of the academic pipeline debate is the financial aid discussion and the impact of financial need on access to higher education.

In addition to potential academic obstacles to college access, financial capital remains a significant influence on access to higher education for many students. The gap in college participation rates between students in the lowest-income quartile and those in the highest-income quartile is much larger than it was 30 years ago (Heller, 2004), and it continues to widen (Heller, 2003; St. John, 2002). One of the most significant roles of federal and state governments in postsecondary education in the United States is to close that gap by providing funding in the form of grants and loans to students (Gladieux, Hauptman, & Knapp, 1997/1999). The Higher Education Act, which authorized the majority of all postsecondary financial aid available to students in the United States, was significant in that it shifted the recipient of federal funding from institutions primarily to individual students (Gladieux et al., 1997/1999; Hannah, 1996/1997; Keppel, 1987/1997). Since the 1980s, there has been a dramatic shift from federal postsecondary funding via grants to loans (Ficklen & Stone, 2002; Hannah, 1996/1997; Hearn & Holdsworth, 2004).

Coupled with the shift from grants to loans, has been a move away from financially supporting low-income students to supporting middle-income students, often in the form of merit-based aid (Ficklen & Stone, 2002; Heller, 2004; Sanoff & Powell, 2003; St. John, 2002; St. John, Musoba, & Simmons, 2003). The effect of these dramatic shifts at the federal level, from grants to loans, and from supporting low-income students to supporting the middle class, results in an estimated one-half of high school graduates from low- and middle-income backgrounds being unable to attend four-year institutions because of financial barriers (Ficklen & Stone, 2002). Among the many shifts in financial aid, the need for state-funded grants has increased over the past two decades to provide aid to students who would otherwise be left out of higher education (Heller, 2004). State-funded grant programs, focusing on need-based aid, are a vital tool to promote access to and equity in higher education, especially for low-income and minority students. Too little is known about the subjective experiences of students with financial and academic barriers and how finances may influence choice processes. This chapter focuses on both the academic and financial barriers faced by African American women related to their college choice process.

Research Design

The data presented here are part of a larger critical ethnographic study of women's college experiences and identity at a predominantly White, public, research extensive postsecondary institution, called Midwest University. Critical research makes an explicit link between research methodology and social justice—attempting to uncover oppression where it exists and allowing the voices of often-marginalized groups to be heard (Carspecken, 1996). Because of the link to social justice in this research process, the participants played a key role in developing the research questions and in analyzing and interpreting the study findings.

This chapter presents the African American women's responses to the following general questions, which were asked in the first meeting of every focus group: (a) What was the process that you underwent to attend Midwest University (MU)? (b) How did you make your decision to attend MU? (c) What factors did you consider? The women reflected on these questions, which allowed them an opportunity to consider the factors that may have influenced their decisions and how this process affected their subsequent college experiences, if at all.

Participants and Data Collection

The larger study included 42 African American, Latina, multiracial, and White women, and data were collected over a 9-month period. Appendix A includes the demographics of all of the participants in the larger study. For purposes of this discussion, I am primarily focusing on the 28 women who self-identified as Black (African American, Black, Black Latina, or multiracial with Black as one identity) in the study, most of whom were first-generation college students; that is, their parents were not college educated (23 women). Using purposive sampling (Creswell, 1998), I selected African American women (ages 18–22) from 4 groups on campus (an early–intervention, need-based aid program; a merit-based aid program; a peer-mentoring program; and a living-learning community in the residence halls).

In the full study, I conducted individual interviews, focus groups, and observations. This chapter focuses on data from the eight focus groups. I separated the women into groups of three to five that met regularly (biweekly or monthly) for a period nine months. Each group determined the size of its membership, the location where it met, and the number of times it met. These focus groups were a good technique for gathering data related to racial issues because the group process evoked a feeling of support, which allows for observation of social processes and collective discourses (Morgan, 1997).

Data Analysis and Validation Techniques

Focus groups were audiotaped and transcribed verbatim, using pseudonyms the participants chose to protect confidentiality. Following each session, I wrote field notes, which enabled me to check my own biases and served as a preliminary compilation of trends in the data collection process. I used the field notes to check my interpretation.

I coded data from the focus groups using a combination of themes and subthemes (Carspecken, 1996). Before the coding process, I used a variety of analysis techniques to delve deeper into the meaning in the women's statements. For example, I used meaning field analysis, developed by Carspecken to determine the range of possible meanings for each statement. Then, I used a technique, called reconstructive horizon analysis (Carspecken, 1996), to elucidate the objective, subjective, normative, and identity claims that were both explicit and implicit in the statements.[6] These techniques deepened the meaning of the codes and served as a validation technique to ensure rigor in the analysis process. After meaning field and reconstructive analysis, I used low-level codes to identify explicit categories for the data (e.g., students' experiences, financial aid, college choice decisions, etc.). Then, I coded the data using high-level codes, which identify implicit meaning within the data such as the women's perceptions or experiences with a particular situation. I placed the codes into a master code list, and then I was able to combine the codes into themes and subthemes.

I used a variety of validation techniques to ensure that the data analysis was trustworthy (Carspecken, 1996): peer debriefing (African American colleagues reviewed the analysis); member checks (participants reviewed the analyses and the transcripts); and assessing my own biases and value orientations.

Limitations

The data presented here are primarily representative of only first-generation African American women, many of whom were from lower socioeconomic backgrounds (23 women). Thus, these findings may or may not relate to African American students in general or to Black women from middle or upper-middle socioeconomic backgrounds. The fact that many of the women came from lower socioeconomic backgrounds, primarily from neighborhoods that were often plagued with violence, might have influenced the extreme nature of the findings (e.g., the life or death terms that emerged here). However, even if these life or death terms were not consistent with the larger African American female population, the fact that women saw their college choice as such a monumental decision is noteworthy and merits further consideration.

As is primarily the case with qualitative research, these data cannot necessarily be generalized to larger populations. However, the findings indicate that the college choice processes of African American students, particularly those from lower socioeconomic backgrounds, may be quite different from those from other racial and socioeconomic groups. More research is needed to ascertain between-group and within-group differences in college choice decision-making processes.

Findings: Choosing College as a Life or Death Decision

As the women reflected on their college-related decisions, the process of choosing to attend college was framed in the dramatic terms of life or death. Their reflections emerged in the data as a duality of choosing college (life) versus not choosing college (death). By life or death, I mean both the literal notion of living or dying and the metaphorical idea of giving life or death to one's aspiration of getting a college degree. Here, I present the following themes related to this life or death notion of college choice: (a) Fulfilling a Promise to Attend College; (b) Attending College as Avoiding Death; and (c) Financial and Academic Barriers to College. Related to the Hossler and Gallagher (1987) model of college choice, these findings would be placed in the predisposition phase where a student decides whether to attend college.

Fulfilling a Promise to Attend College

This theme refers to the way in which the women described their college choice process as fulfilling a promise made to a loved one. That is, some of the women made the decision to attend college as part of a promise to someone whom they loved (e.g., a dying friend, mother, etc.), as a way of carrying on that person's legacy.

The decisions of many of the first-generation Black women, especially those from large urban areas, to attend college were affected heavily by the death of a loved one and promises made before these deaths. Michelle, a senior health and recreation major from a metropolitan area, confided a heart-wrenching story about making a promise to attend college to her best friend when she was seven. For her, this promise was literally made because of a death, because her friend was killed. However, attending college was her "way out" or the way to avoid danger because she grew up in fear of being killed in her neighborhood, or of getting in trouble (which is a metaphorical death) if she stayed in the city where she grew up:

> When I was seven, my best friend died. So I promised her that I would go to school. That is really why I decided to go to school [begins to cry].
>
> [Through tears]. It just . . . it was hard. When my best friend died it was just really, really hard because when I saw her in the casket, I was like, "I gotta go, I can't stay here." So, it was hard, but after that. . . . Like, one of the people I grew up with murdered somebody and he was in jail. And then, like, my cousins started packing. And it was rough, so they didn't think that I was going to make it. So . . . that was weird.

Michelle often referred to the lasting impression her friend's death had on her life at such a young age. Her choice to attend college was a long-term way of honoring the last wishes of her childhood friend. In addition, this transformative, personally challenging event made salient to her the desire to "get out" of her neighborhood.

Claudia, a senior psychology major from an urban area, also made the decision to attend college as a way to honor the last wishes of a loved one, her mother. She recalls, "Like, my mother before she died, she wanted me to keep going in school. She wanted me to stay in school. I knew she only finished high school, so she wanted me to go to school . . . to college. So, it was probably because of that I decided to go." Claudia was quite young when her mother died, but the promise made before her mother's death stayed with her through college as a challenge to keep going: "I was three years old when my mother died, so she was, like. . . . Everybody always said that, like, 'You have got to finish because your mom wanted you to go.'" Similar to Michelle, Claudia considered her decision to attend college as a way to honor a loved one's last wishes. This became a motivating factor for her because she wanted to honor her mother's memory. This desire to extend the legacy of her mother was integral to her choice to attend college and to her desire and motivation to persist through her degree.

While some women, like Claudia and Michelle, made their college-going decisions as a direct result of the last wishes of a loved one, others described the college decision-making process as a literal fight between life or death, illustrating the extreme gravity of such decisions in the lives of these women. Next, I describe this process of deciding to go to college to remain safe.

Attending College as Avoiding Death

For some women, attending college was literally enabling them to avoid danger. This theme refers to all comments regarding one's decision to attend college as a decision to remain safe and as overcoming obstacles. Many of the first-generation African American women in this study grew up in urban settings where basic safety was a privilege. For example, Michelle described her childhood as just "trying to stay alive." She remembered having to fight constantly to keep the hope of going to college alive as she learned early on that she was unsafe and her college dream was unsupported in her neighborhood:

> I was, like, "I'm going to college." And they was [*sic*], like, "No, you're not." Because not only was [*sic*] people around me getting in trouble, but I could have gotten in trouble when I was younger because it was the way of survival. Because I used to walk because we never had a car. So I had to walk to work, you know, walk home or take the bus. So, you know, my mom, the first thing she gave me was a wrench [laughs sarcastically] with tape around it, so I could take it with me so I could protect myself. She was, like, "You hit, you run, you scream," and this and this and this. So that is what I learned and that was the mentality that I had of who I am, and it was hard. I guess that is why I wanted to go to school. Because it was really hard for me to get over that. That obstacle of that everybody is about to come out and get you [sniffs]. So, that is why . . . it is just so weird.

For Michelle, the dream of going to college actually may have kept her out of trouble in the neighborhood where she grew up. Attending college provided a path to safety. In Michelle's case, being in college literally gave her a second chance to stay alive:

Going to college . . . that was the mentality. Like, people in my school would get expelled and have to go to juvenile for, like, five days and have to pay a fee at the end. And most people's parents couldn't afford this fee. So, it was tough. I really didn't think I was going to live until I was 18. I was really, really excited for my birthday. I was celebrating for a whole week [laughs]. The whole week is my birthday week! So, it was tough but . . .

Michelle underscores the life and death decision about going to college as she describes simply remaining alive as a privilege. She wanted to leave the challenges of her neighborhood so she could begin a new life, and she saw college as the way out. Thus, attending college became linked to Michelle's very existence, making this choice extremely significant to her life. Another woman, Isis, a senior nonprofit management major who also grew up in an urban area, described being shot twice before the age of 14. She explained how this process changed her by providing the impetus for her desire to attend college. The focus group also began to reflect on this experience, considering the way it might have motivated Isis to attend college. Isis confided to the group:

I got shot when I was in sixth grade. I was 12 years old. I was makin' straight As, honor roll, blah blah blah, and it was, like, why did I get shot? Mindin' my own business, walkin' down the street, I was just outside, playin' with kids, it was, like, me and my friend were playin'. . . . So, then I got shot again when I was 14. So, it was, like . . . what's goin' on?

Michelle responded to Isis's story in a supportive way, asking her, "If you wouldn't have got shot, would you have stayed in? Would you still be in school?" Isis shook her head Michelle continued, "You know what I'm sayin'? Like, my friend being shot was the reason I went to school. So you could think of it as me being shot was a push for me to go to school." Isis nodded again and reflected, "I know that . . . like the one time when I was 12, I thought, I better live my life. You know what I'm sayin'? After that, I was, like . . . I better live my life." Isis continued:

I really believe that. That's somethin' that really drives [emphasis] me. I'm here [emphasis]. That's just somethin' that . . . at that time, that's what I thought. I think about it like this, I thought about it and thought somethin' is not right. I was thinkin' there's gonna be a third time, you know, three strikes I'm out blah blah blah. Because if you are young like that and something like that happen to you. You are just like, what is wrong?

Isis indicated that being shot was something that "drives her," providing her the motivation or the personal challenge to attend college initially, in addition to providing the impetus to remain in there.

Renee, a senior art major, concluded, demonstrating the caring and support that occurred within the focus groups and the long journey Isis and many others made to attend college: "You have come a long way." Renee's comment was a common occurrence among the focus groups with first-generation African American women. They often encouraged one another, finding support in one another and attempting to make sense of negative experiences. In addition, the women encouraged one another to feel a sense of pride at overcoming such tremendous obstacles.

While the decision to attend college was couched in terms of life or death, underscoring the gravity of this decision, especially for first-generation African American women from urban areas, there were often huge academic and financial barriers, making college access difficult. The following section examines some of these challenges.

Financial and Academic Barriers to College

The theme of financial and academic barriers to college teases out the perceptions of the first-generation Black women in the study regarding the accessibility of college, both financially and in terms of their academic preparation. Finances and academic preparation, or lack thereof, created a metaphorical choice between life or death.

The women in this study had varied academic preparation discrepancies and challenges. The vast differences in academic preparation were primarily class-based, that is, first-generation college students often attended high schools that offered fewer college preparatory courses and less college-related counseling than did women whose parents were college educated or who were from higher socioeconomic backgrounds. To overcome these academic challenges, federally funded early-intervention programs such as Upward Bound and Talent Search, along with statewide early-intervention programs, were vital in providing first-generation women the financial and academic support to gain access to college. For example, some programs brought the women to campuses to take classes and acclimate to their surroundings before enrolling. Also, the programs often provided information on how to apply for financial aid or for admission. Without exception, all of the first-generation women in this study attributed their financial and/or academic ability to attend college to the support these programs offered.

Krystal, a first-year sports marketing major from a mid-size, predominantly White town, concluded that the federally funded Talent Search program served the role of her high school counselor because her high school counselor did not take an interest in her. She noted, "[My counselor] didn't really help us." When asked direct questions about her high school counselor, Krystal said that she had little contact with her counselor because the counselor "knew that Mr. Thomas would take care of us." Mr. Thomas was the director of the Talent Search program, and Krystal maintained contact with him well into her first year of college. Mercedes, who went to high school with Krystal, agreed that Mr. Thomas was the primary reason she decided to attend college as well.

Other programs, like the federally funded Upward Bound, were often cited as primary gateways to college during this study. Ryan, a sophomore biochemistry major, recalled that her Upward Bound experience, which brought her to campus in the summers during high school to take classes, was the key reason she attended college. Upward Bound was a supplementary support for the lack of academic preparation that Ryan received in high school. She noted:

> Over the summer we'd have to stay at the university and actually live on campus and take, like, high school prep classes so, like, my algebra class, I was going to take it my freshman year. I took algebra in the summer through Upward Bound, so I basically knew half the stuff before I got there.

The Upward Bound program mitigated the academic barriers that Ryan and many of the other first-generation women faced. Simply stated, without this program and other early-intervention support programs of its kind, the majority of the women in this study would not have been able to attend college, because of poor academic preparation in high school, including poor college counseling, or financial constraints.

The State College Promise Program, which provided vital financial and academic support for many of the women in this study, promised full tuition remission, along with academic support services to students as early as the fifth grade. For their part, the students had to sign a pledge to finish high school, apply for college admission, apply for federal financial aid, and stay off drugs and out of jail. Tina, a senior psychology major who grew up in a predominantly White mid-size town, noted that this program was "*the* most important part of my decision to attend college." Many of the women echoed these sentiments, indicating that the financial assistance, along with the emotional and academic support of this program, was integral to their ability to attend college.

Yet, finances often determined the types of institutions to which the women even applied. Many of the women initially voiced a desire to attend a historically Black college or university (HBCU). However, for many of these first-generation Black women, HBCUs were often perceived as too costly. For example, Mercedes, a first-year undecided major from a mid-size, predominantly White city had wanted to attend an elite HBCU and found that it was "too expensive." She explained, "I wanted to attend Spelman. But, I just couldn't afford it. But, Spelman . . . oooweee, it would have been nice." Many of the first-generation Black women in the study shared this notion that HBCUs were too expensive.

Black women whose parents were college educated described a different college choice process, where financial and academic constraints often were not barriers to, or even issues in, their decision-making processes. Additionally, their process was more detailed as they noted having a lot of information, from both their parents and their high school counselors, about which schools were accessible to and appropriate for them. Many of these women also remembered having had beneficial academic support in the way of college preparatory course work in high school. Financial challenges were generally not as big an issue for students whose parents were college educated. Renee, a multiracial woman who self-identified as Black, had parents who were both college educated. She did not consider Midwest University her first choice. Unlike most first-generation participants, she always knew that she would attend college, so she was placed in college-preparatory course work and extracurricular experiences:

> I didn't come in [with] The Summer Bridge Program. I actually transferred here my sophomore year. I grew up planning to go to Notre Dame because that's where my dad went. So, the family goal was to go Ivy League. So I was, like, the president of everything in high school and the captain of everything. And I was salutatorian, and then I got all kinds of different scholarships to places. But my dad had gone to Notre Dame and I didn't want to be in debt, so, like, I got state scholarships to cover everything and then I qualified for work/study but I wasn't into that. So I was looking at fashion design and most of the schools I was looking into had crappy fashion design programs. Then I came here for art history, because of the program here. And because of the study abroad program here, too, because I took Spanish so I just came here.

Ever since elementary school, I have been in programs where you are, like, getting ready for interviews and all that stuff. And it is, like, choosing your major early, like, already early on, you decide what you are going to major in. So, it was never, like, college or no college. It was, like, what are you going to *study* when you are in college.

Renee takes care to differentiate herself from first-generation students who came to Midwest University with The Summer Bridge Program, a federally funded, early-intervention program. This could indicate that a sort of stigma is associated with some early-intervention programs. Her choice was different in that she "always knew" she would attend college. Thus, her decision was more about which college to attend, rather than whether to attend college at all. Additionally, she applied to more schools and seemed to have more information about college available to her. Finances also were not a significant barrier or challenge for her. When she described her decision, she did not mention finances at all.

Leila, a sophomore business major whose parents are also college educated and who grew up in a predominantly White neighborhood in an urban area, had a similar experience to Renee. She always knew that she would attend college:

In my house, it would be unheard of [emphasis on "heard"] if I didn't go to college. It'd be, like, you are not going WHERE? It would be, like, normal . . . it would be, like, of course you are going to college. It was normal, I mean, of *course* [emphasis added], you are going to college. I mean, there was no talk about it. I just have to go to college. So, that was basically what it was.

Not unlike Renee, the college choice process for Leila was primarily about *which* institution to attend, rather than *whether* she would attend. Again, finances and academic preparation were not significant barriers for her. Leila was tracked into a math and science curriculum in high school; she noted that nearly all of the students in this track attended college. What is more, this track helped her to take some college course work before actually enrolling in college:

Most of them went on to college . . . from math and science. But the rest of the school . . . like, the people that were not in any magnet programs . . . more than likely, they didn't go to college. But, those in the math and science, health professions program. . . . There was, like, one entrepreneurial program or something like that. They definitely had, like, the best chance [stutters] of going to college . . . you know what I mean . . . afterwards. The health professions . . . I had a lot of friends who were in that also . . . a lot of them went to college also. But, some of them just didn't go for some reason or another. But, for the most part, basically those in math and science were the ones who usually went to college.

And my last two years [in high school] through the math and science program, I took [college] classes. And that was Chemistry 1 and 2, with the lab and stuff and Calculus 1. Then, like, from there . . . I mean, like, normally I registered through math and science. I went on my own and I took other [college] classes. Stuff like sociology, psychology, and some other . . . accounting, stuff like that. So, I finished basically started college with 34 credit hours. It was kind of a lot.

Leila was prepared academically for college; in fact, she was able to transfer in almost two semesters' worth of credits when she began her degree. Finances were less of a barrier for Leila, whose parents were college educated, than they were for many of the first-generation students. When Leila discussed the role finances played in her college choice decision, she related, "Like, if I didn't have a scholarship, my parents would find a way." Again, her college choice was more about *which* institution to attend rather than *whether* she would get to go to college.

For those women who began college with significant financial and/or academic challenges, these barriers often did not disappear during college. During one focus group session, some of the women contemplated leaving college to pay off their debts. Many of the women worked two or three part-time jobs while in college, leaving them little time to study.

Discussion and Implications

The first-generation African American women's reflections on their college choice decision-making process highlight the academic, financial, and social backgrounds from which participants came. These backgrounds paved the road for decisions to attend college, acting as supportive influences, and/or they provided significant challenges that the women had to overcome before they arrived on campus. In part, the disparities in the women's backgrounds could relate to the cultural capital literature, which suggests that one's socio-economic background and subsequent social networks and tastes influence one's college choice decisions (Nora, 2004). Certainly, many of the women in this study experienced such dramatic situations in their neighborhoods growing up, due in large part to urban poverty, that their college decision-making process was quite different from that of students growing up in other settings.

The data presented here demonstrate the intersection of race and socioeconomic status. The first-generation African American women's experiences were so extreme, in part, because they were from lower socioeconomic backgrounds and from neighborhoods where most of the people were from lower socioeconomic backgrounds as well. Sociologists, like Thomas Shapiro in his book, *The Hidden Cost of Being African American: How Wealth Perpetuates Inequality* (2004), have recently started to consider the intersections with race and class and the way disadvantages can be cumulative for African Americans. More research is needed to understand how these cumulative disadvantages affect African American students' access to higher education.

The findings presented here provide evidence consistent with the access literature (Ficklen & Stone, 2002; Myers, 2003; St. John et al., 2004), indicating that first-generation African American women face significant social, academic, and financial barriers to higher education. According to this study, early-intervention programs greatly affected these academic, social, and financial barriers, providing the women much-needed support for college access. Scholars have attempted to provide evidence of the positive benefits of these early-intervention programs (Musoba, 2004; St. John et al., 2003; Tierney & Jun, 2001). However, data in this chapter reveal individual experiences with these programs, indicating that these programs were integral to providing access for first-generation African American women. More qualitative work is needed to provide voices on and anecdotes of the importance of early-intervention programs.

Adding to the college choice literature, the college-related decisions of the first-generation African American women in this study were framed in life or death terms, indicating that college can have a monumental effect on the lives of these women. Considering the first, predisposition phase of the Hossler and Gallagher (1987) model of college choice, these data show that greater consideration of the nuances of students' backgrounds is needed. That is, as a Black woman student determines whether to attend college in this first phase, she is greatly influenced by personal challenges, those in her neighborhood, her socioeconomic background (influencing those with whom she comes into contact), and her family. The college choice decision-making process may not be linear or even entirely rational for all students. In particular, the decision whether to attend college, often called the "predisposition phase" of college choice (Hossler & Gallagher, 1987), may be determined by influential moments or events in students' lives. For example, the women in this study indicated that they often made their decision to attend college in moments of high stress, loss, or emotional turmoil—often making the decision to attend college almost a life or death decision.

Conclusion

More work is needed to better understand why higher education may have an extraordinary impact on first-generation African American women. These findings underscore the necessity of early-intervention programs to provide the academic and social support necessary for underrepresented populations. If the goal is to increase access for African American students, one must take into account the unique factors of many of their experiences. For some students, such as many of the women in this study, access is not just about upward social mobility—it is a matter of life and death.

Notes

1. By first-generation, I mean that the students' parents are not college educated. Thus, they are the first in their families to attend college.

2. Throughout this paper, I refer to women as both African American and Black. I use these terms to refer to women who have African, Caribbean, or Hispanic (self-identifying Black as one of their identities) heritage. The women involved in this study used both terms, and there was some disagreement about them. Because the participants did not reach consensus on these terms, I have chosen to use both terms to represent the sentiments of both sides of this issue.

3. Social capital can be defined as a system of social networks.

4. Cultural capital refers to a set of tastes, derived from one's social class, that provide advantages in social institutions (McDonough, 1997; Bourdieu, 1984). It is a property often transmitted by upper- and middle-class families to their children, and it substitutes for economic capital as a means of maintaining class status and privilege (McDonough, 1997).

5. Habitus is a common set of subjective perceptions held by all members of a group or class that shapes attitudes, expectations, and aspirations (McDonough, 1997; Bourdieu, 1984).

6. Subjective or first person claims refer to a person's experiences, thoughts, or opinions. Objective or third person claims relate to multiple access, meaning that many people have access to the same observable characteristics. Normative claims are linked to ethical or moral norms in the socially constructed world.

References

Allen, W., & Jewell, J. O. (1996). The miseducation of Black America: Black education since "An American Dilemma." In O. Clayton Jr. (Ed.), *An America dilemma revisited: Race relations in a changing world.* New York: Russell Sage Foundation, 169–190.

American Association of State Colleges and Universities. (2002). *Filling the pipeline: A look at enrollment and employment trends in public higher education. Special report.* Washington, DC: American Association of State College and Universities.

Berkner, L., & Chavez, L. (1997). Access to postsecondary education for 1992 high school graduates. *National Center for Education Statistics Statistical Analysis Report, 98–105.* Washington, DC: U.S. Department of Education, Office of Educational Research and Improvement.

Blau, J. (2004). *Race in the school: Perpetuating White dominance?* Boulder, CO: Lynne Rienner Publishers.

Bourdieu, P. (1984). *Distinction: A social critique of the judgment of taste.* (R. Nice, Trans.). Cambridge, MA: Harvard University Press.

Carnoy, M. (1995). *Faded dreams: The politics and economics of race in America.* New York: Cambridge University Press.

Carspecken, P. F. (1996). *Critical ethnography in educational research: A theoretical and practical guide.* New York: Routledge.

Creswell, J. W. (1998). *Qualitative inquiry and research design: Choosing among the five traditions.* Thousand Oaks: Sage Publications.

Cureton, S. R. (2003). Race-specific college student experiences on a predominantly White campus. *Journal of Black Studies, 33(3),* 295–311.

Feagin, J. R. (1991). The continuing significance of race: Antiblack discrimination in public places. *American Sociological Review, 56(1),* 101–116.

Feagin, J. R., Vera, H., & Imani, N. (1998). *The agony of education: Black students at White college and universities.* New York: Routledge.

Ficklen, E. & Stone, J. E. (Eds.). (2002). *Empty promises: The myth of college access in America. A report of the Advisory Committee on Student Financial Assistance.* Washington, DC: Advisory Committee on Student Financial Assistance.

Freeman, K. (1997). Increasing African Americans' participation in higher education: African American high-school students' perspectives. *The Journal of Higher Education, 68(5),* 523–551.

Freeman, K. (1999a). The race factor in African Americans' college choice. *Urban Education, 34(1),* 4–25.

Freeman, K. (1999b). Will higher education make a difference–African Americans' economic expectations and college choice. *College and University Journal, 75(2),* 7–12.

Freeman, K. (2005). *African Americans and college choice: The influence of family and school.* Albany, NY: SUNY Press.

Freeman, K., & Thomas, G. E. (2002). Black college and college choice: Characteristics of students who choose HBCUs. *The Review of Higher Education, 25(3),* 349–358.

Fries-Britt, S. L., & Turner, B. (2002). Uneven stories: Successful Black collegians at a Black and a White campus. *The Review of Higher Education, 25(3),* 315–330.

Gladieux, L. E., Hauptman, A. M., & Knapp, G. L. (1997/1999). The federal government and higher education. In L. F. Goodchild, C. D. Lovell, E. R. Hines, & J. I. Gill (Eds.), *Public policy and higher education: ASHE Reader Series* (pp. 103–124). Needham Heights, MA: Simon & Schuster.

Hannah, S. B. (1996/1997). The Higher Education Act of 1992: Skills, constraints, and the politics of higher education. In L. F. Goodchild, C. D. Lovell, E. R. Hines, & J. I. Gill (Eds.), *Public policy and higher education: ASHE reader series* (pp. 84–102). Needham Heights, MA: Simon & Schuster.

Hearn, J. C., & Holdsworth, J. M. (2004). Federal student aid: The shift from grants to loans. In E. P. St. John (Ed.), *Readings on Equal Education, 19, Public policy and college access: Investigating the federal and state roles in equalizing postsecondary opportunity* (pp. 40–59). New York: AMS Press.

Heller, D. E. (2003). *State financial aid and college access: Research report.* Report from the National Dialogue on Student Financial Aid and the Pathways to College Network, RR-4("&"). New York: College Entrance Examination Board.

Heller, D. E. (2004). State merit scholarship programs. In E. P. St. John (Ed.), *Readings on Equal Education, 19, Public policy and college access: Investigating the federal and state roles in equalizing postsecondary opportunity* (pp. 99–108). New York: AMS Press.

Horn, L., & Bobbitt, L. (2000). Mapping the road to college: First-generation students' math track, planning strategies, and context for support. *National Center for Education Statistics Statistical Analysis Report, 2000–153.* Washington, DC: U.S. Department of Education, Office of Educational Research and Improvement.

Hossler, D., Braxton, J., & Coopersmith, G. (1989). Understanding student college choice. In John C. Smart (Ed.), *Higher education: Handbook of theory and research* (Vol. 5, pp. 231–288). New York: Agathon Press.

Hossler, D., & Gallagher, K. S. (1987). Study student college choice: A three-phase model and the implications for policymakers. *College and University, 2,* 207–221.

Keppel, F. (1987/1997). The Higher Education Acts contrasted, 1965–1986: Has federal policy come of age? In L. F. Goodchild, C. D. Lovell, E. R. Hines, & J. I. Gill (Eds.), *Public policy and higher education: ASHE Reader Series* (pp. 189–205). Needham Heights, MA: Simon & Schuster.

Longanecker, D. A., & Blanco, C. D. (2003). Student financial assistance. In *Student success: Statewide P-16 systems.* Denver, CO: SHEEO.

McDonough, P. M. (1997). *Choosing colleges: How social class and schools structure opportunity.* Albany, NY: State University of New York Press.

Morgan, D. L. 1997. *Focus groups as qualitative research.* Thousand Oaks, CA: Sage.

Musoba, G. D. (2004). Postsecondary encouragement for diverse students: A reexamination of the twenty-first century scholars program. In E. P. St. John (Ed.) *Public policy and college access: Investigating the federal and state roles in equalizing post secondary opportunity,* (vol. 19, pp. 181–196). New york: AMS

Myers, R. D. (2003). *College success programs: Executive summary.* Washington, DC: Pathways to College Network Clearinghouse.

Nora, A. (2004). The role of habitus and cultural capital in choosing a college, transitioning from high school to higher education, and persisting in college among minority and nonminority students. *Journal of Hispanic Higher Education, 3*(2), 180–208.

Osyerman, D., Coon, H. M., & Kemmelmeier, M. (2002). Rethinking individualism and collectivism: Evaluation of theoretical assumptions and meta-analyses. *Psychological Bulletin, 28*(1), 3–72.

Pathways to College Network. (2003, August). *A shared agenda: A leadership challenge to improve college access and success.* Washington, DC: Author.

Perna, L. W. (2000). Differences in the decision to attend college among African Americans, Hispanics, and Whites. *The Journal of Higher Education, 71*(2), 117–141.

Roscigno, V. J., & Ainsworth-Darnell, J. W. (1999). Race, cultural capital, and educational resources: Persistent inequalities and achievement returns. *Sociology of Education, 72,* 158–178.

Sanoff, A. P., & Powell, D. S. (2003, Summer). *Restricted access: The doors to higher education remain closed to many deserving students.* Lumina Foundation Focus, Indianapolis, IN: Lumina Foundation for Education.

Shapiro, T. M. (2004). *The hidden cost of being African American: How wealth perpetuates inequality.* Oxford University Press.

St. John, E. P. (2002). *The access challenge: Rethinking the causes of the new inequality. Policy issue report.* Indiana Education Policy Center: Policy Issue Report R-2002–01("&"). Bloomington, IN: Education Policy Center.

St. John, E. P., Chung, C. G., Musoba, G. D., & Simmons, A. B. (2004). Financial access: The impact of state finance strategies. In E. P. St. John, *Readings on Equal Education, 19, Public policy and college access: Investigating the federal and state roles in equalizing postsecondary opportunity* (pp. 109–129). New York: AMS Press.

St. John, E. P., Musoba, G. D., & Simmons, A. B. (2003). Keeping the promise: The impact of Indiana's Twenty-first Century Scholars Program. *The Review of Higher Education, 27*(1), 103–123.

St. John, E. P., & Noell, J. (1989). The effects of student financial aid on access to higher education: An analysis of progress with special consideration of minority enrollment. *Research in Higher Education, 30*(6), 563–581.

Steele, C. M. (1995). Stereotype threat and the intellectual test performance of African Americans. *Journal of Personality and Social Psychology, 69*(5), 797–811.

Steele, C. M. (1997). A threat in the air: How stereotypes shape intellectual identity and performance. *American Psychologist, 52,* 613–629.

Tierney, W. G., & Jun, A. (2001). A university helps prepare low-income youths for college: Tracking school success. *Journal of Higher Education, 72*(2), 205–225.

APPENDIX A
Demographics of Participants in the Full Ethnographic Study

	NUMBER OF PARTICIPANTS
RACE/ETHNICITY	
African American	25
Latina	4
Multiracial	2
White	11
YEAR IN COLLEGE	
First-year	8
Sophomore	10
Junior	11
Senior	12
First-Year Graduate	1
MAJOR BY COLLEGE	
Arts and Sciences	18
Education	7
University Division/Undecided	5
Journalism	1
Business and Marketing	7
Health and Recreation	3
Public Policy/Environmental Affairs	1
FIRST-GENERATION STUDENT	
Students who were first generation	30
Students whose parents had college degrees	12

3

BUOYANT BELIEVERS

Resilience, Self-Efficacy, and Academic Success
of Low-Income African American Collegians

Terrell L. Strayhorn

When you starts measuring somebody, measure him right, child. . . . Make sure you done
take into account what hills and valleys he come
through before he got wherever he is.

—Lorraine Hansberry, *A Raisin in the Sun*, 1959

Abstract: In this chapter, the author presents findings from a multivariate analysis of survey data to describe the relationship among resilience, academic self-efficacy, and academic success among a sample of low-income African American collegians attending a predominantly White institution (PWI). Implications for future research and theory are delineated at the end of the chapter, including a set of evidence-based recommendations for educational practice.

Lorraine Hansberry's 1959 screenplay, *A Raisin in the Sun*, was the first drama written by a Black woman to be produced on Broadway, also with a Black director (Lloyd Reynolds) (Domina & Hansberry, 1998). Inspired by Langston Hughes's (1959) poetic observation ("What happens to a dream deferred? Does it dry up like a raisin in the sun?") (p. 268), the play details the realities of a poor, Black family, the Youngers, as each member struggles to "make it" in the face of difficult, uncertain, and often daunting obstacles. The quotation at the beginning of this chapter is from one of the most intense scenes in the play when Walter Lee Younger (Sidney Poitier) storms out of the room frustrated, on the one hand, by his *dream* of making life better for his poor family in Chicago and, on the other, by the *real* economic disparities that seemingly cripple Black life in America. When his sister is ready to give up on him, claiming, "There's nothing left to love," Mama Younger stares her in the eye and scolds her for "measuring somebody" without taking into account "what hills and valleys he come through before he got wherever he is."

A friend reminded me of this passage just before I started work on this chapter. After several weeks of thinking about how I might open this discussion, I settled on Hansberry's words as they point to the very essence of *resilience*, which is the focus of my analysis. Essentially, Mama Younger reminds us that the "measure of a man" is not only where he ends up, but also what it took to get him there; it's important to note that the same is true for women. That is, for some individuals, and poor families like the Youngers, success is determined by one's ability to *persist* in the face of adversity and to believe amid uncertain circumstances. Under such conditions, one must be a *buoyant believer* with enough resilience to "bounce back" from hardships and must have a reasonable portion of self-efficacy to believe in one's own ability.

Thus, resilience and self-efficacy seemed useful for my work as these theoretical perspectives provide a lens for understanding more clearly how the ability to "bounce back" from hardships and a belief in one's own abilities affect the academic success of low-income African American students, many of whom hail from poor, inner-city, or rural neighborhoods where, according to research (Carter, 2005; MacLeod, 1995), academic success is much more the exception than the rule.

Purpose

The purpose of the study that informs this chapter was to measure the relationship among resilience, academic self-efficacy, and academic success using a sample of low-income African American collegians attending a PWI. Specifically, two questions guided the study: (a) What is the magnitude and direction of relationships among resilience, academic self-efficacy, and academic success? (b) What is the relationship among resilience, academic self-efficacy, and academic achievement, controlling for differences in precollege academic ability? For the purposes of this chapter, I define academic success using three outcome variables: first-year grade point average (GPA), intention to stay in (versus "leaving") college, and sense of belonging, which

reflects the social support that students perceive on campus and the extent
to which they feel that they "matter" (Hurtado & Carter, 1997; Jacoby &
Garland, 2004–2005; Rosenberg & McCullough, 1981).

Significance of the Topic

The focus of this chapter is significant for at least four reasons. First, to date,
much of the research on resiliency has focused on links between resilience
and maladaptive behaviors, such as substance abuse, sexual abuse, and pre-
mature adolescent pregnancy (Day & Livingstone, 2003; Himelein, 1995;
Himelein & McElrath, 1996; Hyman & Williams, 2001; Scott-Jones, 1984;
Valentine & Feinauer, 1993) or experiences with trauma (Banyard & Cantor,
2004). Little research has examined resiliency in terms of academic achievement among economically disadvantaged ethnic minorities. Thus, this chapter extends the existing literature by focusing simultaneously on the
academic success of college students, academic self-efficacy, and resiliency.

Second, by directing attention to affective variables such as resiliency
and self-efficacy, I approach the question of race and economically based
differences in achievement from a vantage point that is atypical of research
in this area. That is, two of the most common explanations for leveled
achievement among historically underrepresented and economically disadvantaged students is (a) lack of educational aspirations (Carter, 2001) and
(b) the amount of social and cultural capital students bring to college. However, Lee, Winfield, and Wilson (1991) argue that this "cultural deficit"
model . . . is of very limited utility" (p. 66). Others have shown that "poverty
and family structure among racial-ethnics continue to be created more by
economic conditions external to the family than by race-specific cultural
patterns" (Zinn, 1987, p. 3). My focus on resiliency and self-efficacy responds
to such concerns by examining social-psychological determinants of academic achievement, over which individuals and policymakers, respectively,
have some degree of internal and programmatic control.

Third, focusing on the social-psychological determinants of students'
success may provide clues to effective strategies and promising practices that
college educators can leverage to improve academic achievement among
racially diverse, economically disadvantaged students who represent one of
America's "untapped" resources (Kahlenberg, 2004). Indeed, this approach
places the responsibility for student success on individual students' efforts as
well as on college student educators. All too often analysts focus exclusively
on students, families, and neighborhood characteristics, which, in effect,

exonerates colleges and universities of any duty to help students achieve. I did not write this chapter to shift blame but rather to offer suggestions for nurturing resilience and self-efficacy among students who, according to research (Hare, 1988; Horn, 1997; Schreiner, 1991), are considered at risk for failure in college.

Last, in recent years, scholars have called for more research that goes beyond explaining academic success from "demographic and academic variables" (Pritchard & Wilson, 2003, p. 18). While such variables are important to our understanding of student achievement, they offer little insight into how student achievement can be manipulated or changed through policy or practice. By focusing on resilience and self-efficacy, this chapter provides information that can be used to fashion interventions that effectively alter student achievement and facilitate resiliency among low-income ethnic minorities.

Theoretical Framework

Before I could conduct a study on resiliency and self-efficacy, I found it necessary to identify scholarly sources that describe each of these constructs and explain their relation to other educational outcomes. Thus, I adopted a social-psychological theoretical framework in this chapter consisting of both self-efficacy and resiliency. As Kerlinger (1986) explains, "[T]heory is a set of interrelated constructs, definitions, and propositions that presents a systematic view of phenomena by specifying relations among variables, with the purpose of explaining and predicting phenomena" (p. 9).

Resiliency

Resiliency refers to "success in school [settings] despite personal vulnerabilities, adversities brought about by early and ongoing environmental conditions and experiences" (Wang & Gordon, 1994, p. 38) or to academic achievement when achievement is rare for those facing similar conditions (Gayles, 2005). While a number of scholars describe individuals who persist in the face of obstacles as *resilient*, some use the term *resiliency* to imply an ability to "bounce back" successfully from hardship or failure (e.g., Cappella & Weinstein, 2001; McDermott, 1987). For instance, Scott-Jones (1984) conducted a critical review of the literature and found that social support from family, community members, and school officials is critical to the academic success of young adolescent parents who are prone to drop out of school.

To persist in the face of threatening and often uncertain conditions, research has shown that persons must draw on all of their available resources, including economic, environmental, and psychological factors (Gordon, 1993), one of which is self-efficacy.

Self-Efficacy

Self-efficacy generally refers to a belief in one's competence to perform a task (Bandura, 1986). Accumulated empirical evidence suggests that self-efficacy is domain-specific, such as mathematics self-efficacy (see Hackett & Betz, 1989), and related to behaviors such as career choice (Creamer & Laughlin, 2005; Lent, Brown, & Larkin, 1986). Self-efficacy beliefs regulate educational goals, too, as people tend to set goals based on their confidence in their abilities and the odds of achieving such goals (Zimmerman, Bandura, & Martinez-Pons, 1992). Based on this literature, it seemed reasonable to hypothesize that *academic self-efficacy*—that is, students' feelings about their ability to accomplish academically oriented tasks—is associated with students' academic success in college.

A number of studies have demonstrated that self-efficacy may fuel one's resiliency (Gordon Rouse & Cashin, 2000; Luthar, 1991; Waxman, Huang, & Pardon, 1997). For instance, Gordon Rouse and Cashin analyzed survey data from 64 urban, Caucasian high school sophomores to study their self-concept and motivational patterns. They found that resilient students have several goals and environmental support beliefs that are related to academic achievement. In addition, resilient students have higher cognitive ability and more positive self-beliefs than do their non-resilient peers.

So, in sum, this study used resiliency and self-efficacy as theoretical constructs to predict the academic success of students who, for all intents and purposes, must "overcome the odds" to succeed in college (Geary, 1988; Levine & Nidiffer, 1996).

The Study

This chapter is based on findings from a larger mixed-methods study of the experiences of economically disadvantaged undergraduates at PWIs. The larger study used a two-phase, sequential, mixed-methods design (Creswell, 2003) to obtain statistical, quantitative data from a sample of low-income students, and then followed up with willing individuals to probe or explore those results in more detail using in-depth interviews (Kvale, 1996). Only findings from the survey are reported here, as they allowed me to answer the questions under investigation.

I wanted to gather information about resilience, academic self-efficacy, and achievement among low-income African Americans, so I sought out individuals who had these characteristics. Participants were drawn from two university scholarship programs that provided financial aid to students from (a) poor urban or rural counties within a single state (program #1), and (b) families with annual income levels below federal poverty guidelines (program #2). Specially, the sample consisted of 124 first-year students, the majority of whom were women. For more information about the study, sample, and variables, see Strayhorn (2008a).

Key Findings

Descriptive statistics reveal several important data points to characterize the study's sample. On average, students performed better in high school than they did during the first year of college, although the group's average was still just above 3.0. This is probably due to a number of factors, one of which is university progress requirements. To maintain their scholarship, students are required to maintain at least a 2.5 grade point average (GPA) while enrolled.

Generally speaking, participants reported low to moderate levels of sense of belonging on a composite scale, ranging from 3 ("no sense of belonging at all") to 12 ("very much a sense of belonging"). Despite modest levels of a sense of belonging on campus, a large majority of students expected to "stay in" college and had no intentions to leave before earning their degree. Table 3.1 presents additional information to describe the sample.

In response to the first question, I conducted correlation analyses to estimate the magnitude and direction of relationships. Some relationships were rather intuitive. For instance, high school GPA and first-year GPA were statistically related. Adelman (1999) and others have emphasized that high achievement (and preparation for college) in high school often begets achievement in college. Still, I uncovered several other linkages with practical and theoretical significance. For instance, low-income African American students who reported a higher sense of belonging intended to stay in college. This adds to a growing line of scholarship about sense of belonging's relation to college student retention (e.g., Strayhorn, 2008b).

Those who rated higher on academic self-efficacy had higher high school GPAs, first-year GPAs, and feelings of belonging than did those with lower

TABLE 3.1
Descriptive Statistics for All Independent and Dependent Variables

Variable	M	SD
High school GPA	3.54	0.39
First-year GPA	3.01	0.69
Intent to leave college	1.94	0.24
Sense of belonging	8.05	2.04
Academic self-efficacy	20.73	4.49
Resilience	7.31	1.46

Note. GPA = grade point average.

levels of self-efficacy. And students who, according to their scores, were more resilient also had higher high school GPAs, were more self-efficacious, and intended to remain enrolled more than did their less resilient counterparts. Table 3.2 summarizes the results of all correlation tests.

As stated earlier, I hypothesized that academic self-efficacy and resilience predict academic achievement, as measured by first-year GPA, in the sample. Given the importance of academic preparation for college and its bearing on subsequent achievement, which the literature has shown consistently (Adelman, 1999; Riehl, 1994; Warburton, Bugarin, & Nuñez, 2001), I controlled for differences in high school GPA to reduce, if not eliminate, inflation

TABLE 3.2
Correlations Among All Variables

	1	2	3	4	5	6
1. HS GPA	—					
2. FY GPA	0.25**	—				
3. INTENT	0.07	0.07	—			
4. SOB	0.34**	0.14	0.35**	—		
5. ASE	0.34**	0.29**	−0.09	0.33**	—	
6. RES	0.42**	0.04	0.27**	0.22*	0.15	—

Note. HS GPA = high school grade point average; FY GPA = first-year grade point average; INTENT = intent to leave college; SOB = sense of belonging; ASE = academic self-efficacy; RES = resilience.
* $p < 0.05$.
** $p < 0.01$.

of the statistical estimates (Koljatic, 2000). Regression results indicate that academic self-efficacy and resilience powerfully predict first-year GPA above and beyond one's precollege academic ability. Accounting for approximately 30% of the variance in first-year GPA, the final model suggests that low-income Black students with high levels of academic self-efficacy and resilience earn higher GPAs during the first year of college. Consistent with previous research (e.g., Adelman, 1999), high school GPA was the most powerful predictor of college GPA. Adding to this line of inquiry, I found that academic self-efficacy (β = 0.29) was the next most powerful predictor of college achievement, followed by resilience (β = 0.22). Table 3.3 presents a summary of the analysis.

Limitations

Before discussing the relevance of the study's findings, I should present a number of limitations. First, all participants were drawn from a single institution. It is possible that low-income Black students at this institution differ in some important ways from students at other colleges and universities. If so, this might limit the generalizability of findings to similar student samples.

Second, while 30% of the variance is explained by high school GPA, academic self-efficacy, and resilience, other factors that contribute to students' achievement are left unexplained by the model. For instance, in a previous study of first-generation college students (Strayhorn, 2006), I found

TABLE 3.3
Relationship Among Academic Self-Efficacy, Resilience, and First-Year GPA, Controlling for Differences in Precollege Academic Ability

Variables	B	SE	β
Constant	− 0.90	0.58	
High school GPA	0.62	0.14	0.36**
Academic self-efficacy	0.05	0.01	0.29**
Resilience	0.10	0.04	0.22**

R = 0.544
R^2 = 0.296

Note. GPA = grade point average; F (3, 123) = 16.82; $p < 0.01$.
** $p < 0.01$.

that college grades are influenced by time elapsed between college entry and degree receipt, number of undergraduate institutions attended, taking remedial courses, and educational aspirations, to name a few. Excluding these variables may have a confounding effect on the study and limit the predictive ability of the model. Despite these limits, this study represents an important contribution to our literature on African American collegians.

Discussion

The primary purpose of the study on which this chapter is based was to measure the relationship among resilience, academic self-efficacy, and academic success, using a sample of low-income African American collegians attending a PWI. Specifically, two questions guided the study: (a) What is the magnitude and direction of relationships among resilience, academic self-efficacy, and academic success? (b) What is the relationship among resilience, academic self-efficacy, and academic achievement, controlling for differences in precollege academic ability? Results suggest several important conclusions.

First, academic self-efficacy and resilience correlate with students' sense of belonging on campus. Findings suggest that students who might otherwise perceive themselves as marginal to campus life actually report feeling a sense of "connectedness" when they are confident in their academic abilities and are able to overcome difficulties. Recall that the correlation coefficients for sense of belonging and academic self-efficacy ($r = 0.33$) and resilience ($r = 0.22$) were statistically significant. Indeed, this chapter augments related studies (e.g., Hurtado & Carter, 1997) but shifts the focus to a group of students that is often rendered "invisible" in the literature.

Results presented in this chapter provide substantial support for scholars who argue for the central importance of academic preparation in shaping at-risk students' success in college. Remember that high school GPA was the most powerful predictor of first-year college GPA for low-income African American collegians. This lends support to the notion that good academic preparation for college may have a compensatory effect for those students who enter college with the least amount of social and cultural capital (Strayhorn, 2006; Terenzini, Springer, Yaeger, Pascarella, & Nora, 1996). Indeed, more college preparatory courses must be offered in low-income and/or high-minority high schools. One attractive policy argument is to extend students' opportunity to learn (OTL) by increasing hours in the classroom, offering before- and after-school academic enrichment activities, and spending more time reading, studying, and doing homework, to name a few

(Oakes, 1995). Indeed, additional research is warranted on OTL and its impact on students' postsecondary success.

In sum, this study offers fairly compelling evidence to suggest that academic self-efficacy and resilience influence achievement during the first year of college for low-income African Americans. And it is important to note that, while these students face challenges in college as do any other students, their experiences often involve unique academic, social, and cultural transitions (Rendón, 1994; Rendón, Hope, & Associates, 1996) that may require them to be bicultural, self-confident, and resilient (Carter, 2005). We can use this information to assist them in navigating campus environments that may, at times, seem culturally incongruent and fraught with challenges.

Implications

This study was significant for several campus constituencies. One group that might benefit from the results of this study includes those who work in academic advising. Advisors can assist in one of two ways. First, they provide important information (e.g., major requirements, financial aid, etc.) to students, which, in turn, may affect their degree of self-confidence, because those who have sufficient information about academic matters are usually better positioned to evaluate their options.

That resilience predicts academic achievement for low-income African Americans, controlling for precollege academic ability, has implications for college admission officers. Results presented here indicate that highly resilient students earn higher grades in college than do their less resilient peers. Admission counselors might consider these findings when evaluating student applications. Any evidence that a student has had to overcome adversity may suggest that he or she will do well in college and, thus, should be admitted, especially if the student did well in high school despite obstacles. For instance, last year, when working with an admissions office to train staff members for holistic review, I ran across an application from a 15-year-old, low-income African American female (fictitiously named "Laurice") who had done exceptionally well in high school (GPA ~ 3.8) despite living with a physical disability, working 15 hours per week, and taking care of her younger brother. Initially, the admissions committee had concerns about Laurice's youth and the difficulties she might face in adjusting to the social life of college. But Laurice's personal essay exuded resilience, which reduced our concerns and demonstrated a strong capacity to overcome difficulties.

We admitted Laurice without condition and offered her a university scholarship for her high achievement. Admissions officers are urged to use such information when making holistic decisions.

These findings also hold significance for postsecondary faculty members and counselors. Some low-income African Americans may possess a sense of "learned hopelessness" (Seligman, 1990) caused by negative school experiences or other difficulties in life; as a result, they may have little to no confidence in their abilities to perform well academically. Educators should support such students to adopt a positive view of "self" by encouraging them whenever possible, highlighting their positive attributes, and praising their achievement. I am not suggesting that educators should fall prey to students' "woe is me" antics. Instead, I am arguing for a consistent, smooth blend of praise and critique that provides such students with positive affirmations as well as necessary "truth." But, as Emily Dickinson once wrote, "The truth must dazzle gradually or every man be blind." Harsh critique of students who lack confidence, without an appropriate level of support, is likely to be misunderstood and further reduce, if not extinguish, one's motivation to succeed. Faculty might consider these words when working with such students.

The present study also has significance for future research. For instance, this study explored the relationship among resilience, self-efficacy, and academic achievement, broadly conceived, for low-income African American collegians. Future studies might examine differences in resilience among African Americans, including differences by age, gender, and year in school. Such studies may expand on the information available about resilient college students. Additionally, future researchers might use qualitative methods, such as interviewing, observation, and document analysis using reflective essays, to further study the resilience of underserved populations in higher education.

Finally, the study is significant in terms of future theory. To date, resiliency theory has focused primarily on resilience as an educational concept and how it relates to motivation (e.g., Griffin, 2006). This study offers insight into the effect of resilience on Black students' achievement during the first year of college. One might use these data to expand existing theory (e.g., retention, see Tinto, 1993) to include information about the influence of resilience and self-efficacy on African American students while they are in college.

Turning again to the quotation that began this discussion, I urge educators to consider students' resilience and their perceived agency over educational outcomes when determining the likelihood of their success. The take-home message is that some students, such as low-income African Americans, can succeed with the appropriate level of support, confidence, and resiliency. Educators should remember this when "measuring" students' odds for success in college. Quite often, consciously or subconsciously, educators make judgments about students based on pre-existing stereotypes, previous interactions, and what we think or "see" as possible for them. While taking into account these students' academic preparation for college, don't forget to take into account the "hills and valleys" they've overcome to get where they are.

Recommendations for Educational Practice

Resiliency is not a fixed attribute; instead, it is a characteristic that can be developed, nurtured, and activated over time. Therefore, it is highly responsive to programmatic intervention. So, building on the results presented here, I offer several explicit recommendations for those who are interested in improving the academic achievement of low-income African Americans.

First, educators would do well to design environments in which low-income Black students can engage in educationally purposeful activities that nurture their resiliency and improve their academic self-efficacy. This is particularly true for educators who work at PWIs as such environments tend to be perceived as unsupportive, threatening, and unwelcoming to Black students (Feagin & Sikes, 1995; Fleming, 1984). For instance, students with low levels of academic self-efficacy should have multiple chances for incremental success on academic tasks such as homework or quizzes and should receive appropriate feedback from their instructors (Deci & Ryan, 1985).

Second, earlier research has shown that social support from families, community members, and peers fuels one's resiliency (Jackson, Smith, & Hill, 2003; Wilson-Sadberry, 1991). Thus, opportunities to build positive, supportive relationships with others on campus are likely to enhance one's ability to persist in the face of challenges. Learning communities, faculty-student research collaborations, and fraternities and sororities, as well as well-designed mentoring programs, seem to be effective means for establishing relationships that might foster resilience (Strayhorn, 2008c).

Third, books in the popular press, such as that by Brooks and Goldstein (2002), outline several strategies for nurturing resilience in youth, which can be translated and applied to collegiate settings. For instance, the authors argue that empathy is necessary to nurture resilience in youth. Empathy is the capacity to "view the world" through others' eyes. Administrators, then, might exercise empathy by reserving judgment about students' actions or decisions and simply validating their point of view, where appropriate and reasonable.

Another popular strategy for building resilience is rewriting negative scripts. Quite often students who face adversity develop self-defeating thoughts that, if left unchallenged, become self-fulfilling prophecies (Steele, 2000). College student educators can help students rewrite negative scripts by teaching them to recognize unhealthy thoughts (e.g, "I'm not good enough," "This college isn't for me") and to replace and *rewrite* them with positive responses (e.g., "Things will work if I try," "I'm smart enough," "I can do this," "I belong here"). Practicing such activities frequently is likely to yield the best results.

College professors can play a role in nurturing resilience and enhancing self-efficacy among low-income African Americans. Students who need to increase their skills in these areas will benefit from meaningful learning activities that are "doable" and progressively challenging such as those characterized by problem-based learning. Moreover, professors should provide students with frequent opportunities for success, which are likely to engender academic self-efficacy.

Conclusion

This study extends our understanding about the relationship among resilience, self-efficacy, and the academic success of disadvantaged ethnic minorities such as low-income African Americans. While much is still unresolved, it is clear that self-efficacious, resilient, economically disadvantaged African American students tend to fare better in college than do their peers who lack confidence in themselves and their ability to overcome challenges. Indeed, this chapter provides a framework for designing effective educational environments that facilitate their success in college. And it is the first of several attempts to understand *buoyant believers* and the "hills and valleys [they] come through" to get to where they are.

References

Adelman, C. (1999). *Answers in the toolbox: Academic intensity, attendance patterns, and bachelor's degree attainment.* Washington, DC: U.S. Department of Education, Office of Educational Research and Improvement.

Bandura, A. (1986). *Social foundations of thought and action: A social cognitive theory.* Englewood Cliffs, NJ: Prentice Hall.

Banyard, V. L., & Cantor, E. N. (2004). Adjustment to college among trauma survivors: An exploratory study of resilience. *Journal of College Student Development, 45*(2), 207–221.

Brooks, R., & Goldstein, S. (2002). *Nurturing resilience in our children.* Lincolnwood, IL: NTC Publishing Group.

Cappella, E., & Weinstein, R. (2001). Turning around reading achievement: Predictors on high school students' academic resilience. *Journal of Educational Psychology, 93*(4), 758–771.

Carter, D. F. (2001). *A dream deferred? Examining the degree aspirations of African American and White college students.* New York: RoutledgeFalmer.

Carter, P. L. (2005). *Keepin' it real: School success beyond Black and White.* New York: Oxford University Press.

Creamer, E. G., & Laughlin, A. (2005). Self-authorship and women's career decision making. *Journal of College Student Development, 46*(1), 13–27.

Creswell, J. W. (2003). *Research design: Qualitative, quantitative, and mixed methods approaches* (2nd ed.). Thousand Oaks, CA: Sage.

Day, A. L., & Livingstone, H. A. (2003). Gender differences in perceptions of stressors and utilization of social support among university students. *Canadian Journal of Behavioural Science, 35,* 73–83.

Deci, L., & Ryan, M. (1985). *Intrinsic motivation and self-determination in human behavior.* New York: Plenum.

Domina, L., & Hansberry, L. (1998). *Understanding* A Raisin in the Sun*: A student casebook to issues, sources, and historical documents.* Detroit, MI: Greenwood Publishing Group.

Feagin, J. R., & Sikes, M. P. (1995). How Black students cope with racism on White campuses. *Journal of Blacks in Higher Education, 8,* 91–97.

Fleming, J. (1984). *Blacks in college: A comparative study of students' success in Black and White institutions.* San Francisco: Jossey-Bass.

Gayles, J. (2005). Playing the game and paying the price: Academic resilience among three high-achieving African American males. *Anthropology & Education Quarterly, 36*(3), 250–264.

Geary, P. A. (1988). *Defying the odds? Academic success among at-risk minority teenagers in an urban high school.* Paper presented at the annual meeting of the American Educational Research Association, New Orleans, LA.

Gordon, K. A. (1993). *Resilient African American high school students' self-concept and motivational patterns: Sources of strength.* Unpublished doctoral dissertation, Stanford University, Stanford, CA.

Gordon Rouse, K. A., & Cashin, S. E. (2000). Assessment of academic self-concept and motivation: Results from three ethnic groups. *Measurement and Evaluation in Counseling and Development, 33,* 91–102.

Griffin, K. A. (2006). Striving for success: A qualitative exploration of competing theories of high-achieving Black college students' academic motivation. *Journal of College Student Development, 47*(4), 354–400.

Hackett, G., & Betz, N. E. (1989). An exploration of the mathematics: Self-efficacy/mathematics performance correspondence. *Journal for Research in Mathematics Education, 20,* 261–273.

Hare, B. (1988). African American youth at risk. *Urban League Review, 12,* 25–38.

Himelein, M. J. (1995). Childhood sexual abuse and the academic adjustment of college women. *Child Abuse and Neglect, 19,* 761–764.

Himelein, M. J., & McElrath, A. V. (1996). Resilient child sexual abuse survivors: Cognitive coping and illusion. *Child Abuse and Neglect, 20,* 747–758.

Horn, L. J. (1997). *Confronting the odds: Students at risk and the pipeline to higher education* (NCES Report 98–094). Washington, DC: U.S. Department of Education, National Center for Education Statistics.

Hughes, L. (1959). *Selected poems of Langston Hughes* (1st ed.). New York: Alfred A. Knopf.

Hurtado, S., & Carter, D. F. (1997). Effects of college transition and perceptions of campus racial climate on Latino college students' sense of belonging. *Sociology of Education, 70*(4), 324–345.

Hyman, B., & Williams, L. (2001). Resilience among women survivors of child sexual abuse. *Affilia, 16,* 198–219.

Jackson, A. P., Smith, S. A., & Hill, C. L. (2003). Academic persistence among Native American college students. *Journal of College Student Development, 44*(4), 548–565.

Jacoby, B., & Garland, J. (2004–2005). Strategies for enhancing commuter student success. *Journal of College Student Retention: Research, Theory, & Practice, 6*(1), 61–79.

Kahlenberg, R. D. (2004). *America's untapped resource: Low-income students in higher education.* New York: Century Foundation Press.

Kerlinger, F. N. (1986). *Foundations of behavioral research* (3rd ed.). New York: Holt, Rinehart, & Winston.

Koljatic, M. (2000). *A longitudinal assessment of college student perceptions of good practices in undergraduate education.* Unpublished doctoral dissertation, Indiana University, Bloomington.

Kvale, S. (1996). *InterViews: An introduction to qualitative research interviewing.* Thousand Oaks, CA: Sage.

Lee, V. E., Winfield, L. F., & Wilson, T. C. (1991). Academic behaviors among high-achieving African-American students. *Education and Urban Society, 24,* 65–86.

Lent, R. W., Brown, S. D., & Larkin, K. C. (1986). Self-efficacy in the prediction of academic performance and perceived career options. *Journal of Counseling Psychology, 33*(3), 265–269.

Levine, A., & Nidiffer, J. (1996). *Beating the odds: How the poor get to college.* San Francisco: Jossey-Bass.

Luthar, S. (1991). Vulnerability and resilience: A study of high-risk adolescents. *Child Development, 62,* 600–616.

MacLeod, J. (1995). *Ain't no makin' it: Aspirations and attainment in a low-income neighborhood.* Boulder, CO: Westview Press.

McDermott, R. (1987). The explanation of minority failure again. *Anthropology & Education Quarterly, 18*(4), 361–364.

Oakes, J. (1995). Two cities' tracking and within-school segregation. *Teachers College Record, 96*(4), 681–690.

Pritchard, M. E., & Wilson, G. S. (2003). Using emotional and social factors to predict student success. *Journal of College Student Development, 44*(1), 18–28.

Rendón, L. I. (1994). Validating culturally diverse students: Toward a new model of learning and student development. *Innovative Higher Education, 19*(1), 33–51.

Rendón, L. I., Hope, R. O., & Associates. (1996). *Educating a new majority: Transforming America's education system for diversity.* San Francisco: Jossey-Bass.

Riehl, R. J. (1994). The academic preparation, aspirations, and first-year performance of first-generation students. *College and University, 70*(1), 14–19.

Rosenberg, M., & McCullough, B. C. (1981). Mattering: Inferred significance and mental health among adolescents. *Research in Community Mental Health, 2,* 163–182.

Schreiner, L. A. (1991). *The college student inventory: Accurately identifying students at risk.* Iowa City, IA: Noel-Levitz Centers for Institutional Effectiveness and Innovation, Inc.

Scott-Jones, D. (1984). Family influences on cognitive development and school achievement. *Review of Education Research, 11,* 259–304.

Seligman, M. E. P. (1990). *Learned optimism.* New York: Alfred A. Knopf.

Steele, C. M. (2000, February). "Stereotype threat" and Black college students. *AAHE Bulletin, 52,* 3–6.

Strayhorn, T. L. (2006). Factors influencing the academic achievement of first-generation college students. *The NASPA Journal, 43*(4), 82–111.

Strayhorn, T. L. (2008a). Buoyancy in success: Academic resilience among African American male collegians. *Illinois Committee on Black Concerns in Higher Education* (ICBCHE) *Voices,* 10–11.

Strayhorn, T. L. (2008b). Fittin' In: Do diverse interactions with peers affect sense of belonging for Black men at predominantly White institutions? *The NASPA Journal, 45*(4), 501–527.

Strayhorn, T. L. (2008c). The role of supportive relationships in facilitating African American males' success in college. *The NASPA Journal, 45*(1), 26–48.

Terenzini, P. T., Springer, L., Yaeger, P. M., Pascarella, E. T., & Nora, A. (1996). First-generation college students: Characteristics, experiences, and cognitive development. *Research in Higher Education, 37*(1), 1–22.

Tinto, V. (1993). *Leaving college: Rethinking the causes and cures of student attrition* (2nd ed.). Chicago: University of Chicago Press.

Valentine, L., & Feinauer, L. L. (1993). Resilience factors associated with female survivors of childhood sexual abuse. *The American Journal of Family Therapy, 21,* 216–224.

Wang, M. C., & Gordon, E. W. (1994). *Educational resilience in inner-city America: Challenges and prospects.* Hillsdale, NJ: Lawrence Erlbaum.

Warburton, E. C., Bugarin, R., & Nuñez, A. M. (2001). *Bridging the gap: Academic preparation and postsecondary success of first-generation students* (NCES Report 2001–153). Washington, DC: U.S. Department of Education, National Center for Education Statistics.

Waxman, H. C., Huang, S. L., & Pardon, Y. N. (1997). Motivation and learning environment differences between resilient and nonresilient Latino middle school students. *Hispanic Journal of Behavioral Sciences, 19*(2), 137–155.

Wilson-Sadberry, K. R. (1991). Resilience and persistence of African-American males in postsecondary enrollment. *Education and Urban Society, 24*(1), 87–102.

Zimmerman, B. J., Bandura, A., & Martinez-Pons, M. (1992). Self-motivation for academic attainment: The role of self-efficacy beliefs and personal goal setting. *American Educational Research Journal, 29*(3), 663–676.

Zinn, M. B. (1987). *Minority families in transition.* Flint, MI: University of Michigan.

4

FOCUSING ON ACHIEVEMENT
African American Student Persistence in the Academy

Fred A. Bonner II

Abstract: In this chapter, the author weaves together findings from studies of the relationship between academic achievement and African American student persistence in higher education. Implications for strengthening future research and policy are presented at the end of the chapter, as well as evidence-based recommendations for shaping educational practice.

At the heart of many debates concerning the role and status of American higher education are conversations about college student achievement. Whether the focus of these debates highlights the importance of improving education at the P–12 level or emphasizes the need to ratchet up the rigor of the postsecondary curriculum, what provides seemingly limitless fodder for these discussions is how to identify viable approaches and methods to improve achievement. Some researchers (Allen, 1988, 1992; Allen & Haniff, 1991; Astin, 1993; Fleming, 1981, 2000; Hughes, 1987; Pascarella & Terenzini, 1979, 1991, 2005; Tinto, 1975) have dedicated their life's work to studying the complexities associated with this topic. What their research has consistently revealed is that achievement does not have a singular nature. Much like grand bodies of water, comprising multiple and competing tributaries, so, too, is achievement affected by a number of influences. Influences such as faculty mentoring, institutional demographic profile, peer support, and psychosocial development all contribute to how college students define and subsequently experience academic success.

Despite the plethora of research literature on college student achievement (Allen & Haniff, 1991; Awad, 2007; Bonner, 2001; Cokley, Komarraju,

King, Cunningham, & Muhammad, 2003; Cuyjet, 1997, 2006; Hughes, 1987) and its many contributing influences, information about whether and how achievement-related variables influence the college matriculation experiences of students of color in general and African American students in particular has been conspicuously limited. For example, a search for achievement-related literature focusing on the experiences of African American males from low socioeconomic backgrounds who choose to attend a selective, predominantly White institution (PWI) yields few returns. An even more dire example is a database search for literature that identifies the factors affecting the achievement of African American females not only in PWIs but in historically Black college and university (HBCU) contexts as well. These examples reveal the vast amount of work that is left to be done.

This chapter has a major and a minor theme. Although, the minor theme serves as background to the larger foreground discussion, it is nonetheless important. Achievement is the major theme for investigation, while the minor theme, persistence, functions as the means by which achievement is attained. As a point of departure, I begin the chapter by investigating how current African American student cohorts, referred to as *Millennials*, negotiate their achievement in the academy. Following this discussion I discuss a number of other key topics presented for examination: college choice; academic and social integration; institutional climate; and identity and achievement. Finally, I offer a number of recommendations for both academic and student affairs practitioners as well as policymakers who are vested in providing the challenge and support necessary for African American collegians to achieve their potential.

Millennial College Student Culture

Generational influences on college student success are not a new phenomenon. The most recent conceptualization was offered by Howe and Strauss (2000), who cite examples of how age, peer, situational, and other variables coalesce to produce certain generational cohort behaviors. Today's generation of college students has been termed *Millennials*. According to Coomes and DeBard (2004), although there is some debate about the year marking the beginning of this generation, most researchers define Millennials as individuals who were born during and after 1982. In addition to Millennials' stronghold in undergraduate representation in colleges and universities,

Coomes and DeBard also report that they are the most educationally ambitious and diverse (e.g., at least one in five Millennials has at least one immigrant parent [McGlynn, 2005]) collegiate cohort the nation has ever witnessed.

In describing the Millennial generation, Howe and Strauss (2000) provide a set of characteristics that reveal some of the "central tendencies" endemic to this group. They report that Millennials feel, want to feel, or perceive that they are

1. Special—Because they have been told all their lives by their Baby Boomer parents that they are special, they tend to feel a sense of importance.
2. Sheltered—As the "baby on board generation," they have grown up under the intense and watchful gaze of doting and often overly protective parents.
3. Confident—Highly optimistic, this generation has been rewarded for its behavior. Millennials have also been told consistently that they are extremely capable of achieving any goal they set their minds to.
4. Conventional—Accepting of social rules and order promoted by members of the Baby Boomer generation, they tend to be more conservative than many people realize.
5. Team-Oriented—The axiom, "We rise and fall together" is an apt description of this group's attitude about collaboration and working together.
6. Achieving—Since they are no strangers to accountability standards and high-stakes testing, they tend to be very achievement-oriented and driven.
7. Pressured—Because they are achievement-oriented and their intellectual prowess has been affirmed consistently, they tend to feel pressured to perform at optimal levels at all times.

Although Howe and Strauss (2000) provide useful fodder for discussions about this generation, there are a number of gaps and shortcomings in their work. One in particular has been their lack of focus on Millennials of color. In referring to the Millennial generation in its entirety, Coomes and DeBard (2004) are quick to point out that, "the big picture seldom contains images of marginalized groups" (p. 14). Bonner and Hughes (2007), in their recently coedited special-theme edition of the *National Association of Student Affairs Professionals (NASAP) Journal*, assert that recent higher education literature highlighting this generational cohort has lacked a specific emphasis on critical issues such as culture, ethnicity, and race, thereby leaving a number of questions unanswered, such as the role pop culture plays in the identity of this population. Additionally, within the same coedited volume of the *NASAP Journal*, Dilworth and Carter (2007) lament that "terms such as 'hip hop,' 'baby boomers,' 'generation X,' and 'Millennial' are recognized as acceptable and standard social labels used to categorize and compare young people relative to prior generations, [although] such labeling does not always consider the diverse cultural experiences of the many groups that make up society" (p. 75).

For the higher education official, it will become ever more prudent to develop competencies based on what Millennials in general and African American Millennials in particular bring to the institutional context. Seeking a universal template to address the myriad issues this generational cohort is experiencing is a mistake. When attempting to understand the range of Millennials' experiences, previous works have provided clear and concise information, but they have lacked the comprehensiveness needed to understand individual group behaviors and idiosyncratic cultural proclivities. This statement is not meant to be overly critical of previous contributions, but rather to be a clarion call to all who seek to provide the supports African American students need. Essentially, what Howe and Strauss (2000); Coomes and DeBard (2004); and DeBard (2004) have provided are general road maps, particularly as this research addresses populations of color. What is needed now is to add to this road map by providing necessary details, landmarks, facts, and figures that will expand our collective knowledge and provide a more comprehensive view if taken in from a topographical perspective.

College Choice

Ongoing research in college choice has led to a greater understanding of the processes postsecondary aspirants use to select an institution of matriculation. According to Smith and Fleming (2006), "The term *college choice* represents a process that captures the academic, social, economic, and familial influences that shape a child's journey from kindergarten to post-high school" (p. 76). A litany of scholars (Cabrera & La Nasa, 2001; Hossler, Braxton, & Coopersmith, 1989; McDonough, 1994, 1997; Stordahl, 1970) has sought to better understand what variables are included when high school students initiate their search and subsequently select the college or university they will attend. One clear example is taken from the college choice model developed by Litten (1982) and Hossler and Gallagher (1987), which identified three distinct phases of the college choice process: predisposition, search, and choice. This is but one of several frameworks that have been advanced to demonstrate that college choice is a far more complex experience than many thought.

Despite the emphasis on better understanding college choice processes among students seeking entrance to higher education, much is left to discover concerning how African American student populations engage in these same experiences. The questions become: Do African American students draw on a different set of resources from their White counterparts when choosing an institution of higher education? Does race play significant roles in how African American students make their selections? Also, what do African American students' background and culture contribute to the final decision-making process? These are only some of the questions that have gone virtually unanswered, which may be due to the fact that earlier research in this area is largely based on the experiences of majority (White) college students. As with other topics related to the college experiences of African American students, it is important to study the whole issue (e.g., college choice) by looking at the sum of its parts (e.g., predisposition, search, choice). The research has viewed college choice holistically, so a deconstruction of this issue to better understand the unique contributions of individual parts is critical, especially for African American students.

Roughly eight years ago, Freeman (1999) advanced her notions about college choice among African American students by stating,

> Perhaps the problem has been that few studies have given voice to African American students who are in the best place to assess the influences on their decision processes. By all accounts, the college choice process for African American high school students is a complicated one that necessarily has to take into consideration the context of their culture. Otherwise, any programs or solutions developed by educational institutions possibly might be based on models that may not fit the circumstances of these students. (p. 38)

Freeman's (1999) statement articulates what has been most discouraging about the college choice literature; namely, the models used in this area were derived from research investigations involving White student populations and, thus, are ill-suited to interpret how African American students negotiate this process. She further reports that, "Although it could be argued that who and/or what are influences on students to choose or not to choose college participation are similar across cultures, the depth and meaning (the perception of reality) each culture attaches to these influences differs . . ." (p. 40). Hence the question posed earlier regarding the relative influence of race on the decision-making processes of African American students is one that Freeman's research sought to answer but also one that continues to beg contemporary examinations and theoretical responses.

To further roil the college choice waters, it is critical to look at the host of issues often imbedded or subsumed within larger discussions. Just as Freeman's research (1999) uncovered an umbrella issue, race, a host of other topics for investigation relate to African American students that might not be readily perceived as important. Questions posed in the first part of this section illuminate the need to highlight race as well as culture and background, but this list is not exhaustive. And, perhaps the best way to uncover these remaining issues will be to engage in research that lends voice (Freeman, 1999) to African American students while concomitantly recognizing how choice intersects with critical variables like parental influence (Holloman & Strayhorn, this volume) and support as well as academic self-efficacy (Smith & Fleming, 2006; see chapter 3).

Academic and Social Integration

Notwithstanding the fact that academic and social integration represent different aspects of the same root issue (Tinto, 1993), it is necessary to address both to ensure that African American students are adequately prepared to manage the rigors of academe. Academic and social integration of African American students into the college life represents another line of needed research. Bonner and Evans (2004) submitted to audiences invested in better understanding the academic integration process for African American college students the idea that, "All students who seek scholarly success need to be integrated into the fabric of the institution. Like many other minority students, African American students enrolled in PWIs often find this process of integration difficult" (p. 11). These authors go on to say, "African American students encounter multiple difficulties in academe—poor academic preparation, lack of proper advising, and inadequate financial resources" (p. 11). Readily apparent in both of these statements about academic integration is that they parallel the gamut of statements made about achievement and persistence; that is, these problems are complex, so they defy singular solutions. These are all concepts that for African American student populations in the academy present multiple and competing *challenges* that have to be addressed, sometimes in tandem, at other times in turn. But they all must be addressed.

Further investigation of the academic integration experiences of African American students reveals that they, much like their White peers, achieve better and persist longer when critical supports are present. Invariably, for both groups, and particularly for African American students who are negotiating myriad integration issues, establishing a relationship with a faculty member is often the critical factor in their success. Booker's (2007) study involving African American students' perceptions of belonging finds that interpersonal relationships between these students and faculty members are essential—that when faculty are engaged with and committed to students, with respect to instructional technique and interpersonal sentiment, they have a positive impact on students. Similarly, Fischer (2007) states, "More extensive involvement with professors outside of class may indicate mentoring on the part of professors, which has been shown in previous work to be predictive of academic success" (p. 138).

Thus, one supportive factor contributing to the academic integration and subsequent success of African American students in higher education is the relationships they are able to establish with faculty members (Strayhorn, 2008b). According to Astin (1993), second only to relationships established with peer groups, faculty-student interaction represents the most salient factor in student success at the undergraduate level. Faculty relationships provide opportunities for these students to connect and to overcome several of the difficulties they encounter that I presented earlier in this section. Additionally, Black college students benefit from participating in educationally purposeful activities with faculty members such as undergraduate research experiences (see chapter 10, this volume).

Social integration presents yet another set of circumstances that provide the support necessary for African American students to achieve. African Americans who attend PWIs, as opposed to their peers who elect to attend HBCUs, find that social integration plays a unique role in their pursuit of academic success. Whereas in the HBCU context, social integration enables social networking, in the PWI context, social integration enables survival (Bonner, 2001). Hausmann, Schofield, and Woods (2007) go so far as to assert that, "sense of belonging is most often implied as the result of social and academic integration . . ." (p. 806).

Just as the successful academic integration of African American students depends on developing some sense of understanding of these students' academic backgrounds, so, too, must social integration reflect the experiences these students bring to the institution. According to Bonner and Evans (2004),

> Colleges and universities must be cognizant of who these African American students are and what they bring to the institutional context. Institutions must not assume that social integration processes are the same for African American and White students. In essence, the social integration experiences for these collegians must be purposeful, exhibiting an institutional willingness to explore differences honestly. (p. 13)

Individuals and institutions must approach social integration differently from academic integration. Although there is variety among the curriculum, disciplines, learning styles, and other academically related variables, at its core, college life embraces a number of unifying concepts—academic degree plans, course units, and the core curriculum are but a few of these variables. Similarly, a montage of different interests and motivations exist on the college campus. Student motivations are just as varied as the collegians who bring with them diverse social cultures, mores, and traditions.

Institutional Climate and Environment

The institutional climate and environment in higher education has often been described by people of color and women as "chilly," "inhospitable," and "unwelcoming" (Aguirre, 2000; Bonner & Evans, 2004; Smith, 1997; Strayhorn, 2008b). Although many of these authors focus on the experiences shared by faculty of color in higher education contexts, the experiences of students of color do not vary considerably from those shared by faculty. Bonner and Evans (2004) reported that, "An important factor in the success of African American collegians on the predominantly White campus is the actual institutional environment, campus climate, or institutional ecosystem" (p. 9). What continues to matter to students of color in general and African American students in particular is finding some sense of belonging in environments that quite often greet them with indifference and even hostility (Strayhorn, 2008a). Additionally, for African American collegians, identifying with higher education settings that are often woefully incongruent with their background experiences, whether culturally, financially, ethnically, or racially, can constitute a formidable challenge during their four- or five-year matriculation experience, which underscores the importance of support.

Establishing some sense of agency as both a college student and as a person of color in a context that is at best misaligned and at worst totally incongruent with one's background experiences represents a serious challenge for many African American college students. Watson et al. (2002) reveal that many students of color enter the college and university setting with a number of erroneous preconceived notions about the campus culture and environment they will experience. These authors find that colleges and universities themselves often contribute to the misguided notions that African Americans construct regarding their campus experiences. For instance, while every institution strives to put its best foot forward via marketing and recruitment efforts, what invariably happens is that they falsely represent the actual climate for diversity at their respective schools. This notion of climate for diversity moves beyond mere numbers and success in recruiting greater numbers of students of color; it speaks to the prevailing ethos surrounding diversity and multiculturalism issues on campus.

Campuses do not confront, and students do not ask, questions such as, "*How does it feel* to be an African American student on campus?" Instead, they ask, "*How many African American students do you have* on campus?" These students unknowingly become caught in the institution's game of promoting progress related to diversity through greater numbers of students of color. By bringing a cohort of students of color to campus on interview days, or by showcasing minority student organizations via marketing campaigns, students are seduced by the thought of experiencing what they perceive to be diverse and accepting campus environments—the exact opposite of what they actually find once enrolled. In Watson et al. (2002), several students of color offer the following comments, in response to a question about the institutional environment on their respective predominantly White campuses:

> Hickory College "talks the talk"; they don't "walk the walk." This multicultural thing to them is a big game. That's just a word to them. It's a façade.—Student "A"

> Well, outside the classroom, I try to tell students who are interested in coming here that if they want a social life to pop out at them, that this is not the school and you may have to make your own fun here and that's one of the first questions students ask.——Student "B"

> I feel like they act like they're so diverse and multicultural. . . . This is not a representation of how it is for people who go here.—Student "C"

These examples reflect how the institutions these students attend lacked the diversity and multicultural focus they had represented or reported. Also, these statements speak to the students' perceived incongruence with these environments, the implication being that these settings did not support their interests. For African American students, research studies and extant literature (Allen, 1992; Bonner & Murry, 1998; Cheatham, Slaney, & Coleman, 1990; Cokley, 2001; Davis, 1994; DeSousa & Kuh, 1996; Fleming, 1981, 1984; Flowers, 2002; Harper, Carini, Bridges, & Hayek, 2004; Pascarella & Terenzini, 1991) have suggested ways to improve the college campus environment for this group. From the perspective of creating more welcoming environments from a human aggregate perspective, perhaps Smith (1997) said it best: "student involvement with campus groups that reflect personal, cultural, or service interests have a strong impact on helping students feel that they belong on the campus, are contributing to the campus culture, and have their interests reflected in the institutional structure" (p. 29). However, creating institutional environments that are welcoming and meet the needs of African American students does not happen solely by addressing human aggregate concerns; these concerns represent only a piece of the puzzle. These students need to see themselves reflected in physical, organizational, and perceptual spaces on campus as well.

Identity Development, Self-Esteem, and Self-Concept

To fully comprehend the experiences of African American students in academic contexts like colleges and universities, one must look at all of the variables that affect their success. Cokley et al. (2003) state that, "Noncognitive variables such as motivation as well as different percepts of the self such as self-esteem, self-efficacy, and academic self-concept, have all been examined to determine the nature of their relationships with academic achievement" (p. 707). How these students perform in such venues has as much to do with who they are and how they identify themselves, as it has to do with their academic competencies. Hence, without launching into an exhaustive discussion of racial identity development models, two in particular provide useful insights on identity development processes experienced by African American college students: Asante's (1988) *Afrocentric Cultural Identity* and Cross's (1971, 1991) *Negro to Black Conversion* models.

In framing discussions related to racial identity development processes for African Americans, Cross (1971) introduces a provocative model. The four stages or themes his model identifies include: pre-encounter, encounter, immersion/emersion, and internalization—"each describes 'self-concept' issues concerning race and parallel attitudes that the individual holds about Black and White as a reference group" (p. 169). Noteworthy is that each theme represents an ever-increasing sense of self as a racial being and an ever-deepening sense of understanding regarding the establishment of a healthy identity (Bonner, Jennings, Marbley, & Brown, 2008). According to Asante's (1988) Afrocentric model, it is important to recognize problems associated with cultural misalignment. His model promotes a worldview aimed at constructing a collective Black consciousness that ultimately leads to a new sense of empowerment and identity. According to Bonner et al. (2008), the cultural values identified in Asante's Afrocentric model are congruent with the fundamental principles identified in the literature highlighting the African American worldview: interdependence, cooperation, unity, mutual responsibility, and reconciliation.

African American college students who seek to establish some sense of identity in these contexts often encounter social enclaves that are ill-suited and uncomfortable with this unfolding process. What often results from this stunted identity development process is that this lack of identity spills over into areas such as self-esteem and self-concept. According to Awad (2007), "Given the presumed connection between identity development and academic outcomes for African Americans, an important variable that may be related to academic achievement for African Americans is racial identity" (p. 189). What higher education must find is not only viable ways to encourage and promote healthy identity development among these students but also viable means of recognizing the critical connections among such constructs as identity development, self-esteem, and self-concept. College student educators and higher education practitioners must be ready to answer difficult questions that often defy simple solutions. For example, how does racial identity affect student success? Does academic self-esteem affect self-concept? What role does stereotype threat play in matriculation experiences? These are but a few of the myriad questions academics must investigate to address the attendant problems these students experience.

Mentoring and Role Modeling

Identifying a mentor or role model to help navigate and negotiate the higher education terrain has been touted as one of the most important supportive factors in ensuring the retention of students in colleges and universities (Bowser & Perkins, 1991; Patton & Harper, 2003; Sutton, 2006). For African

American students, finding an individual, especially someone who is attuned to the nuances of the academy (e.g., a faculty member), becomes an even more important reality for their socialization into the academy (see chapter 10, this volume; Strayhorn & Terrell, 2007). Much like the scholars and researchers of past decades, my research speaks to the critical need for African American students to make these important links and connections to mentors and role models who are familiar with the challenges and pitfalls as well as the opportunities and supports For example, in speaking to the needs of African American males, particularly in terms of the relationships they establish with faculty members, a colleague and I concluded: "To circumvent many of the problems African American males are experiencing in college, purposive initiatives aimed at pairing these students with viable faculty mentors are essential" (Bonner & Bailey, 2006, p. 30). These same needs are critical to African American females as well—actually all students, regardless of race, have been found to benefit from key relationships with mentors or role models who assist them with their matriculation experiences.

Common to discussions associated with mentors and role models for African American students is the view that to be a viable mentor or role model requires the individual to come from the same cultural community as the African American student. Some believe that only African Americans can meet the needs of African American students in a mentoring relationship. However, what the literature (Bonner & Bailey, 2006; Patton & Harper, 2003; Sutton, 2006) reveals is that, while the cultural, ethnic, or racial status of the mentor may play some role, it is not the only factor and often not the most important factor in the protégé receiving what is needed to be successful (Crutcher, 2007). According to Sutton (2006), "Regardless of the mentor's gender or ethnicity, it is imperative that the mentoring experience of the protégé foster learning from an active rather than a passive mode" (p. 97). Sutton's work reveals the importance of focusing on the content of the mentoring relationship rather than on the identity of the mentoring participants. Additionally, Bonner and Bailey (2006) assert that, in PWIs, finding an African American mentor for each African American student presents a challenge that necessitates a more flexible approach to these pairings.

Notwithstanding the function that mentors and role models play in the lives of African American students, investigations are needed that focus on how the nature of these relationships has changed or should change to accommodate a different generational cohort. Earlier I discussed Millennial student cultures; conversations focused on the different needs and expectations that this group brings to higher education and to these mentoring relationships is critical. Perhaps earlier arguments regarding the salience of factors such as race in mentoring relationships are less important to this cohort than are other factors. A prime example is the recent work of F. M. Nave, assistant professor of chemical engineering at Prairie View A&M University (personal communication, December 18, 2007) with a population of high-achieving, African American Millennial college students enrolled in science, technology, engineering, and mathematics (STEM) disciplines in an HBCU. Researchers found that questions they posed to this group about the importance they ascribed to relationships with faculty revealed somewhat different responses from the literature. Additionally, they discovered that although *some* students recognized the importance of establishing relationships with faculty members, *many* did not readily see their benefits, preferring to get what guidance and mentoring they need from peer relationships. Thus, new mentoring frameworks colleges and universities implement may need to take into account this generation's preference for peer mentoring.

Family Relationships and Support

Across the educational continuum, the family is a principal source of support for African American students. Whether these relationships buttress confidence and esteem or act as a buffer against the vicissitudes of lives spent in enclaves that are diametrically opposed to one's background and upbringing experiences, they constitute a major staple in the lives of African American students. In their discussion of African American male students, White and Cones (1999) report that the family meets needs for safety, emotional security, affection, and guidance for these students—factors that are also important for African American female students. According to Bonner and Evans (2004),

> The relationships maintained between collegians and their families are a linchpin holding together an often precarious existence. The student must negotiate life and school circumstances simultaneously with growth and development issues. The overload that can occur often leads to despair and frustration, and sometimes to stopping-out or dropping-out of higher education. The family is invaluable in combating this sense of overload and bewilderment. (p. 15)

What higher education institutions must recognize is that for African American student cohorts, much like their peers from other communities of color, going to college is a collective endeavor that includes family, friends, church, and community (Bonner & Evans, 2004). Therefore, "[a]ny effort to reach the student must accommodate these varied discourse communities who feel some sense of responsibility for the student's ultimate success" (p. 15). Again, if one uses generational cues as a source of information, it becomes readily apparent that this generation, the Millennials, is more connected to parents and extended family members than was any previous generation (Bonner & Hughes, 2007; Coomes & DeBard, 2004; Howe & Strauss, 2000). Thus, to exclude family members from the African American college-going equation could be unfruitful.

Additionally, colleges and universities must determine how best to include family members in their efforts to support the success of African American students. The connections these students make throughout their undergraduate experiences are apparent, so inclusion initiatives should not simply occur at the front end of the higher education experience, but should be provided at key points throughout the college years. Also, culminating decisions (e.g., career, graduate school, professional school) made at the end of the undergraduate career should include family members as well.

The model of family inclusion occurring solely during orientation or other first-year experience programming is not enough for many African American students. And, in many ways, this truncated approach to parental inclusion shows a lack of respect for the needs of these students who want family access and input. Whether institutions provide the necessary support structures to facilitate these relationships is, on the one hand, critically important, and, on the other, is in many ways a moot point. Millennials have shown that they will make these connections regardless of institutional support. However, what a powerful message it would send to this generation that institutions support their efforts to remain connected to family.

Conclusion

This chapter has focused on a range of issues that are part and parcel of the experiences of African American students in academe. While no chapter, compendium, monograph, or volume can ever capture all of the experiences and nuances associated with any student demographic, attempts to bring to light at least a portion of the *challenges* are still critically necessary. As stated in the introduction, this chapter focuses on both a major and minor theme: academic achievement and persistence are the organizing anchors for discussion. What becomes readily apparent in this chapter is that no issue stands in isolation. These factors overlap and connect in ways that create a dynamic collection of issues.

If academe is truly committed to improving the experiences of all students, especially African Americans, developing a set of action plans that pay homage to what students view as critical to their success, while at the same time becoming cultural anthropologists who cull information about students' experiences that often goes unspoken, becomes critical. So, too, is it necessary to routinely (re)visit the issues that have been determined to be salient over the years. A past issue may not be of contemporary importance or it might be operationalized in new and different ways. Perhaps the best example provided in this chapter is the observation made earlier on mentoring and role modeling. Applying age-old approaches or relying solely on data collected more than two decades ago might not work in this particular instance.

Scrutinizing the approaches, data, and findings suggested here should be applied to the themes identified earlier and to other themes as well. More important, these themes should be the starting point in investigating what makes African American students—for lack of a better term—tick. The beauty in identifying themes, as I have done in this chapter, is that this process illuminates and reinforces and validates the research cited here. In contrasting, the downside of using these identified themes is that they can force all of the issues into predetermined boxes. What then happens is that new and competing themes and solutions remain unidentified. It is much easier to force all problems into frameworks that researchers in the field already identified.

For many, simply writing, "according to," replaces the need to go out and conduct original research. Yet, the result is again that all findings have to be rationalized and fit into an existing template. What this chapter has attempted to do is provide a forum to begin the dialogue on African American student achievement and persistence, a dialogue that offers plausible information but does not try to force a particular paradigmatic approach. What will prove most helpful to institutions attempting to understand African American student success is to adopt a flexible stance that accommodates multiple perspectives. Otherwise, academia will rely erroneously on traditional methods that are not applicable to; it will rely instead on the old axiom: *When all you have is a hammer, then every problem begins to look like a nail.* This chapter, along with others in this volume, sheds light on the challenges and supports that affect African American collegians' higher education success. Armed with this information, educators can identify new tools and creative solutions.

References

Aguirre, A., Jr. (2000). Academic storytelling: A critical race theory story of affirmative action. *Sociological Perspectives, 43*, 319–339.

Allen, W. R. (1988). The education of Black students on White college campuses: What quality the experience? In M. T. Nettles (Ed.), *Toward Black undergraduate student equality in American higher education* (pp. 57–86). New York: Greenwood Press.

Allen, W. R. (1992). The color of success: African American college student outcomes at predominantly White and historically Black public colleges and universities. *Harvard Educational Review, 62*(1), 26–44.

Allen, W. R., & Haniff, N. Z. (1991). Race, gender, and academic performance in U.S. higher education. In W. R. Allen, E. G. Epps, & N. Z. Haniff (Eds.), *College in Black and White: African American students in predominantly White and in historically Black public universities* (pp. 95–110). Albany, NY: State University of New York Press.

Asante, M. K. (1988). *Afrocentricity.* Trenton, NJ: Africa World Press.

Astin, A. W. (1993). What matters in college. *Liberal Education, 79*(4), 4–15.

Awad, G. H. (2007). The role of racial identity, academic self-concept, and self-esteem in the prediction of academic outcomes for African American students. *Journal of Black Psychology, 33*, 188–207.

Bonner, F. A., II. (2001). *Gifted African American male college students: A phenomenological study.* Storrs, CT: National Research Center on the Gifted and Talented.

Bonner, F. A., II, & Bailey, K. W. (2006). Enhancing the academic climate for African American men. In M. J. Cuyjet & Associates (Eds.), *African American men in college* (pp. 24–46). San Francisco: Jossey-Bass.

Bonner, F. A., II, & Evans, M. P. (2004). Can you hear me?: Voices and experiences of African American students in higher education. In D. Cleveland (Ed.), *Broken silence: Conversations about race by African American faculty and students on the journey to the professorate* (pp. 3–18). New York: Peter Lang.

Bonner, F. A., II, & Hughes, R. L. (Eds.). (2007). African American millennial college students [Special issue]. *National Association of Student Affairs Professionals Journal, 10*(1).

Bonner, F. A., II, Jennings, M., Marbley, A. F., & Brown, L. (2008). Capitalizing on leadership capacity: Gifted African American males in high school. *Roeper Review, 30*(2), 93–103.

Bonner, F. A., II, & Murry, J. R., Jr. (1998). Historically Black colleges and universities: A unique mission. *National Association of Student Affairs Professionals Journal, 1*(1), 37–49.

Booker, K. C. (2007). Perceptions of classroom belongingness among African American college students. *College Student Journal, 1*(41), 178–186.

Bowser, B. P., & Perkins, H. (1991). Success against the odds: Young Black men tell what it takes. In B. P. Bowser (Ed.), *Black male adolescents: Parenting and education in community context* (pp. 183–200). New York: University Press of America.

Cabrera, A. F., & La Nasa, S. M. (2001). On the path to college: Three critical tasks facing America's disadvantaged. *Research in Higher Education, 42*(2), 119–150.

Cheatham, H. E., Slaney, R. B., & Coleman, N. C. (1990). Institutional effects on psychosocial development of African-American college students. *Journal of Counseling Psychology, 37*(4), 453–458.

Cokley, K. O. (2001). Gender differences among African American students in the impact of racial identity on academic psychosocial development. *Journal of College Student Development, 42*(5), 480–487.

Cokley, K., Komarraju, M., King, A., Cunningham, D., & Muhammad, G. (2003). Ethnic differences in the measurement of academic self-concept in a sample of African American and European American College Students. *Educational and Psychological Measurement, 63*, 707–722.

Coomes, M. D., & DeBard, R. (2004). A generational approach to understanding students. *New Directions for Student Services, 106*, 5–16.

Cross, W. E. (1971). Negro-to-Black conversion experience: Toward a psychology of black liberation. *Black World, 20*(9), 13–27.

Cross, W. E. (1991). Negro to Black conversion experience: Toward a psychology of Black liberation. *Black World, 20*(9), 13–27.

Crutcher, B. N. (2007). Mentoring across cultures. *Academe Online.* Retrieved September 5, 2008, from www.aaup.org/AAUP/pubsres/academe/2007/JA/Feat/crut.htm

Cuyjet, M. J. (Ed.). (1997). *Helping African American men succeed in college.* San Francisco: Jossey-Bass.

Cuyjet, M. J. (2006). *African American men in college.* San Francisco: Jossey-Bass.

Davis, J. E. (1994). College in Black and White: Campus environment and academic achievement of African American males. *Journal of Negro Education, 63*, 620–633.

DeBard, R. (2004). Millennials coming to college. *New Directions for Student Services, 106*, 33–45.

DeSousa, D. J., & Kuh, G. D. (1996). Does institutional racial composition make a difference in what Black students gain from college? *Journal of College Student Development, 37*(3), 257–267.

Dilworth, P. P., & Carter, S. M. (2007). Millennial versus hip hop: Exploring Black undergraduate students' perspective on socially constructed labels. *National Association of Student Affairs Professionals Journal, 10*(1), 70–84.

Fischer M. J. (2007). Settling into campus life: Differences by race/ethnicity in college involvement and outcomes. *Journal of Higher Education, 78*, 125–161.

Fleming, J. (1981). Special needs of Blacks and other minorities. In A. W. Chickering & Associates (Eds.), *The modern American college: Responding to the new realities of diverse students and a changing society* (pp. 279–295). San Francisco: Jossey-Bass.

Fleming, J. (1984). *Blacks in college.* San Francisco: Jossey-Bass.

Fleming, J. (2000). Affirmative action and standardized test scores. *Journal of Negro Education, 69*(1/2) 27–37.

Flowers, L. A. (2002). The impact of college racial composition on African American students' academic and social gains: Additional evidence. *Journal of College Student Development, 43*(3), 403–410.

Freeman, K. (1999). My soul is missing: African American students' perceptions of the curriculum and the influence on college choice. *Review of African American Education, 1*(l), 31–43.

Harper, S. R., Carini, R. M., Bridges, B. K., & Hayek, J. (2004). Gender differences in student engagement among African American undergraduates at historically Black colleges and universities. *Journal of College Student Development, 45,* 271–284.

Hausmann, L. R. M., Schofield, J. W., & Woods, R. L. (2007). Sense of belonging as a predictor of intentions to persist among African American and White first-year college students. *Research in Higher Education, 48*(7), 803–840.

Hossler, D., Braxton, J., & Coopersmith, G. (1989). Understanding student college choice. In J. Smart (Ed.), *Higher education: Handbook of theory and research* (pp. 231–288). New York: Agathon Press.

Hossler, D., & Gallagher, K. (1987). Studying college choice: A three-phase model and the implication for policy makers. *College and University, 2,* 207–221.

Howe, N., & Strauss, W. (2000). *Millennials rising: The next great generation.* New York: Vintage Press.

Hughes, M. S. (1987). Black students' participation in higher education. *Journal of College Student Personnel, 28,* 532–545.

Litten, L. H. (1982). Different strokes in the applicant pool: Some refinements in a model of student college choice. *Journal of Higher Education, 53,* 383–402.

McDonough, P. M. (1994). Buying and selling higher education: The social construction of the college applicant. *Journal of Higher Education, 65,* 427–446.

McDonough, P. M. (1997). *Choosing colleges. How social class and schools structure opportunity.* Albany, NY: State University of New York Press.

McGlynn, A. P. (2005, October 10). Teaching millennials, our newest cultural cohort. *The Hispanic Outlook in Higher Education.* Retrieved November 9, 2009, from http://www.hispanic.outlook.com

Pascarella, E. T., & Terenzini, P. T. (1979). Student-faculty informal contact and college persistence: A further investigation. *Journal of Educational Research, 72,* 214–218.

Pascarella, E. T., & Terenzini, P. T. (1991). *How college affects students.* San Francisco: Jossey-Bass.

Pascarella, E. T., & Terenzini, P. T. (2005). *How college affects students, Vol. 2, A Third Decade of Research.* San Francisco: Jossey-Bass.

Patton, L. D., & Harper, S. R. (2003). Mentoring relationships among African American women in graduate and professional schools. *New Directions for Student Services, 104,* 67–78.

Smith, D. G. (1997). *Diversity works: The emerging picture of how students benefit.* Washington, DC: Association of American Colleges and Universities.

Smith, M. J., & Fleming, M. K. (2006). African American parents in the search stage of college choice. *Urban Education, 41*(1), 71–100.

Stordahl, K. J. (1970). Student perceptions of influence on college choice. *Journal of Educational Research, 63*(5), 209–212.

Strayhorn, T. L. (2008a). Sentido de pertenencia: A hierarchical analysis predicting sense of belonging among Latino college students. *Journal of Hispanic Higher Education, 7*(4), 301–320.

Strayhorn, T. L. (2008b). The role of supportive relationships in facilitating African American males' success in college. *NASPA Journal, 45*(1), 26–48.

Strayhorn, T. L., & Terrell, M. C. (2007). Mentoring and satisfaction with college for Black students. *The Negro Educational Review, 58*(1–2), 69–83.

Sutton, M. (2006). Developmental mentoring of African American college men. In M. J. Cuyjet (Ed.), *African American men in college* (pp. 69–94). San Francisco: Jossey-Bass.

Tinto, V. (1975). Dropout from higher education: A theoretical synthesis of recent research. *Review of Educational Research, 45,* 89–125.

Tinto, V. (1993). *Leaving college: Rethinking the causes and cures of student attrition* (2nd ed.). Chicago: University of Chicago Press.

Watson, L. W., Terrell, M. C., Wright, D. J., Bonner, F. A. II, Cuyjet, M., Gold, J., et al. (2002). *How minority students experience college: Implications for planning and policy.* Sterling, VA: Stylus.

White, J. L., & Cones, J. H. (1999). *Black man emerging: Facing the past and seizing a future in America.* New York: W. H. Freeman.

5

TRIPLE THREAT

Challenges and Supports of Black Gay Men at
Predominantly White Campuses

Terrell L. Strayhorn, Amanda M. Blakewood,
and James M. DeVita

Man cannot remake himself without suffering, for
he is both the marble and the sculptor.

—Dr. Alexis Carrel

Abstract: In this chapter, the authors share new findings from a qualitative study of Black male undergraduates who identify as gay/bisexual. Major findings were organized into two broad categories: challenges and supports. Specifically, participants spoke in detail about the academic and social challenges they faced in college (e.g., lack of sense of belonging, coming out, homophobia and racism, multiple minority status), as well as factors that provided much-needed support (e.g., relationships with peers). Implications for improving campus experiences for Black gay male undergraduates are presented at the end of the chapter, as well as evidence-based recommendations for shaping educational practice.

I t has been said that college is a time of self-exploration, a time to learn about oneself and to develop the confidence to stand on one's own, despite adversity. However, as many who have navigated this process can attest, it is not always easy. It can be especially complicated if one's identity is multidimensional, thereby requiring an individual to manage and negotiate multiple developmental tasks simultaneously that, at times, may be in conflict (Jones, 1997; Jones & McEwen, 2000).

Several theorists have attempted to explain identity development for various subgroups, including racial/ethnic minorities (Cross, 1971, 1995;

Helms, 1990); women (Gilligan, 1982; Josselson, 1987); and people who identify as lesbian, gay, bisexual, and transgender (Cass, 1979; D'Augelli, 1994).
However, these theories are not necessarily applicable for gay students of
color (Evans & Broido, 1999; Evans & Wall, 1991).

Indeed, some evidence suggests that identity development is a more complex process when multiple identities are developing simultaneously (Stevens,
2004); managing multiple developmental processes at one time can be difficult,
and such developmental crises may compromise student success. And while we
know a good deal about identity development in general, and for particular
subpopulations such as gays and lesbians, we know comparatively little about
how multiple dimensions of identity affect students' experiences in college.
The study on which this chapter is based addresses this gap.

This chapter presents key findings from stories shared by seven participants. Each participant is an African American male college student who
identifies as gay or bisexual and who, according to theory, is trying to resolve
issues of personal identity. Through the participants' voices we learn of factors that were critical to their success and their challenges and supports. By
giving voice to their experiences, we hope we might learn how to better
support this largely invisible population through more informed campus
policies, programs, and educational practices.

What We Know From Theory

To start, let us look at existing literature on identity development. As mentioned earlier, identity development theory generally focuses on a single
dimension of identity (e.g., race) and seeks to explain the stages through
which development occurs. Thus, we organized this section into two separate
categories that relate to the chapter's focus: racial identity theory and lesbian,
gay, bisexual, and transgender (LGBT) identity theory.

Racial Identity Theory

Cross (1971, 1995) proposes a model of African American racial identity
development, known as Nigresence Theory; that is, the process by which
persons "become Black." Specifically, he defines five stages of development: (a) pre-encounter, (b) encounter, (c) immersion, (d) emersion, and
(e) internalization-commitment. In Cross's first stage, Black individuals view
race as unimportant and may even have an anti-Black perspective. In the
"encounter" stage, an individual faces a situation where he or she can no
longer ignore race as a factor. Consequently, the individual's worldview is

shaken and his or her current identity is challenged. In Stage 3, immersion-emersion, the individual must shed his or her old identity (e.g., race as unimportant) and adopt a new one that acknowledges the salience of race to the individual's existence. The fourth stage, internalization, begins the process by which the individual starts to resolve his or her identity, gaining a sense of self-confidence about being Black. Internalization-commitment is marked by the individual's commitment to helping other African Americans and oppressed peoples address issues of social justice.

In sum, Nigrescence is a "resocializing experience" (Cross, 1995, p. 97). Individuals *resocialize* by moving from a stage of non-Afrocentrism to Afro-centrism and, finally, resolving their identity in a state of multiculturalism. As they grow and develop racially, Blacks also acquire skills to balance both internal and external responses to racism.

Theoretically based research on racial identity development specific to Black college students is relatively scant compared to the vast number of studies that focus on Black students' campus involvement and engagement in educationally purposeful activities without explicit reference to developmental theory. A few studies, however, have uncovered some important findings. For example, one study indicated that pre-encounter Black students tend to have lower self-esteem, whereas students in advanced stages tend to have higher, more positive views of self (Parham & Helms, 1981). Another study linked participation in cultural and noncultural campus organizations to one's level of identity development. Results of this study indicate that students in advanced stages of "becoming Black" are more likely to be involved in cultural organizations (e.g., Black student union, Black political groups) than are those students who are in the beginning stages of development (Mitchell & Dell, 1992). In addition to these studies, several others have begun to explore the experiences of Black males, including work on African American male collegians (e.g., Davis, 1994; Strayhorn, 2008a, 2008b); student athletes (e.g., Messer, 2006); and even Black male student leaders (e.g., Harper, 2003).

Lesbian, Gay, Bisexual, Transgender (LGBT) Identity Theory

Cass (1979) developed the first identity development theory on gay individuals. She proposed that gay individuals negotiate their identity by progressing through six stages, beginning at identity confusion and, ultimately, ending with identity synthesis. To resolve his gay identity successfully, an individual must understand his role as a gay male, acknowledge he exists in a heterosexual world, be willing to tolerate and accept his role as a sexual minority, and balance the internal and external pressures by taking pride in his sexual identity (Cass, 1979, 1984). Although Cass provided the first enduring theory on gay individuals, her theory has been criticized because it assumes that development occurs through linear stage-like progressions (Stevens, 2004) and is perhaps most applicable to gay White males only (Wall & Washington, 1991). More recent models of sexual identity development have attempted to account for the limitations of Cass's theory, most notably D'Augelli's framework (1994). D'Augelli posits a lifetime span model that underscores the importance of disclosure of one's sexual identity (i.e., coming out) and integration into the gay community. Additionally, his model allows for more flexible movement or "developmental plasticity" through six interactive processes. A growing number of scholars (e.g., Jones & McEwen, 2000), however, suggest that identity development is too complicated a process to be illustrated by two-dimensional, linear models; thus, they have proposed multidimensional models.

While most prevailing theories posit an orderly stage-wise progression from a private sense of self as nonheterosexual to a public acknowledgment or acceptance of one's LGBT identity, one theory focuses on the intersectionality of multiple socially constructed identities (i.e., race, gender, sexuality) into the "core self" (Jones & McEwen, 2000). Theories that account for multiple dimensions of identity have been aptly applied in previous studies on women college students (Jones, 1997) and lesbian college students (Abes, 2003; Abes & Jones, 2004), but no studies were readily uncovered that use such theoretical understandings to study the experiences of Black gay undergraduate men in college. This is the space this chapter seeks to fill.

In the following section we describe the study that provided data for the chapter. Then we present themes, challenges, and supports identified by African-American gay male undergraduates as they worked to resolve their identities and come to terms with themselves as "Black," "gay," and "male."

The Study

To investigate this issue, we interviewed seven African American male college students who identify as either gay or bisexual. Most participants were members (or attended a meeting) of the on-campus organization for LGBT students at some point in their college career. Researchers sent e-mails to the president of the organization that explained the study, any associated risks, and invited participants who met the criteria to enroll in the study. We located additional participants using a form of snowball sampling, where we asked participants to recommend other potential participants.

The final sample consisted of seven "information rich" (Patton, 1990, p. 169) participants. Since we wanted the interviews to be candid, we promised them anonymity. However, they can be described in "rich, thick" terms (Geertz, 1973). Table 5.1 summarizes the sample.

Each participant was allowed to choose his interviewer from the three members of the research team, which comprised an African American male faculty member, a gay White male doctoral student, and a White female doctoral student. One-on-one interviews were conducted with each participant using a semistructured interview protocol; each interview lasted 50–90 minutes, on average. All interviews were audiotaped and later transcribed verbatim by a professional. Each researcher read the transcripts several times to identify emerging themes. Once all themes were identified, researchers met to argue out their differences. For more information about the study and its procedures, see Strayhorn, Blakewood, and DeVita (2008).

Discussion of Findings

This section is organized into two major categories: challenges and supports. In some instances, participants reported a single factor as both a challenge and a support. Verbatim quotes are presented, where possible, to illustrate the in vivo meaning and significance of themes.

Challenges

Sense of belonging. Findings suggest that, like other students (e.g., Osterman, 2000), Black gay males (BGMs) at PWIs need to establish a connection to the institution that makes them feel comfortable and as if they belong in college. Establishing meaningful friendships with others is one way Black gay males facilitate a sense of belonging, although many reported difficulty in doing so. Participants described several strategies they used to negotiate such friendships. For example, Blake, a finance major who aspires to coach cheerleaders, described how joking makes his friends comfortable with him and helps him fit in among his White friends:

> For the most part my friends are comfortable with my being [a Black gay male] . . . because I always make a joke about it. I'm so used to being the only Black guy in a room. So I'm always making, like, "the Black joke," that everyone is thinking but not really saying. It's just humorous to me

TABLE 5.1
Description of Study Participants ($N = 7$)

Pseudonym	Major	Minor	Clubs & Activities	Mom's Job	Dad's Job	Career Aspiration
Terrance	Spanish	Dance	Dance Company	Office Manager	Shift Supervisor	Business or Education
Leon	Vocal Performance	Theater	All Campus Theater	State Internal Revenue Specialist	Owner of a Construction Company	Musical Theater Performance
Blake	Finance	Accounting Collateral	Cheerleading	House Manager for Girls' Program	Manager	Coaching Cheerleading
Lamont	Journalism & Electronic Media and French	N/A	Orientation Leader, Model UN, College Democrats	Nurse	Manager	Media Management
Lawrence	Architecture	Japanese	Employee: Fast Food & Retail	Self-Employed	IT Specialist	Business Architecture
Desmond	Public Relations, Psychology	Business Administration	NAACP, Honor Societies, Black Cultural Programming Committee	County Health Inspector	City Clerk's Office	Lifestyle Public Relations Practitioner
Sidney	Opera	Dance	Campus Opera/ Theater	—	—	Famous Opera Singer

for me to be the only Black guy, or the only "gay guy." So I crack jokes all the time so they don't really have a problem with it.

Blake's comments also reveal several challenges he encountered in college. First, he used self-deprecating humor, which may suggest a level of discomfort in being around certain individuals (i.e., friends) on whom he relies for support. Additionally, Blake admitted that he sometimes felt a tremendous burden in these situations to "play down" his race and/or sexuality for his friends. By colluding in the perpetuation of stereotypes about his identities, Blake may do unconscious and unnecessary harm to his own development and prevent his friends from ever knowing his "core self." Thus, struggling to fit in is clearly one challenge Black gay males at PWIs face, and while similar, in general, to the challenges of their same-race heterosexual peers, whom Strayhorn (2008a) studied, there may be serious developmental consequences for Black gay men who are working to resolve issues of race and sexuality. This is fertile ground for future research and innovative educational practices.

Coming out. Virtually all participants expressed the desire to come out during their time in college. Lawrence, for example, said that "coming to [college] was basically coming out for [me] because back home only a select few knew." Statements like his affirm that college is viewed as a time of self-discovery, of new beginnings, of coming out for BGMs.

Other participants linked the disclosure of their sexual orientation to their happiness. Blake stated:

> Like, I came to college knowing that I knew sometime in freshman year that I would be out. And I know a lot of Black people aren't. And if you can live with that, sure, go for it. But I couldn't. Just accept that. Try to be yourself as much as you can, because there are ways that you can do it.

Unlike his discomfort among White friends discussed in the previous section, Blake seemed quite comfortable with himself and the prospect of coming out. His statement also points to a tension between his two identities. Blake is clearly aware of other African Americans who are not out, and many out gay men who are not Black. He realized that he could not live "in the closet" in terms of his sexual orientation. Several other participants shared these sentiments.

The need for disclosure and the tensions between Blake's two or three social identities create unique challenges for him, challenges that many college student educators probably are unprepared to support. For instance,

Blake, along with a few others, shared how difficult the coming out process was for them because they lost friends who found their sexuality unacceptable, grew distant from family members who found their sexuality embarrassing or sinful, and struggled to make new friends who accepted their sexuality. These difficulties may be the "struggle" to which Alexis Carrel refers in the quotation that began this chapter.

While Blake diffused this challenge by exercising his agency to "live out," other students, particularly other BGMs, may not have the personal strength or capacity (i.e., self-authorship) to openly identify as gay in the face of others' opinions—even though other students are aware of their sexual identity. Thus, the desire to come out during college presents unique challenges for BGMs as well as opportunities for educators to support such students.

Be True to Thyself. For our participants, enrolling in college allowed them to disclose their sexual orientation. Such disclosure contributed to each student's ability to be free from the psychological oppression of hiding his sexual orientation, even if it did not allow him to be fully comfortable in all settings with all people. Not all BGMs in the study share Lawrence and Blake's sense of self, however. Leon, for example, said that he is frequently unable to be himself around friends:

> When I'm talking with somebody about something, especially with relationships, [I] have to watch . . . how [I] say things, [and] stuff like that. It gets tiring at times because at the end of the day . . . it's basically . . . you're telling a lie, but it's a lie to yourself. . . . [Sometimes I] feel like [I'm not] being totally [me] in a conversation with friends who may not know [I'm gay]. Or still friends who may know but they . . . they might not know everything.

Leon's discomfort stems directly from his unwillingness to disclose his sexual orientation unconditionally. Simply put, he struggles to be his true self because he is not out to everyone, and he believes that some people, especially his Black peers, "are not ready to handle him being out."

The challenge represented here is related directly to the issue of coming out. Although coming out is often described as a one-time event or final destination (D'Augelli, 1994), evidence from our studies suggests that it is actually an ongoing process where selections regarding disclosure must be made on a day-to-day, case-by-case basis for BGMs. While Lawrence and Blake chose to disclose their sexuality regardless of the situation, Leon and Desmond were more selective. This results in what Leon referred to as "not being totally me"; instead he constantly reflects on whom he has told, how much he has disclosed, and "who knows what when." Some explained that this process of juggling lies can be physically and mentally exhausting and may distract a student from his academic responsibilities. For instance, some participants talked about avoiding group settings such as tutoring or study sessions where some people might know about his sexual identity while others might not.

Depression. Research has shown that internalized oppression and marginalization could result in more serious psychological problems, such as depression, if left untreated. D'Augelli (1993) found that gay and lesbian college students are at high risk for mental health problems because of issues they encounter managing their personal development. While one solution D'Augelli recommends is the support of individuals who are experiencing similar problems, this may be less possible for Black gay undergraduate men given the paucity of African American men in higher education (Cuyjet, 2006), not to mention those who openly identify as gay (Icard, 1986). It is not surprising, then, that Lamont described his battle with depression from early adolescence:

> Yeah, I've had depression for a long time; from middle school until sophomore year of high school, is when I stopped going to a psychiatrist. And it wasn't because he said that I didn't need to, but I just stopped because I felt, like . . . , you know, I don't want to [do this forever]. And it's time for me to get away from it. So sometimes—especially the first day it got really cold. It was really hot for a long time, and then one day it was like freezing. And that day, I felt THE [emphasis added] worst possible ever.

Recently, colleges and universities have invested considerable time and resources in offering more programs and services that address the mental health challenges that students face. However, colleges must also be prepared to address the mental health issues of those who may face multiple challenges or developmental crises simultaneously, such as BGMs. For example, study participants reported that *going to college* provoked or encouraged their desire (and willingness) to *come out*. This decision presented them with new, as well as previously resolved, developmental questions (e.g., Who am I? Who matters most? How do others perceive me?). Struggling to resolve these issues required participants to question unexamined assumptions of race and sexuality; consider perspectives that were different from those inherited from or taught at home and even use coping strategies to navigate various social settings. College student educators should consider these findings when working with BGMs and similar students because such individuals may require support from others (e.g., counselors, mentors, advisors) to work through this process.

Teaching Heterosexual Individuals. Many participants expressed difficulty interacting with heterosexual nonminority individuals because of the burden of teaching them about their identities. In many cases, the participants had to inform them not only about their gay identity, but also about how race and sexual orientation interact. While this burden is a challenge for BGMs, Leon was proud of his ability to inform some of his friends:

> I've gotten more people to be aware of [what it's like to be gay] . . . [and I'm proud] of my getting people, certain friends, mainly the ones who I doubt whether [they're] comfortable because [I'm gay and Black]. . . . My freshman year, last year, when I met them [they weren't comfortable at all], but now who actually can have conversation about being gay or being gay and Black. Some who know about me and some who don't . . . it's just the fact that I've gotten them to engage in conversation and I feel comfortable [enough to] have a conversation with them about it.

Leon viewed his experiences talking with heterosexual individuals as a success. However, other participants characterized this burden as a major challenge they have had to overcome. To support African American gay males, college campuses might develop educational initiatives on sexuality (including gay issues), which are likely to attract a broader audience. Additionally, educational programs should include discussions of how social identities can intersect and compound one's challenges and should offer strategies for managing such issues as well.

Multiple Minority Status. It is not surprising, that nearly all of the participants described feeling as if they already had "two strikes against them" as a double-minority, given the challenges described earlier regarding their racial identity (i.e., being Black) and sexual orientation (i.e., being gay). Leon poignantly explains, through tears, this notion of double- or triple-minority status:

> Now as a Black gay man, I haven't seen anything done towards it, so that's kind of a difficult field to cater to because that's a combination of some of probably two of the hardest things on this campus that need to be addressed, which is kind of hard to fix. So you can't really fix it right there, or take some time, and then fix it, [you] have to change a lot of things within the university. . . . Unfortunately as a Black gay man, I mean it's

just you're already coming in with . . . you're already coming in with two strikes against you . . . maybe even three.

Careful analysis of Leon's statement suggests that some Black gay undergraduate men feel as if they are in double jeopardy as Black males. Being gay adds a third strike against Black men, according to some of our participants. Facing triple threats places them at risk for failure in educational and social settings, especially in environments that are largely incongruent with or unaccepting of one or all three of their social identities.

Findings demonstrate that supporting African American gay males is critical to their success in college. While Leon has seen "nothing done" to support his group, he also acknowledges that it is hard to address multiple social pathologies (e.g., racism, homophobia) at once. Perhaps the best advice one can offer is to start "somewhere, even with one issue," realizing that "isms" rarely exist in isolation. Attempts to dismantle injustice anywhere are a threat to injustice everywhere.

Homophobia and Racism. As anticipated, several participants described experiencing harassment, or knowing others who have been harassed, on campus. These findings are consistent with other studies, which have found that as many as 50% of all gay college students face harassment (Rankin, 1998). African American gay males discussed harassment based on both identities from multiple individuals; Desmond's description was particularly troubling:

> If one decides to [go to college], I'd just tell [a prospective Black gay male] to be ready to face racism and homophobia . . . like White people here don't really respect Black students . . . it's not everyone but a lot of them, especially White faculty, and there's all this stuff going on with racist remarks on campus. . . . On the other hand, he's gonna deal with homophobia from Black people . . . it's like they're mistreated so now they want to mistreat somebody . . . even the ones who are [gay] . . . they do it too.

The frankness of his comments demonstrates how overt racism and discrimination can be at PWIs for BGMs. As Blacks, they may face racism from their White peers; as gay men, they may face homophobia from their Black peers. And those who perpetrate these offenses are not limited to peers, but may include faculty members as well. Colleges should ensure that mechanisms are in place for reporting and addressing such incidents in a timely manner. Working together, Blacks and gays must try to reduce, if not eliminate, homophobia and racism by "engaging in dialogue with . . .

advocates . . . , confronting and correcting homophobic [and racist] attitudes, and understanding how these attitudes prevent the liberation of the
total being" (Clarke, 1999, p. 43). Establishing coalitions across groups,
cosponsoring campus events that address the mutual concerns of both
groups, and turning attention to issues of social (in)justice rather than divi-
sive political and religious views are several ways to work together. Given the
power differential between faculty members and students, campuses should
implement new or reinforce existing policies that support students who experience faculty harassment. Transparent and timely action in the face of
harassment is the best way to support students, or any individuals, facing it.

Supports

The final section of this chapter explores both on- and off-campus support
systems for African American gay males. Participants identified these systems
as either valuable to their success or challenges they encounter. Some offer
opportunities for colleges to provide greater support, while others require
more creative initiatives to counteract their negative influences. In either
case, institutions need to be aware of how students perceive and respond to
these specific support systems.

Relationships With White Peers. African American students are often
expected to get support from other African American individuals on campus.
However, for African American gay males, relationships with White individuals, both socially and romantically, were significant. Sidney, for example,
says that most of his friends are White:

> For most of my life, the way I've just been raised, and the situations I've
> been in, the groups and the interests I've had and whatnot. It's just put
> me around more White people. It's just the way it's been for me.

Sidney's experience is consistent with Harris's (2003) findings that African
American gay males from predominantly White communities tend to be
more comfortable around White individuals when they arrive at college.
Thus, while establishing meaningful connections between African American
and White students at PWIs is often viewed as a challenge, this does not
seem true for BGMs, who report facing more difficulty socializing with
Black heterosexual males than with White or gay peers.

Similar to Sidney's comfort with White individuals as friends, several
participants expressed a desire to have romantic relationships with White
males exclusively. For instance, Blake stated:

First of all, because I've not been around a lot of other Black people, it's like I'm normally attracted to White guys. So I don't know how much of that is actually based on me just not being around Black guys. I don't think that I have. . . . Like, is there a typical White outlook on Black guys? But I'm just normally attracted to White guys. We're in the South and a smaller community. So it's hard to find another stay-in-shape White guy who's in college, or around my age at least, that likes Black guys—which is what I'm looking for. That's really hard to find. I almost found it once, but it just never took off.

Blake, like Sidney, attributes his attraction to White males to his socialization in a predominantly White community while growing up. Although clearly Black, the young men with whom we spoke tended to feel more comfortable socializing with their White, often gay, peers. Since many supports for African American students on college campuses seem to provide opportunities for African Americans to interact with each other, this finding underscores an often missing piece of information—namely, the supportive role White students can play in the success of their Black peers, especially those who may be marginalized even within oppressed groups. Creating spaces where BGMs can interact in meaningful ways with White, gay, or heterosexual peers may be helpful. Also, findings remind college student educators that one-size-fits-all approaches may not work well, especially for students whose experiences are shaped by multiple dimensions of identity and those who live at multiple margins (hooks, 2004).

Affinity Groups. Many colleges have student organizations that provide emotional, psychological, and social supports to their members. These organizations help students meet others who are like them and get integrated into campus culture. Participants reported involvement in several organizations: Black student union, NAACP, historically Black fraternities, LGBT student group, and gospel choir. While participants acknowledged each of these as critical to participants' academic success, some also identified several challenges. Sidney had this to say about the LGBT group on campus:

I was involved in [the LGBT group] second semester of my freshman year and, like, a year after that. But [it] is just not a society for me. It's very politically driven. And for better or for worse, I'm not that political of a person. I know I should be, but my interests and my involvement just lies elsewhere. Especially in that group, where—I don't know—it's just a weird dynamic. I just don't really, you know. They're just very political, and they get very irritated over small things. And it just seems like they just want to, like, make a noise and make a commotion. And it's, like, "Yeah, we understand you want to say we're gay or we can do what we want." And, you know, we want to fight for rights, but I think there's a more productive way of going about it. But that's just me.

Several participants reported involvement in affinity groups that were religious in nature, one of which is the campus gospel choir. Although some research underscores the role gospel choir involvement plays in supporting African American college students (e.g., Strayhorn, in press), the benefits of gospel choir involvement are not the same for all Black students. BGM gospel choir members, in our study, described how they masked their sexuality when interacting with other choir members (e.g., pretending to have girlfriends), endured negative comments or "sermons" about sexuality from other choir members or pastors, and struggled to negotiate spaces where they were forced to make decisions about "which aspect of [my]self could be expressed." Participants explained in detail that they felt uncomfortable as "Black and Christian" in gay environments, "gay and Christian" in some Black environments, and gay in Christian environments. This is an important finding to note as it demonstrates that marginalization, alienation, and oppression can even occur *within* marginalized communities.

Thus, identity-based organizations can be unappealing to the very students they intend to serve. This is an important caveat for college student educators to keep in mind as they consider how to meet the needs of an increasingly diverse and heterogeneous student population. Not all Black students aspire to be involved in Black organizations. And it's equally true that not all gay organizations are of interest to all gay students. As the student body grows and changes over time, this caveat is likely to become more the rule than the exception.

One reason why BGMs may feel as if they don't fit into gay, African American, or Christian student organizations is that the organization focuses on one aspect of their identity only, without bridging multiple concerns. Sidney, for example, does not have a strong desire to be politically active, so he did not find the LGBT organization suitable, but he might have been more involved in the LGBT student group if the organization catered to other dimensions of his identity (e.g., tackled homophobia in the Black community). Here we see an example of an intended support that fails to fulfill its goal. Colleges should encourage student organizations to provide a variety of programs and initiatives that meet the needs of diverse student populations. Additionally, if institutions could successfully model and encourage collaborations between organizations with distinct missions, students belonging to multiple identities might feel more comfortable getting involved with one, the other, or both groups.

Religion. Many college campuses provide opportunities for students to maintain their involvement in religious and spiritual pursuits. These opportunities can be powerful sources of support for students from diverse backgrounds (see Stewart, this volume). Several participants identified as Christian, despite the issues they encounter practicing religion as African American gay males. Religion has become particularly problematic in Sidney's life:

> My Dad recently decided he's been called to minister, so he's becoming a Minister. My mom's secretary of a church who sends me about five forwarded e-mails from like the Purpose Driven Life and all these religious things, and I am a religious person, but just growing up in the church, my parents being so involved, and hearing all the . . . like, the back story about issues of people, it's kind of turned me off to these religious people in this church. But, since my parents are so religious and already giving me hell about just not going to church as often as I should and all this stuff—[it's difficult for me to be comfortable with religion].

Although religion has been an ongoing influence in Sidney's life, and continues to play a significant role in his family's life, it is clearly a site of intrapersonal struggle. Other participants expressed similar tensions, but related them more directly to discomfort with religious views, tradition, and Christian views about homosexuality. For example, Lawrence said he "can tell that some people in the church . . . [are not okay with my being gay]." His excitement about being involved in church activities is diminished by the lack of support he receives from fellow parishioners.

To ensure that campus-based organizations are supportive and inclusive of all individuals, institutions must consider how campus policies and practices affect *all* students. For instance, campus policies that assume heterosexual relationships (e.g., family housing, roommate assignments) might privilege some students while disadvantaging others. Once again, collaborative initiatives might be an effective solution, as having many voices at the decision-making table can reduce the odds of overlooking the interests of particular groups. This need not require enormous human or fiscal resources but rather a will to think outside the box about creating an environment that is conducive to the development and success of all people, even those whose voices are often unheard and whose experiences are often unseen.

Family. The most significant off-campus support our participants described was undoubtedly their families. Brothers, sisters, parents, and grandparents all had a major influence on the lives of the African American gay males in this study. As expected, some participants found their families to be very supportive, while others presented challenges. Terrance described the support network from his siblings:

> My sister and I are very close—I don't know how, even though there are 12 years apart between us. I think it's just because, I don't know . . . we were close because she was still at home when I was born. My brother, he was, like, going to college when I was born, so we're not that close. It's just always, like, "Oh, if you need anything, call me."

In contrast, Blake's family is a challenge to his happiness at times:

> Well, the only reason I told my Mom [I was gay] was because in sopho-more year I got sick. . . . And she was, "OK." She didn't really blow up at me, but I think that's because she's already dealt with it once with my Dad, because my Dad is gay, too. . . . So that's really messed her [up] . . . all the animosity between her and my dad or any that she might have with me, even though I don't think she had any, is because of [his coming out to her]. I still kind of blame him for all the problems that I've had family-wise. Not getting along, why I had to move thousands of miles away from where I was, it was because of him. I haven't actually said that to him, but I still kind of blame him for a lot of stuff. Other than that, he's just never been there. He's never been around. It's like, if I want something, I really have to ask him for it. Like every time. It doesn't matter if it's, like, a birthday gift. . . . And we've never even really talked about the being gay thing with each other. Like, when I came out, he asked me if my mother blamed him for me being gay.

The contrast between Terrance and Blake's family lives represents the breadth of experiences the African American gay males in this study shared. Additionally, they represent the various challenges and supports that must be balanced for these young men to succeed in college.

Indeed, family can greatly facilitate or hinder one's development, as illustrated earlier. One of the most surprising findings was that Blake's father, who was also gay, provided no support for him in his transition to college. Not only did his father offer little financial support, but he also failed to provide the emotional support that Blake reported as necessary to his success in college. Additionally, the impact of his father's sexual orientation on his mother probably affected Blake's adjustment to college and his willingness to come out to his mother. Although no institution could possibly be aware of such a unique situation, appropriate supports (e.g., counseling, LGBT resource center, safe zone) should be available for students who are otherwise left to shoulder such formidable challenges on their own. Institutions should also take special care to publicize widely the availability of such services.

Conclusion

This chapter has identified several challenges for African American gay males. It is important to note that, although these challenges have been experienced by a group of African American gay males, they were limited to just one campus. Even though we have discussed a broad range of challenges, including everything from internalized, psychological issues to stereotypes and fear of harassment, Black gay men face other challenges as well (see Strayhorn, Blakewood, & DeVita, 2008). Future studies should use similar methods to identify additional challenges and new supports.

We also discussed throughout this chapter potential supports that colleges could offer to counteract the negative effects of the challenges described. Obviously, some of these are easier to implement than others. Many of the ideas for potential support, in fact, came from the African American gay males interviewed. Thus, colleges should be willing to engage Black gay undergraduate men in conversations about their experiences on campus. By doing so, they probably will be able to understand these students' experiences better, but they also will learn about best practices for supporting them. Increased awareness, collaborative initiatives, and improving campus climates for racial/ethnic minorities and LGBT students are a few supports recommended for colleges. Enhancing current support systems, most notably counseling services, is also important, but it must be accompanied by efforts to publicize their availability to LGBT communities of color, especially Black gay undergraduate men who face triple threats in predominantly White collegiate environments.

References

Abes, E. S. (2003). *The dynamics of lesbian college students' multiple dimensions of identity.* Unpublished doctoral dissertation, The Ohio State University, Columbus.

Abes, E. S., & Jones, S. R. (2004). Meaning-making capacity and the dynamics of lesbian college students' multiple dimensions of identity. *Journal of College Student Development, 45,* 612–632.

Cass, V. C. (1979). Homosexuality identity formation: A theoretical model. *Journal of Homosexuality, 4*(3), 219–235.

Cass, V. C. (1984). Homosexuality identity formation: Testing a theoretical model. *Journal of Sex Research, 9*(1–2), 105–126.

Clarke, C. (1999). The failure to transform: Homophobia in the Black community. In E. Brandt (Ed.), *Dangerous liaisons: Blacks, gays, and the struggle for equality* (pp. 31–44). New York: The New Press.

Cross, W. E. (1971). Toward a psychology of Black liberation: The Negro-to-Black conversion experience. *Black World, 20*(9), 13–27.

Cross, W. E. (1995). The psychology of Nigrescence: Revising the Cross model. In J. G. Ponterotto et al. (Eds.), *Handbook on multicultural counseling* (pp. 93–122). Thousand Oaks, CA: Sage.

D'Augelli, A. R. (1993). Preventing mental health problems among gay and lesbian college students. *The Journal of Primary Prevention, 13*(4), 245–261.

D'Augelli, A. R. (1994). Identity development and sexual orientation: Toward a model of lesbian, gay, and bisexual development. In E. J. Trickett, R. J. Watts, & D. Birman (Eds.), *Human diversity: Perspectives on people in context* (pp. 312–333). San Francisco: Jossey-Bass.

Davis, J. E. (1994). College in Black and White: Campus environment and academic achievement of African American males. *Journal of Negro Education, 63*(4), 620.

Evans, N. J., & Broido, E. M. (1999). Coming out in college residence halls: Negotiation, meaning making, challenges, supports. *Journal of College Student Development, 40,* 658–668.

Evans, N. J., & Wall, V. A. (1991). *Beyond tolerance: Gays, lesbians, and bisexuals on campus.* Washington, DC: American College Personnel Association.

Geertz, C. (1973). Thick description: Toward an interpretive theory of culture. In C. Geertz (Ed.), *The interpretation of cultures* (pp. 3–30). New York: Basic Books.

Gilligan, C. (1982). *In a different voice.* Cambridge, MA: Harvard University Press.

Harper, S. R. (2003). Most likely to succeed: The self-perceived impact of involvement on the experiences of high-achieving African American undergraduate men at predominantly White universities. *Dissertation Abstracts International, A64*(6), 1995.

Harris, W. G. (2003). African American homosexual males on predominantly White college and university campuses. *Journal of African American Studies, 7*(1), 47–56.

Helms, J. E. (1990). *Black and white racial identity.* Westport, CT: Greenwood Press.

hooks, b. (2004). *We real cool: Black men and masculinity.* New York: Routledge.

Icard, L. (1986). Black gay men and conflicting social identities: Sexual orientation versus racial identity. *Journal of Social Work and Human Sexuality, 4*(1–2), 83–93.

Jones, S. R. (1997). Voices of identity and difference: A qualitative exploration of the multiple dimensions of identity development in women college students. *Journal of College Student Development, 38*(4), 376–385.

Jones, S. R., & McEwen, M. K. (2000). A conceptual model of multiple dimensions of identity. *Journal of College Student Development, 41*(4), 405–414.

Josselson, R. (1987). *Finding herself: Pathways to identity development in women.* San Francisco: Jossey-Bass.

Messer, K. L. (2006). African American male college athletes. In M. J. Cuyjet & Associates (Eds.), *African American men in college* (pp. 154–173). San Francisco: Jossey-Bass.

Mitchell, M. L., & Dell, D. M. (1992). The relationship between Black students' racial identity attitude and participation in campus organizations. *Journal of College Student Development, 33*, 39–43.

Osterman, K. F. (2000). Students' need for belonging in the school community. *Review of Educational Research, 70*(3), 323–367.

Parham, T. A., & Helms, J. E. (1981). The influence of Black students' racial identity attitudes on preference for counselor's race. *Journal of Counseling Psychology, 32*, 431–440.

Patton, M. Q. (1990). *Qualitative evaluation and research methods* (2nd ed.). Newbury Park, CA: Sage.

Rankin, S. (1998). Campus climate for lesbian, gay, bisexual and transgendered students, faculty, and staff: Assessment and strategies for change. In R. Sanlo (Ed.), *Working with lesbian, gay, and bisexual students: A guide for administrators and faculty* (pp. 277–283). Westport, CT: Greenwood Press.

Stevens, R. A., Jr. (2004). Understanding gay identity development within the college environment. *Journal of College Student Development, 45*(2), 185–206.

Strayhorn, T. L. (2008a). Fittin' in: Do diverse interactions with peers affect sense of belonging for Black men at predominantly White institutions? *NASPA Journal, 45*(4), 501–527.

Strayhorn, T. L. (2008b). The role of supportive relationships in facilitating African American males' success in college. *NASPA Journal, 45*(1), 26–48.

Strayhorn, T. L. (in press). Singing in a foreign land: An exploratory study of gospel choir participation among African American undergraduates at a predominantly White institution. *Journal of College Student Development.*

Strayhorn, T. L., Blakewood, A. M., & DeVita, J. M. (2008). Factors affecting the college choice of African American gay male undergraduates: Implications for retention. *National Association of Student Affairs Professionals Journal, 11*(1), 88–108.

Wall, V. A., & Washington, J. E. (1991). Understanding gay and lesbian students of color. In N. J. Evans & V. A. Wall (Eds.), *Beyond tolerance: Gays, lesbians, and bisexuals on campus.* Alexandria, VA: ACPA Media Board.

6

CHALLENGES AND SUPPORTS OF STUDENT-TO-STUDENT INTERACTIONS

Insights on African American Collegians

Belinda B. McFeeters

Abstract: In this chapter, the author presents findings from a multivariate analysis of survey data to describe the influence of student-to-student interactions on change in opinion, with a focus on interactions of African American students with their diverse peers at predominantly White institutions (PWIs). A set of evidence-based recommendations for educational practice, including implications for diversity, is delineated at the end of the chapter.

One of the primary functions of higher education is to create campus environments that foster learning for future generations of leaders. Colleges and universities are charged with producing students capable of proactively developing positive settings for others and conducting business in an ethically responsible manner (Clark, 2001; Cooper, Scandura, & Schriesheim, 2005). To this end, higher education institutions have educated each new generation of leaders in business, government, science, medicine, law, and many other professions (Astin & Astin, 2000).

Much of this education takes place through physical, intellectual, social, and student-to-student interactions (Terry, 1992). Student-to-student interactions are defined by activities such as socializing with other students from the same or different racial or ethnic groups, working on group projects for classes, tutoring other students, discussing course content with other students, discussing hot topics or political issues, participating in campus protests, being elected to a student office, and being a member of a student organization (Astin, 1993a).

Though various outcomes are associated with student-to-student interactions on college campuses, we know relatively little about the benefits of these encounters for African American students, given the challenges they face when interacting with diverse others at PWIs (Chang, 1999). This chapter highlights the challenges African American college students face when interacting with others who are different from them. Additionally, the discussion concerns the influence of these interactions on one measure of development, change in opinion.

Conceptual Framework

The present chapter is based on the social influence network theory, which implies that opinions may be changed and/or informed as a result of interactions with others. Developed to address instances of individual differences in interpersonal influences and opinions, it also considers special cases in which individual differences are constrained (Friedkin & Johnsen, 1999).

The typical understanding of opinions is that they are verbal expressions of attitudes that influence behavior on various issues. Opinions help people know who they are and what they stand for, and they help give meaning to the world around them. In addition, opinions serve as the medium for expressing core feelings, beliefs, and values (Bogue, 1994; Kouzes & Posner, 1987; Woodard & Denton, 1988).

One can describe opinion formation in terms of a network paradigm with inputs, outputs, and a process to link the two. Individual and group characteristics are the inputs, and settled opinions of individuals are the outputs. The inputs are transformed into outputs through the opinion formation process, which can be divided into time periods. During these periods, a change of opinion can take place (Friedkin & Johnsen, 1990).

Changes in opinion can be conceptualized in terms of forces operating along a continuum. Social influences are designed to force fields induced by person A on to person B, and the strength of these forces is assumed to vary, depending on the power of A over B. When person A expresses his or her opinion or argues for it in a manner that influences person B, the force field operating on person B pushes his or her position to one that more closely corresponds with person A's position along the continuum of opinion. The result is a change or shift in opinion for person B (French, 1956).

However, people have their own unique personalities, intellectual and emotional characteristics, and perceptions of the world, and they may form their opinion based on personal factors. When individuals come into contact with others in their physical and social world, such interactions also increase the potential for opinion change (Glynn, Herbst, O'Keefe, Shapiro, & Lindeman, 2004).

Review of the Relevant Literature

Like anyone else, students are influenced by others as well, particularly within the college environment. Students learn not only through academic programs or contact with faculty members, but also from various student-to-student interactions that take place in and outside of the classroom (Terenzini, Pascarella, & Blimling, 1996). A consistent body of research suggests that the intellectual development students experience while in college is, at least in part, a result of the role their peers play in their lives. In fact, some research suggests that interactions with peers may be just as influential as formal classroom experiences, if not more so (Astin, 1993a; Terenzini, Springer, Yaeger, Pascarella, & Nora, 1994).

Student-to-student interactions, like peer tutoring or peer teaching, are almost always beneficial to students when they involve educationally purposeful activities (Annis, 1983; Astin, 1993a; Terenzini, Pascarella, & Blimling, 1996). Astin (1993a) suggests that student-to-student interactions are the single most important source of influence on most college campuses and generally influence an extensive range of college outcomes, both academic and nonacademic.

Academic Outcomes

Academic outcomes have varied. Some research suggests that student-to-student interactions influence positive outcomes on writing and thinking skills, understanding the arts and humanities, and reading comprehension and mathematics (Whitt, Edison, Pascarella, Nora, & Terenzini, 1999). Other research suggests that student-to-student interactions, like peer teaching or tutoring, influence student learning (Annis, 1983; Astin, 1993a; Bargh & Schul, 1980; Benware & Deci, 1984; Goldschmidt & Goldschmidt, 1976). In this respect, student involvement in the learning process is enhanced.

For example, student-to-student interactions in the form of peer counseling influence academic outcomes for students. In a cross-institutional study, peer counseling programs compared the performance of students (counselees) involved in the program to that of a control group of students (i.e., students with similar precollege enrollment characteristics but who did have peer counselors). Students who participate in peer counseling programs earn higher grade point averages (GPAs), than do comparable groups of students who do not participate in peer counseling programs (Gúon, 1988).

The research that discusses cognitive outcomes has looked at student-to-student interactions and influences on thinking and writing skills. Students at 23 colleges and universities participated in the National Study of Student Learning (NSSL), a longitudinal examination of the factors that influence learning and cognitive development in college. Course-related and non-course-related activities involving student-to-student interactions that occurred in and outside of the classroom were assessed. The results showed that the more students interact with peers, the greater their cognitive growth (Whitt et al., 1999). Peer interactions are associated with other outcomes.

Nonacademic Outcomes

The literature on student outcomes suggests that students also experience nonacademic outcomes as a result of student-to-student interactions. When asked which aspects of the college experience were most influential in promoting their learning and development, alumni overwhelmingly said that their most significant learning took place outside the classroom and was heavily influenced by their interactions with peers (Marchese, 1990; Murphy, 1989).

The literature also examines outcomes associated with involvement in student organizations and clubs. These organizations serve key developmental functions, provide opportunities for personal growth, promote social responsibility, and offer venues for socialization and developing a sense of community (Winniford, Carpenter, & Grider, 1995). Student-to-student interactions within student organizations influence the development of leadership skills more than does any other aspect of the college student experience (Astin, 1993a). These interactions influence students' aspirations and goals for college (Astin, 1993a; Pascarella & Terenzini, 1991).

Other research suggests that student learning and personal development are often influenced by student-to-student interactions outside the classroom. For example, 149 seniors from 12 institutions were interviewed about interpersonal relations, cultural differences, academics, and other topics.

Self-awareness (self-examination, spirituality), interpersonal and practical competence, and critical thinking are all associated with student-to-student interactions (Kuh, 1993).

Race and Ethnic Background

Given the lack of ethnic awareness and understanding of diversity with which many students matriculate, it is reasonable to expect that their college experiences play some role in shaping their attitudes toward members of other racial or ethnic groups (Hurtado, Enberg, Ponjuan, & Landerman, 2002; Saddlemire, 1996). In fact, Kuh (1995) suggests that interactions with peers from different cultural backgrounds are powerful out-of-class experiences. These interactions have positive influences on various aspects of students' development, particularly their cognitive and personal development.

For example, interracial interactions tend to take the form of discussing racial and ethnic issues with students from different racial/ethnic groups. These discussions seem to influence students' overall academic development, gains in general knowledge, critical thinking, analytical and reflective judgment, and problem-solving skills (Astin, 1993b; Kitchener, Wood, & Jensen, 2000; Kuh, 1995). Overall academic development is enhanced, students gain knowledge in specific disciplines, and their critical thinking skills are improved when such discussions occur (Astin, 1993a; Terenzini, Springer, Yaeger, Pascarella, & Nora, 1994).

Openness to diversity and challenge is also influenced by student-to-student interactions with peers from different racial/ethnic backgrounds. Data from 3,331 students who took the Collegiate Assessment of Academic Proficiency (CAAP) revealed that student-to-student interactions influence growth and development. Openness to diversity and challenge at the end of students' first year is positively influenced by interracial student interactions.

Challenges for African American Students

Though studies find that there are valuable benefits for students who interact with others different from themselves, engaging in these interactions is not always easy for students, especially African American students on predominantly White campuses. Several factors make it difficult for African American students to interact with diverse others, including a reluctance to accommodate a new "group" of students, perceptions of prejudice and discrimination, a general feeling of being unwelcome, and a history of oppression for minorities.

In 1954, some PWIs began to admit minority students only after government mandated them to do so (Allen, 1992; Easley, 1993). Little thought, consideration, or action was taken into account to accommodate the "strangers" (Saddlemire, 1996; Taylor, 1989), so tension between cultures escalated because there was no real change within the campus setting. This unchanging nature sent a message to African American students that White institutions considered themselves superior, and students who wanted to attend must assimilate to the PWI culture (Taylor, 1989).

Nora and Cabrera (1996) add that, during the 1980s, college attendance in general declined for African American students, who exhibited the lowest rates of participation among other groups and were more prone than others to drop out. Building on Astin's involvement theory, Nora and Cabrera argue that perceptions of prejudice-discrimination affect the cognitive and affective development of African American students by discouraging them from becoming involved with faculty, students, campus organizations, and, thus, leadership opportunities.

With this type of campus climate, both in and outside the classroom, African American students are slow to interact with others different from themselves (Woodard & Sims, 2000). As late as the 1970s, African American students experienced direct acts of social alienation on PWI campuses, and even today, in many indirect, nonviolent, and subtle ways, these students continue to be subject to many demeaning and damaging experiences. The chilly climate is expressed in African American students' statements that they feel increasingly like outsiders, isolated, and unwelcome on the campuses of predominantly White institutions. To this end, social alienation plays a major role in the adjustment to college for African American students.

Coupled with social alienation, African American students have to deal with ignorance about their culture (Allen, 1992), and the curriculum, teaching styles, available student services, and the campus as a whole typically cater to White students rather than a diverse student body. Most of the curriculum, for example, mirrors the perspective of the dominant culture and tends to exclude other minority cultures and perspectives (Taylor, 1989). As a result, when African American students attempt to engage their White peers at PWIs, they face difficulty in becoming integrated into the institution's social systems (Easley, 1993).

Given the difficulty many African American students at PWIs experience, it is reasonable to assume that low levels of interaction with others different from themselves will continue. But why is it important for African American students to interact with others who are different?

Not only do students gain a greater sense of ethnic awareness (Hurtado et al., 2002), as discussed previously, peer student interactions also foster various academic and nonacademic outcomes, including writing and thinking skills, reading comprehension, personal development, and leadership skills (Astin, 1993a; Kuh, 1993; Whitt et al., 1999). However, African American students at PWIs are at risk of losing opportunities to gain these skills and eventually may fail to persist as a result of feelings of isolation and a lack of a sense of belonging (Bean & Hull, 1984; Strayhorn, 2006, 2008). Tinto (1975, 1993) suggests that students who do not become a part of the academic fabric of the campus culture end up leaving college.

In addition, one vital reason for fostering student interactions with diverse others, the focus of my study, is the ability to generate informed opinions based on diverse perspectives. One of the goals of higher education is to create student leaders who are contributing members of society and who are able to generate informed opinions. In the next section, I briefly summarize a study I conducted to explore this issue, followed by a discussion of key findings and implications.

Methodology

I was interested in studying how opinions are generated and what influences change in opinion, so I analyzed survey data from 2,000 respondents to the 2004 College Student Experiences Questionnaire (CSEQ). White/Caucasian students represented the majority of the sample (74.4%), and African Americans accounted for 6.4% of respondents. Frequency data about participants are reported in table 6.1. Given the focus of this chapter, I am presenting the findings of the complete national study but I limit my discussion to implications for African American students. For a full discussion of the national study, see Bennett, 2006.

The purpose of this study was to explore the influence of student-student interactions on change of opinion among student leaders (SLs) and non-student leaders (NSLs). This study compared differences between student leaders and non-student leaders and examined which types of discussions with students different from themselves best predict change in opinion. Data were analyzed via logistic regression and t-tests. The next section outlines the main findings.

Key Findings

National data revealed that discussions with other students who are different from themselves in terms of political values and country of origin lead to

TABLE 6.1
Demographic Characteristics of the Sample ($N = 1992$)

Characteristics	SLs (n = 1428)		NSLs (n = 564)			
	N	% n	Missing Data	N	% n	Sample Total %
Gender			.4			
Female	958	66.8		346	61.1	65.2
Male	470	32.8		218	38.5	34.4
Race/Ethnicity			1.4			
White/Caucasian	1056	73.6		412	72.8	74.4
Asian/Pacific Islander	171	11.9		63	11.1	11.9
Black/African American	80	5.6		46	8.1	6.4
Mexican American	54	3.8		24	4.2	4.0
Other	57	4.0		13	2.3	3.5
Other Hispanic	28	2.0		14	2.5	2.1
American Indian/Other Native	27	1.9		8	1.4	1.8
Puerto Rican	17	1.2		6	1.1	1.2

higher levels of opinion change for both student leaders and non-student leaders. In this case, leadership status is not a factor when it comes to whether these student-to-student interactions influence opinion change. While opinion change, then, is influenced by specific types of discussions, discussions have an even greater influence on SLs than they do on NSLs. In addition, findings suggest that highly involved SLs engage in discussions with others different from themselves significantly more often than do less involved SLs for each of the seven types of discussions. The most significant predictors for SLs in the current study were discussions with students who have different political values and discussions with students from different countries. The same two predictors that were the most significant for SLs were also the most significant for NSLs.

Last, I found that highly involved SLs, on average, engage in discussions with students who have different interests, philosophies of life or personal values, political opinions, and religious values, and are from a different race or ethnic background, country, or family background, significantly more often than do less involved SLs.

Overall, this investigation provided answers to the study's questions. Discussions with students who have different political values, or are from a different country, have the strongest influence on change in opinion for both SLs and NSLs. In addition, highly involved SLs engage in discussions with students who are different from them significantly more often than do less involved SLs, and there are significant differences between less involved SLs and highly involved SLs for each discussion type.

Limitations

The findings from this research have several implications for future practice, research, policy, and diversity. However, there are also some limitations associated with this study.

The first limitation involves the process used to determine which students were considered student leaders. Students were identified as SLs based on their responses to items on the 2004 CSEQ (Pace, 1984) about how often they attended certain activities on campus (i.e., a meeting of a campus club, organization, or student government group), or how often they managed or provided leadership for a club or organization on or off the campus. Many definitions describe a leader; if a different definition had been used, results might have been different.

A second limitation involves the unequal sample sizes used for SLs and NSLs. The sample consisted of 1,400 SLs and 523 NSLs. Though problems occasionally occur when using unequal sample sizes, I chose not to randomly select a smaller sample from the SL sample to correlate with the NSL sample due to possible issues this approach might create related to sampling error when running inferential statistics.

Next, limitations exist related to the factors used to predict opinion change. I chose seven factors from the CSEQ instrument to examine influences on opinion change. If I had chosen other factors that were a part of the CSEQ instrument, the final results of the regression model used to predict change in opinion might have been different.

Finally, interactions with students different from themselves were identified by two different types of items on the CSEQ, discussion and acquaintance items, but both were treated as general interaction items. For example, some items were phrased, "Discussions with students from a different country," and others were phrased, "Acquainted with students of different backgrounds." If respondents interpreted these items differently, results may be skewed to some extent.

Despite the limitations, this study provided valuable information about the influence of student-student interactions on change of opinion among SLs and NSLs, particularly African American collegians.

Discussion of Study's Relevance

This chapter addresses the challenges African American students face when interacting with individuals who are different from themselves, and highlights the benefits of such interactions. Earlier literature has focused on the purpose of higher education institutions and how leaders have been trained to serve the community. Various qualities and skills necessary to be an effective leader have been discussed in the literature as well but with no specific focus on African American students, their attempt to build on these qualities and skills, and the influence of their interactions with diverse others on opinion change.

The uniqueness of this study, however, is that results identified specific types of discussions educators can encourage SLs and NSLs, including African American students, to have with diverse others that will influence changes in opinion. This study challenges the argument that leaders are born; instead, it suggests that, through peer interactions, leaders can be taught to develop an informed opinion and to influence opinion change in others. Findings from this study suggest that these leadership skills can be intentionally developed. If this is the case, higher education can help students be more effective and be better prepared leaders.

Overall, these findings imply a number of things. First, exposure to different political ideas influences opinion change. College students are often involved in discussions about politics in class and during campus elections. These interactions might explain why political discussions would influence change in opinion. Likewise, with the increasing emphasis on internationalization in the higher education curriculum, college students are socialized to look at global issues and to hold international experiences in high regard. This might explain the finding that discussions with others from different countries influence change in opinion. Last, the finding that highly involved SLs engage in discussions with others different from themselves significantly more often than do less involved SLs might be explained by assuming that less involved SLs only attend meetings of campus clubs and organizations and perhaps do not lead them or hold leadership positions in them. Alternatively, less involved SLs may be active in only one organization versus the multiple student organizations in which highly involved SLs, who hold leadership positions within multiple organizations, are active. Generally, highly involved SLs are exposed to more opportunities than are less involved SLs. Being a SL clearly provides greater opportunities, which may lead to opinion change.

In light of the chapter's findings, I offer some recommendations to higher education and student affairs professionals who wish to enhance the quality of peer interactions between African American students and majority students. First, the campus environment is one of the most difficult challenges for African American students at predominantly White institutions to master. Leadership at PWIs must first realize that individuals generally develop more effectively in surroundings where they are comfortable; feel valued, accepted, and safe; and can easily develop positive social networks (Allen, 1992). Administrators must recognize when Black students perceive the institution as having a "chilly" climate and act appropriately. A true commitment to diversity from executive leadership is vital (D'Augelli & Hershberger, 1993), and these individuals must support African American students and make them feel more comfortable on PWI campuses. Diversity celebrations held not only during Black History Month, but throughout the year, will help warm the chilly climate on campus, and renew African American students' perceptions of the institution's commitment to diversity.

STUDENT-TO-STUDENT INTERACTIONS   *115*

Findings from this study suggest that highly involved student leaders engage in discussions with students who are different from themselves significantly more often than do less involved SLs for all seven discussion types. Therefore, administrators who work with multicultural programs and services could design programs that target specific groups of diverse student leaders, both highly involved and less involved, for different forms of dialogue. For example, administrators in multicultural programs and services might consider developing Sustained Dialogue programs, which are student-driven initiatives in which the focus is on changing relationships within a community that suffers from ethnic, racial, religious, or other deep-rooted differences based on identity, power, misconceptions, or interaction issues. Within Sustained Dialogue, the responsibility of shaping and reshaping perceptions of climate issues rests with the students (Parker, 2006). Considering the findings that less involved SLs interact with others different from themselves less often than do highly involved SLs, administrators might have less involved African American SLs lead the dialogue. This could help encourage them to become more involved and would allow them more exposure to others different from themselves. These interactions are also good opportunities for students to engage in the democratic process, add to their toolbox of leadership skills, and play a role in improving multicultural issues on campus and, especially, in informing opinions.

Student organization advisors might evaluate their student recruitment efforts and reconsider the design of some of their student organization meetings to create opportunities for effective student interactions in governance student organizations. For example, findings from this study suggest that discussions with others who have different political opinions influence change in opinion for SLs. Student affairs administrators who advise governance student groups, such as the SGA, the Young Democrats, the College Republicans, and others, typically work with student leaders. African American students on PWI campuses, however, often choose not to become involved in student governance groups. Based on the small number of minority group representatives in U.S. government, African Americans may perceive these positions as reserved for the majority and not for members of the minority. Therefore, they shy away from joining governance groups or taking leadership roles while in college (Sutton & Terrell, 1997). Administrators might use findings from this study to recruit more African American students to student organizations and encourage debates between opposing sides on various political issues. The more students are exposed to different viewpoints, the broader their perspectives may become about various issues.

These findings can help guide the work of student activities profession-als, particularly those who work with SLs in student organizations. One of the findings suggests that discussions with students from different countries influence opinion change for SLs. Staff might encourage African American SLs to participate in events sponsored by international student organizations and, likewise, encourage international SLs to attend African American stu-dent organization events. In addition, opinion change research reveals that individuals have opinions that are contingent on the context in which they are formed. The manner in which individuals work things through in their minds can vary and can be influenced by personal values and assumptions based on experiences (Cantril & Davis Cantril, 1999). Attending events sponsored by those from other countries might spark dialogue between stu-dent organization members and, therefore, better inform their opinions about cultural issues and perspectives.

Academic faculty also might use these findings to enhance the involve-ment of African American student leaders, both highly involved and less involved, with others different from themselves. Findings from this study suggest that highly involved SLs engage in discussions with students who are different from themselves significantly more often than do less involved SLs. Because faculty are often able to identify the highly involved and less involved student leaders, they could place SLs in positions to interact with others different from themselves based on the students' typical levels of involvement. For less involved SLs, interactions could enhance their expo-sure to others different from themselves and facilitate their involvement in clubs and activities.

Policymakers who manage funding for higher education programs should pay attention to these findings. Discussions with people from a differ-ent country are the most significant predictors of opinion change for all students (SLs and NSLs). This finding is insightful because it implies that cross-cultural education is important. Given that African American students rarely take advantage of study abroad and similar programs due to limited funding, policymakers might consider this when allocating funding for such programs or enhanced opportunities for students to travel abroad. This finding might also inform policies related to international students.

Policymakers who monitor institutional assessment activity may find value in this research as well. Findings emphasize the fact that highly involved student leaders are exposed to diverse individuals significantly more often than are less involved SLs. This fact provides policymakers with more information about the impact of college student involvement. Woodard and

Sims (2000) found that low student leader participation among African American students on PWI campuses can be attributed to a number of climate issues. For example, White faculty at PWIs perceive African American students differently, provide them with less consistent reinforcement, and have poor communication with them (Sedlacek, 1987). Given what we know about the challenges African American students face, it might be beneficial to establish institutional policies that promote Black student involvement to provide them with opportunities to interact with diverse others. These opportunities might enhance their involvement and potentially increase their acceptance of diverse viewpoints and perspectives.

One of the student acquaintances items on the CSEQ asks students how often they have had "serious" discussions with students who were different from themselves, based on various characteristics (e.g., political views, religious beliefs). With each of the previously mentioned recommendations that encourages higher education and student affairs professionals to design opportunities for diverse student interactions, attention should be given to the seriousness of these interactions. Administrators must ensure that student discussions not only take place, but also that students clearly understand the purpose of the interactions, how serious they should be, and how powerfully they affect learning outcomes.

Concluding Thoughts

My findings suggest that certain types of discussions are good measures to predict opinion change. These findings have implications for diversity in general. Social psychologists define student diversity interactions as exchanges with diverse others and exposure to diverse ideas, experiences, and information. They assert that the more interaction people have with others who hold different views, or the more people learn about different aspects of human diversity, the more effectively they will be able to respond to differences (Umbach & Kuh, 2003). Findings that highlight the influence that discussions have on opinion change relate to these assertions.

Due to the chilly climate on PWI campuses, African American students may not take advantage of opportunities to interact with diverse others, thereby gaining the skills needed to inform opinions and become more informed. If this happens, they may eventually fail to persist (Bean & Hull, 1984; Strayhorn, 2006). If African American students fail to persist, the country will continue to have fewer leaders with diverse perspectives.

To the extent that change in opinion or openness to change and difference (Chang, 1999) is a goal of higher education and a necessary condition for participation in a democratic society (Astin, 1993b), diversity-related interactions or conversations with a diverse group of peers is important and is worth continuing to ensure that all students are supported and have equal opportunities.

This chapter addresses the challenges African American students face when interacting with individuals who are different from themselves, and highlights the benefits of such interactions. If these findings are applied, we may some day imagine a world of leaders who are free from Eurocentricity, bigotry, prejudice, close-mindedness, and ignorance. These talents can be transferred to professional leadership positions and can equip leaders to bring about change in government, business, communities, and the world. With these skills, future leaders, particularly African Americans, of tomorrow can help transform the nation to the true and just democratic society we all strive for, and can have a fair opportunity to change the world.

References

Allen, W. R. (1992). The color of success: African American college student outcomes at predominantly White and historically Black public college and universities. *Harvard Educational Review, 64*(1), 26–44.

Annis, L. (1983). The processes and effects of peer tutoring. *Human Learning, 2,* 39–47.

Astin, A. W. (1993a). *What matters in college? Four critical years revisited.* San Francisco: Jossey-Bass.

Astin, A. W. (1993b). Diversity and multiculturalism on the campus: How are students affected? *Change, 25,* 44–49.

Astin, A. W., & Astin, H. S. (2000). *Leadership reconsidered: Engaging higher education in social change.* Battle Creek, MI: W. K. Kellogg Foundation.

Bargh, J., & Schul, Y. (1980). On the cognitive benefits of teaching. *Journal of Educational Psychology, 72,* 593–604.

Bean, J. P., & Hull, D. F., Jr. (1984). *The determinants of Black and White student attrition at a major southern state university.* Paper presented at the Annual Meeting of the American Educational Research Association, New Orleans, LA.

Bennett, B. R. (2006). *The influence of student interactions on college student leader change in opinion: Differences by frequency of involvement.* Unpublished doctoral dissertation, Virginia Polytechnic Institute & State University, Blacksburg.

Benware, C., & Deci, E. (1984). Quality of learning with an active versus passive motivational set. *American Educational Research Journal, 21,* 755–765.

Bogue, E. G. (1994). *Leadership by design: Strengthening integrity in higher education.* San Francisco: Jossey-Bass.

Cantril, A. H., & Davis Cantril, S. (1999). *Reading mixed signals: Ambivalence in American public opinion about government.* Washington, DC: Woodrow Wilson Center Press; Baltimore, MD, & London: Johns Hopkins University Press.

Chang, M. J. (1999). Does racial diversity matter? The educational impact of a racially diverse undergraduate population. *Journal of College Student Development,* 40(4), 377–395.

Clark, G. (2001). *Student leadership and higher education: A Review of the literature.* Retrieved from http://asstudents.unco.edu/students/AE%2DExtra/2001/2/Student.html

Cooper, C. D., Scandura, T. A., & Schriesheim, C. A. (2005). Looking forward but learning from our past: Potential challenges to developing authentic leadership theory and authentic leaders. *The Leadership Quarterly, 15,* 475–493.

D'Augelli, A. R., & Hershberger, S. L. (1993). African American undergraduates on predominantly White campus: Academic factors, social networks, and campus climate. *Journal of Negro Education, 62*(1), 67–81.

Easley, N. (1993). *Black student retention at Colorado State University.* Unpublished manuscript, Colorado State University at Fort Collins.

French, J. R. P. (1956). A formal theory of social power. *Psychological Review, 63,* 181–194.

Friedkin, N. E., & Johnsen, E. C. (1990). Social influence and opinions. *Journal of Mathematical Sociology, 15,* 193–205.

Friedkin, N. E., & Johnsen, E. C. (1999). Social influence networks and opinion change. *Advances in Group Processes, 16,* 1–29.

Glynn, C. J., Herbst, S., O'Keefe, G. J., Shapiro, R. Y. & Lindeman, M. (2004). *Public opinion.* Cambridge: Westview Press.

Goldschmidt, B., & Goldschmidt, M. (1976). Peer teaching in higher education: A review. *Higher Education, 5,* 9–33.

Guon, D. G. (1988, April). *Minority access and retention: An evaluation of a multi-university peer counseling program.* Paper presented at the annual meeting of the Midwestern Psychological Association, Chicago, IL.

Hurtado, S., Enberg, M., Ponjuan, L., & Landerman, L. (2002). Students' precollege preparation for participation in a diverse democracy. *Research in Higher Education, 43,* 163–186.

Kitchener, K., Wood, P., & Jensen, L. (2000, August). *Promoting epistemic cognition and complex judgement in college students.* Paper presented at the meeting of the American Psychological Association, Washington, DC.

Kouzes, J. M., & Posner, B. Z. (1987). *The leadership challenge: How to get extraordinary things done in organizations.* San Francisco: Jossey-Bass.

Kuh, G. D. (1993). In their own words: What students learn outside the classroom. *American Educational Research Journal,* 30, 277–304.

Kuh, G. D. (1995). The other curriculum: Out of class experiences associated with student learning and development. *Journal of Higher Education, 66,* 123–155.

Marchese, T. J. (1990). A new conversation about undergraduate teaching: An interview with Professor Richard J. Light, convener of the Harvard Assessment Seminars. *AAHE Bulletin, 42,* 3–8.

Murphy, R. O. (1989). Academic and student affairs in partnership for freshman success. In M. L. Upcraft, J. N. Gardner & Associates (Eds.), *The freshman year experience* (pp. 375–384). San Francisco: Jossey-Bass.

Nora, A., & Cabrera, A. F. (1996). The role of perceptions in prejudice and discrimination and the adjustment of minority students to college. *Journal of Higher Education, 67*(2), 119–148.

Pace, C. R. (1984). *Measuring the quality of college student experiences: An account of the development and use of the College Student Experiences Questionnaire.* Los Angeles: UCLA Graduate School of Education.

Parker, P. N. (2006). Sustained dialogue: How students are changing their own racial climate. *About Campus, 11,* 17–23.

Pascarella, E. T., & Terenzini, P. T. (1991). *How college affects students.* San Francisco: Jossey-Bass.

Saddlemire, J. R. (1996). Qualitative study of White second semester undergraduates' attitudes toward African American undergraduates at a predominantly White university. *Journal of College Student Development, 37*(6), 684–691.

Sedlacek, W. E. (1987). Black students on White campuses: 20 years of research. *Journal of College Student Personnel, 28,* 484–495.

Stewart, G., Russell, R. B., & Wright, D. B. (1997). The comprehensive role of student affairs in African American student retention. *Journal of College Admission, 154,* 6–11.

Strayhorn, T. L. (2006). Involvement matters: Differences by race. *Interchange, 34*(3), 2–5.

Strayhorn, T. L. (2008). The role of supportive relationships in facilitating African American males' success in college. *NASPA Journal, 45*(1), 26–48.

Sutton, E. M., & Terrell, M. C. (1997). Identifying and developing leadership opportunities for African American men. *New Directions for Student Services, 80,* 55–64.

Taylor, C. A. (1989). *Effective ways to recruit and retain minority students.* Madison, WI: Praxis Publications, Inc.

Terenzini, P. T., Pascarella, E. T., & Blimling, G. S. (1996). Students' out-of-class experiences and their influence on learning and cognitive development: A literature review. *Journal of College Student Development, 40,* 610–623.

Terenzini, P. T., Springer, L., Yaeger, P. M., Pascarella, E. T., & Nora, A. (1994, November). *The multiple influences on students' critical thinking skills.* Paper presented at the annual meeting of the Association for the Study of Higher Education, Tucson, AZ.

Terry, E. F. (1992). Values systems change and the collegiate environment: The freshman experience. *NASPA Journal, 29*, 261–268.

Tinto, V. (1975). Dropouts from higher education: A theoretical synthesis of recent research. *Review of Educational Research, 45*, 89–125.

Tinto, V. (1993). *Leaving college: Rethinking the causes and cures of student attrition.* Chicago: University of Chicago Press.

Umbach, P. D., & Kuh, G. D. (2003, May). *Student experiences with diversity at liberal arts colleges: Another claim for distinctiveness.* Paper presented at the 43rd Annual Association for Institutional Research Forum, Tampa, FL.

Whitt, E. J., Edison, M., Pascarella, E. T., Nora, A., & Terenzini, P. (1999). Interactions with peers and objective and self-reported cognitive outcomes across 3 years of college. *Journal of College Student Development, 40*, 61–78.

Winniford, J. C., Carpenter, D. C., & Grider, C. (1995). An analysis of the traits and motivations of college students involved in service organizations. *Journal of College Student Development, 36*, 27–38.

Woodard, G. C., & Denton, R. E. (1988). *Persuasion & influence in American life.* Prospect Heights, IL: Waveland Press, Inc.

Woodard, V. S., & Sims, J. M. (2000). Programmatic approach to improving campus climate. *NASPA Journal, 37*, 539–552.

7

"A HOME AWAY FROM HOME"

Black Cultural Centers as Supportive Environments for
African American Collegians at White Institutions

Terrell L. Strayhorn, Melvin C. Terrell,
Jane S. Redmond, and Chutney N. Walton

Abstract: Black cultural centers (BCCs) have long since served as bulwarks of
cultural identity and solidarity for African American students attending predom-
inantly White institutions (PWIs). However, abiding beliefs in the value added
of BCCs are largely predicated on anecdotal evidence, and relatively few empiri-
cal research studies focus on the role of BCCs in the academic and social lives of
African American collegians at PWIs. In this chapter, we outline the sociohistori-
cal currents that influenced the creation of BCCs at PWIs, summarize the litera-
ture on BCCs and their evolution at PWIs, and, drawing on findings from a
mixed-methods study, illustrate how BCCs provide supports that African Ameri-
can students at PWIs view as critical to their success in college.

College enrollment rates have risen dramatically over the last 50 years, especially for women and racial/ethnic minorities. Today, more women than men enroll in college. and many more racial/ethnic minorities enroll in college than ever before (in the aggregate). For example, while only 943,000 African Americans were enrolled in college in 1976, more than 1.9 million are enrolled today, representing a 103% increase (U.S. Department of Education, 2007). Yet, noticeable gaps persist across racial/ethnic groups. For example, African Americans, are largely concentrated at less-selective, four-year, minority-serving institutions (e.g., historically Black colleges and universities [HBCUs]), and two-year community colleges (Baum & Payea, 2004; Strayhorn, 2008; Thomas & Perna, 2004).

Such disparities are, at least in part, the consequence of long-standing commitments and historic "savage inequities" that affect students' experiences in college. For example, HBCUs have a long history of accommodating the educational needs of African Americans (Strayhorn & Hirt, 2008), and, despite the lack of resources (Brown, Donahoo, & Bertrand, 2001; Drewry & Doermann, 2004), these institutions remain committed to their historical role of preparing Black leaders for the Black community (Barthelemy, 1984), which may explain why so many Black students attend HBCUs, graduate from them, and assume prestigious occupations (Strayhorn, 2008).

While HBCUs still award the majority of their bachelor degrees to African Americans, approximately 75% of African American collegians currently attend predominantly White institutions (PWIs) (U.S. Department of Education, 2006). In addition, research has shown consistently that Blacks report feeling marginalized, culturally isolated, and socially alienated at PWIs (Fleming, 1984; Gossett, Cuyjet, & Cockriel, 1998). Additionally, Black students often perceive the campus as chilly and unwelcoming (Bonner & Bailey, 2006; D'Augelli & Hershberger, 1993). Unlike their White peers, most African American students experience the added burden of representing the "voice of difference" or serving as spokespersons for their entire race (Gossett et al., 1998), which often leads to psychological stress: "the stress of racial tension and inadequate social lives borne by Black students in White schools generates feelings of alienation that often lead to serious adjustment problems" (Fleming, 1984, p. 3).

The weight of evidence suggests that these problems have threatened the success of Black collegians at PWIs for a long time—today (Cuyjet, 2006); in the 1980s (Fleming, 1984); and as early as the 1930s (Clark, 1930). Indeed, the 1960s marked a critical turning point in the history of Black higher education in America. In consonance with the wider social movement (i.e., Civil Rights) that instigated resistance to power, privilege, and the status quo, Black collegians at PWIs often demanded institutional support and services that affirmed their cultural identity and reduced, if not eliminated, obstacles to their success (Roseboro, 2006; Williamson, 2003). In response to these protestations and racial agitations at White campuses, college student educators established Black cultural centers (BCCs) as a way of promoting, protecting, and affirming African American culture (Young & Hannon, 2002).

History and Purpose of Black Cultural Centers

The first BCCs were established in the 1960s (Anderson, 1990; Young & Hannon, 2002). Later, other BCCs were founded at large, public, predominantly White campuses. For instance, the University of Missouri's BCC opened in 1972 and cost approximately $2.4 million ("University of Missouri renames . . .," 2002). Other centers were created at The Ohio State University (Frank W. Hale Jr. Black Cultural Center); The University of Tennessee, Knoxville; Pennsylvania State University; Northern Illinois University (Center for Black Studies); University of Florida (Institute of Black Culture); Wabash College (Malcolm X Institute of Black Studies); and, perhaps most recently (i.e., 1990s), the University of North Carolina-Chapel Hill (Sonja Haynes Stone Black Cultural Center). Given the social milieu of states south of the Mason Dixon line during the 1960s, it should come as no surprise that most BCCs were established at southern PWIs initially.

The "cultural center was to be the place where attitudes, values, knowledge, and skills could be compared, debated, and shared. For some students, it was to be a safe haven, a place to retreat from the perceived hostility of an unwelcoming campus community" (Young & Hannon, 2002, p. 104). For this reason, BCCs, by definition, were established as both an *academic* and a *social* support. Historically, BCCs were a place where "African American students could feel secure in a world still outwardly hostile toward them . . . [where] the social ethos was a constant reminder of the need for Black pride and solidarity" (Hefner, 2002, p. 22). Thus, BCCs became a symbol of cultural solidarity, diversity, and Black pride (Roseboro, 2006; Young & Hannon, 2002).

From their inception, BCCs were multifaceted organizations with several broad goals, including fostering a positive environment for cross-cultural/cross-racial interactions; infusing the structure, curriculum, and campus with diversity, especially African American perspectives; and serving the academic and social-psychological needs of Black students on campus (Stewart, Russell, & Wright, 1997; Young & Hannon, 2002). BCCs also offered social programs, cultural workshops, and a "safe space" for students at PWIs (Williamson, 2003).

By all accounts, since their initial development, BCCs have become "the symbol of . . . inclusiveness" (Roseboro, 2006; Young & Hannon, 2002) and represent a vehicle through which diversity can be promoted on campus. According to the Association of Black Cultural Centers (ABCC), there are about 400 Black and multicultural centers on college campuses today, and approximately 50% of these are BCCs (Hefner, 2002).

Brief Literature Review

Until 2006, there had been "no published empirical research . . . [examining] ethnic and multicultural centers, much less BCCs" (Patton, 2006b, p. 629). Two qualitative dissertations focused exclusively on BCCs—one completed in 2004 (Patton, 2006b), the other a year later (Roseboro, 2005). For instance, Patton (2006b) conducted semi-structured interviews, using a phenomenological case study approach, with 31 African American undergraduates at three campuses to examine the role BCCs play in the experiences of Black students at White campuses. She derived five themes from her data: campus climate perceptions, initial perceptions of the BCC, "something" in the atmosphere, to be or not to be involved, and the roles of BCCs.

Later, Patton (2006b) published a portion of her dissertation, drawing on interviews with 11 students who were involved in the Institute of Black Culture at the University of Florida. Four themes emerged from her study: a climate of covert racism, learning about the center, using the center, and why we need the BCC. Specifically, she reported that students described encounters with covert and subtle forms of racism, they learned about the center during summer orientation, and their initial impressions were shaped by individuals with whom they interacted and the actual structure/physical location of the BCC.

Using first-person narratives, newspapers, and archival records, Roseboro (2005, 2006) analyzed 10 interviews plus information from secondary sources to understand the student movement that led to the construction of the BCC at the University of North Carolina-Chapel Hill. He argued that Black students inherited an interpretive framework of resistance (i.e., collective consciousness) from the 1960s Civil Rights Movement, which empowered them to protest until the university erected a freestanding BCC in honor of Dr. Haynes Stone.

While the empirical research on Black cultural centers is severely limited, anecdotal evidence consistently points to the virtues of BCCs (e.g., Hefner, 2002). Authors have argued that BCCs help retain students of color, ensure diversity of ideas and representation of culture on campus, and sustain the integrity of the academic experience for African American collegians (Bennett, 1971; Pittman, 1994; Young & Hannon, 2002). In addition, BCCs have been described as safe spaces (hooks, 1994); homes away from home (Patton,

2006b); and fortresses (Hefner, 2002) for students of color, especially African Americans, at PWIs; indeed, BCCs have been deemed places where students can go to counter the resistance to Blacks on White campuses.

Although we know a good deal about the history and intended purposes of BCCs in general (e.g., Hefner, 2002; Roseboro, 2006; Young & Hannon, 2002), we know far less about the supportive role they play in the academic and social success of African American students at PWIs. Additionally, much of what we believe about BCCs (e.g., Hefner, 2002) awaits empirical support. The study on which this chapter is based addresses this gap.

The Study

Findings presented in this chapter were drawn from a larger study that focuses on the role ethnic student organizations (ESOs) play in the academic and social success of racial/ethnic minority students, with a particular emphasis on African Americans. To learn more about the experiences of Black students in BCCs, we used qualitative methods for data collection and analysis; qualitative approaches are most appropriate when "little is known" about a phenomenon (Hill, Thompson, & Williams, 1997; Strauss & Corbin, 1998). Indeed, "qualitative data are sexy; they are a source of well grounded, rich descriptions . . ." (Miles & Huberman, 1994, p. 1).

Specifically, we conducted one-on-one in-depth interviews with 26 African American students, mostly women, at a single institution (table 7.1 summarizes the sample). The university is a large, selective, research-extensive institution located in the southeastern United States. A public land-grant university, its average total enrollment is 26,000, with African Americans accounting for approximately 7%. It is important to note that the BCC was established after Black students protested to campus administrators to build a space they could consider uniquely theirs.

We used purposive sampling methods to recruit a sample of "information rich" (Patton, 1990) African American students who would provide keen insights into the Black cultural center. We conducted one-on-one, in-depth interviews using one of three techniques: face-to-face conversations, group interviews, and electronic mail open-ended responses. All of these are widely accepted methods for conducting qualitative interviews (Guba & Lincoln, 1989; Lincoln & Guba, 1985; Manning, 1992). Interviews, each of which lasted 45–90 minutes, were conducted in the spirit of Kvale's (1996) belief that "an interview is literally an *inter* view, an inter-change of views between two persons conversing about a theme of mutual interest" (p. 14).

TABLE 7.1
Demographics of the Sample

Characteristic	%
Gender	
Male	31
Female	69
Year started attending college	
1968–1982	19
1983–1993	54
1994–2000	19
Undergraduate major	
Engineering	15
Business & Economics	23
Education & Human Sciences	19
Math, Science, & Computer Science	8
Social Sciences	23
Other	12

Data were transcribed professionally and prepared for analysis. First, two of us coded all responses after reading transcripts of the interviews several times. At this step, we developed an initial list of categories and themes (Bogdan & Biklen, 1992). Then, working independently, each of us grouped related categories and themes into super themes using a form of axial coding (Creswell, 1994). In cases of disagreement, we argued out our differences in an attempt to reach consensus. Finally, we developed a list of themes, which is reported in the next section.

In consonance with qualitative research, we took steps to enhance the trustworthiness and accuracy of data. We achieved trustworthiness through triangulation (i.e., method, investigator, and data source), expert review, and peer debriefing. Method triangulation enhances the assets and diminishes the liabilities of using a single method; thus, we employed multiple methods (i.e., interviews, observations, content analysis); multiple investigators; and multiple data sources (i.e., transcripts, field notes, demographic data sheets, websites, etc.). In addition, we subjected our interview protocol and research questions to expert review by two faculty members whose primary focus is qualitative research and we, as a team, met regularly to talk about the study, our presuppositions, and decisions. All of these steps should assist readers in evaluating the validity of our research process (Arminio & Hultgren, 2002).

Key Themes

Five key themes emerged from data analysis. Participants reported that: (a) the BCC serves as a surrogate "home away from home"; (b) the BCC provides academic, social, and emotional support to Black students; (c) the BCC is a "safe place" to study and interact with peers; and (d) the BCC is perceived as a symbol of "mattering" to others on campus. Additionally, participants identified a number of benefits they experienced as a result of participating in the BCC. In the sections that follow, we present additional information to explain the meaning and significance of these findings, along with illustrative quotes from participants; in all cases, we use pseudonyms to protect the confidentiality of participants.

Home Away From Home

Most of the students identified the BCC as a surrogate "home away from home"; that is, a place that acts as a substitute for the "real home" in which they grew up with their parent(s) and sibling(s), if any. Tyrell, a first-year marketing major, explained:

> The BCC is *the place* [emphasis by participant]. It's like a second home to me. I mean, I'm here all the time [laughing] . . . and my friends know if they can't find me in the dorm, I'm probably here. I just like it . . . it's clean, it's comfortable, and it's about the only place you can go on campus where you'll see more than one or two Black faces.

Not only did participants describe the BCC as a surrogate home, but many of them also described BCC staff members as surrogate family members (i.e., "like a mom") and often referred to staff members using familial references (e.g., "Mama Jo," etc.). Belinda, fighting back tears, recounted a powerful illustration of the "family-like" role some BCC staff members play in the lives of students:

> I was having a really rough semester . . . academically and socially. Like, two weeks after I failed a chemistry test—I mean blew it—my boyfriend, who I had been dating ever since high school, broke up with me. I was ready to quit, just drop out of school . . . and since I'm the first in my family to attend college, my parents were ready to receive me back home in Memphis anyway. I went to see Mama Jo [nickname for an associate director of the BCC], and she let me cry on her shoulders for hours. She told me that I needed something to cheer me up so she took me out to

dinner and shopping at the mall . . . we laughed the entire time . . . and when she dropped me off at home later, she looked me in the eye and said, "Now remember this . . . just hang in there 'cuz you can make it."

Voices Heard, Needs Met

According to participants, the BCC offered venues through which the "voices" of African American students could be heard and the academic, social, financial, and emotional needs of students could be met. One mechanism the BCC provided was that it enabled Black students to "voice" their concerns through the Black student programming committee. This committee sponsors educational programs and cultural events that enhance awareness of African Americans and their achievements and contributions to the university and greater society. This group is highly respected on campus and often "gives voice" to the needs of Black students in the presence of state officials, campus administrators, and alumni.

Participants also reported that the BCC provided programs and services through which their academic, social, financial, and emotional needs could be met. For instance, the BCC offered tutorial services to students who needed academic assistance. Noland commented, "I received tutorial services as well as advising and mentoring from the Black cultural center." Those who received academic support through the BCC, in the form of tutoring or mentoring, often excelled as a result. Tiffany's comment is reflective of others': "I obtained excellent tutorial assistance through the BCC's academic support program, which enabled me to earn an A in my course."

Students' financial needs were supported through programs offered by the BCC as well. Several participants talked about the importance of the book loan program, which assists students in paying for their textbooks:

> My financial aid had not been awarded, and I needed immediate funds to purchase books for class. The BCC provided financial support via a student book loan program and purchased my desperately needed books. [Derrick, mechanical engineering major]

A large majority of the participants explained that the BCC and its staff members often provided multiple forms of support over time and even simultaneously, which enabled their academic success. For instance, Black students explained:

> I received help in tutoring. I received help from A. D. Kelley [a pseudonym for a former associate director of the BCC] at the time in getting financial

aid information. I received help from Dr. Smith [a pseudonym for a former director of the BCC] on programs available to me to participate in as a student. I received information of cultural events happening from year to year while I attended. [Keith]

I benefited from the book loan program and the peer mentor program. But the best help I received from the BCC came in less tangible forms. The support, encouragement, and challenge to do, give, and be better are what still remain in my soul. [Crystal]

"Safe Place" to Study and Interact With Others

Nearly all participants described the BCC as a "safe place" or "safe space" for studying and interacting with other African American students. When asked in what ways they found the BCC useful, participants responded with phrases such as "good place to study," "one-stop place where I can work and see friends," and "helps me concentrate on my homework," for example.

Sense of Mattering

Representing a sort of unanticipated finding, participants' responses suggest that they perceive the BCC as a symbol of "mattering" to significant others (e.g., administrators, President, "White folks") on campus. In other words, students understood the existence of the BCC as an affirmation of their presence on campus, which, in turn, fostered a sense of belonging, "mattering," or feeling that they (i.e., Black students) are important to others. This is an important finding as "sense of belonging is fundamental to a member's identification with a group and has numerous consequences for behavior" (Bollen & Hoyle, 1990, p. 484). The following quotation captures the essence of this theme:

Just the fact that we have a BCC at this White school is symbolic . . . it is symbolic of a racist past that once made it difficult for our ancestors to be here. I think it's the campus's way of validating our existence on campus . . . it's a way of saying, "We know you're here, you're welcome to be here, and now we've built this center to meet your needs." I mean, of course, there are still problems . . . but it helps to know that there's a place for you to go on campus.

Benefits of Participation

Finally, students identified several benefits that accrue from their participation in the BCC and its attendant activities. Practical competencies and work experience were the most frequently cited benefits throughout the study. Practical competencies included leadership skills, programming and/or event planning skills, time management, and oral and written communication skills. In addition, participants reported that they gained skills in "building relationships with others on campus," "cultural awareness and diversity," and "networking."

Quite honestly, the number of participants (77%) who reported gaining work experience through the BCC surprised us. Consider the following examples that allude to work experience and other forms of support:

> I received tutorial services as well as advising and mentoring through the BCC. I was also employed by the BCC while completing my degree program.

> I worked in the BCC as an administrative assistant on a temp assignment. [And] the first help I received from the BCC was from a student worker, Edith Levert [a pseudonym] who helped me, an adult old enough to be her mother, through the enrollment process.

> I needed a work study job, and Dr. Smith [a pseudonym for a former BCC director] gave me an opportunity to work in her office. The office staff provided counseling to me on a number of occasions, when the pressures of college life became a bit overwhelming.

Discussion and Recommendations for Educational Practice

As mentioned earlier, the purpose of this qualitative study was to examine the experiences of African American students at PWIs in relation to their involvement in Black cultural centers and the role BCCs play in their academic and social success in college. When we drew on data from a single institution, five themes emerged from our analysis. These findings provide important insights into the experiences of African American students at PWIs and the supportive role BCCs play in helping them to succeed.

Clearly, the BCC acts as a "home away from home" for many Black collegians in predominantly White environments. This finding supports previous research indicating that BCCs have been described as "homes" and fortresses (Hefner, 2002; Patton, 2006a, 2006b). That the BCC serves as a surrogate home for students who may perceive themselves as marginal to the mainstream life of college is important. As such, the BCC seems to provide a comfortable, welcoming environment that may ease Black students' transition to campus, their adjustment to college, and their incorporation into the broader campus community, while also maintaining significant ties to individuals (i.e., peers, staff members, etc.), programs, and activities that reflect their culture of origin (Tinto, 1993; Van Gennep, 1960). Educators might leverage this knowledge to bolster the role and visibility of BCCs in new student orientation, for example.

BCCs also provide the academic, social, financial, and emotional support necessary for Black students to succeed at PWIs. The students with whom we spoke identified several supports provided through the BCC, including tutoring services, mentoring opportunities, supportive interpersonal relationships, and the book loan program. This finding is consistent with the previous research finding that BCCs offer social programs, cultural workshops, and academic assistance to students (Williamson, 2003). However, this study extends our understanding of the ways in which BCCs support students' success by including financial and emotional issues as well.

Results also reveal important findings concerning the role of BCC staff members. These individuals often act as surrogate family members in helping students to overcome academic and personal challenges. Black students often call on BCC staff members to provide support, encouragement, advice, and critiquing, when necessary. A large majority of respondents recalled vivid examples of staff members' devotion to students. And, although devotion to students may seem common for those who work with students—that is, to be student-centered, the results of this study suggest that BCC staff members are much more like parents or extended family members. Staff members are even described using family-like references—"Mama Jo," "Mama Red," and "Brother Tee." Some participants pointed out that the BCC environment operates like a "family." While these findings have not been identified in previous research on BCCs, it is similar to the way in which students view HBCU student affairs professionals and how such professionals talk about themselves (for more, see Hirt, Strayhorn, Amelink, & Bennett, 2006). Campus administrators and BCC directors might consider these findings when developing staff compensation and reward systems, hiring new employees, and evaluating staff members. Our findings suggest that BCC staff members tend to go beyond the call of duty to meet the academic, personal, and financial needs of students. Supervisors might use this information to attract and hire candidates whose talents and professional commitments match that kind of commitment.

BCCs are viewed as safe places to study and congregate with peers. Recall that students reported that the BCC provided a "safe space" where they could "feel safe enough to let their guards down and to be themselves without the fear of offending others or of perpetuating prejudicial stereotypes" (Guiffrida, 2003, p. 315). This finding resonates with earlier research (Patton, 2006b) but also extends our understanding of the experiences of Black students in White environments and the critical supportive role BCCs play. For instance, some of our participants talked about being "the only Black person" in class, on the bus, in the library, or in a residence hall. They also felt that White peers and faculty members questioned their presence on campus. "Sometimes I feel like I have to watch every word that I say, everything that I do, and even the way I dress 'cuz they will assume it reflects all Black people." While references to this sort of "psychological burden" or undue pressure that Black students experience at PWIs are not new, we learned that BCCs provide a "safe space" for Black students to escape such pressures—even if only momentarily—and have their experiences reflected *Black* (Tatum, 1997). So, in a sense, we learned why Black kids sit together in the Black cultural center.

Consistent with previous studies (e.g., Stewart et al., 1997), we found that Black students use BCCs for a variety of purposes. Black students in this study attended student organization meetings, watched TV, took naps, studied, and socialized with friends in the BCC, to name a few activities. Similarly, Patton (2006a, 2006b) points out that BCCs provide students with access to resources (e.g., TV, books, computers) and "support for various Black organizations on campus" (p. 638). What's important here is not merely the *number* of ways in which BCCs are used but the *nature* of such uses. Indeed, Black students use BCCs for academic (e.g., studying) and social (e.g., hanging out with friends) purposes. This is important, as the determinants of student retention have both academic and social roots (Tinto, 1993). Thus, by allocating resources to BCCs, colleges and universities can demonstrate their investment in the retention and success of Black students and their non-Black counterparts who use the center.

Findings indicate that BCCs are often perceived as symbols of "mattering" to others (e.g., administrators) on campus. This corroborates conclusions drawn by Sutton and Kimbrough (2001) who argue that participation in minority student organizations affords Black students a sense of mattering or belonging on campus. Yet, our findings go beyond the boundaries of previous research to suggest that students make significant meaning out of the BCC's existence. In many ways, the BCC represents a collective identity that should be celebrated, affirmed, and preserved. The students with whom we spoke saw the BCC as a cultural artifact, an icon, a symbol of hope that represents inclusiveness (Young & Hannon, 2002). Thus, any attempt to get rid of the BCC is often interpreted as a motion to get rid of Blacks on campus. Senior-level administrators and directors should consider these results and students' perceptions when formulating and implementing policy decisions about cultural centers. These findings are particularly timely in light of recent debates and "pressure to move from 'Black' to multicultural [centers]" (Young & Hannon, 2002, p. 104).

Last, students gain practical competencies and work-related experience from their involvement in the BCC. Our informants shared that they gained important skills from their BCC experiences, including leadership skills, communication (both oral and written) skills, programming opportunities, and jobs. These findings point to an important role of BCCs that is often overlooked in the literature—BCCs are equal partners in achieving the *academic* mission of the university. Directors of BCCs and BCC staff members should be seen as both *academic* and *student affairs* professionals as they provide important supports that enable students to succeed in college. Thus, institutional policies that ensure continuation of these types of programs through the BCC are essential.

References

Anderson, T. (1990). Black studies: Overview and theoretical perspectives. In T. Anderson (Ed.), *Black studies: Theory, method, and cultural perspectives.* Pullman: Washington State University Press.

Arminio, J. L., & Hultgren, F. H. (2002). Breaking out from the shadow: The question of criteria in qualitative research. *Journal of College Student Development, 43*(4), 446–461.

Barthelemy, S. J. (1984). The role of Black colleges in nurturing leadership. In A. M. Garibaldi (Ed.), *Black colleges and universities: Challenges for the future* (pp. 14–26). New York: Praeger.

Baum, S., & Payea, K. (2004). *Education pays 2004.* New York: The College Board.

Bennett, W. (1971). The Afro-American cultural center. *Harvard Journal of Afro-American Affairs, 2*(2), 18–29.

Bogdan, R. C., & Biklen, S. K. (1992). *Qualitative research for education: An introduction to theory and methods.* Boston: Allyn & Bacon.

Bollen, K. A., & Hoyle, R. H. (1990). Perceived cohesion: A conceptual and empirical examination. *Social Forces, 69,* 479–504.

Bonner, F. A., II, & Bailey, K. W. (2006). Enhancing the academic climate for African American men. In M. J. Cuyjet & Associates (Eds.), *African American men in college* (pp. 24–46). San Francisco: Jossey-Bass.

Brown, M. C., Donahoo, S., & Bertrand, R. D. (2001). The Black college and the quest for educational opportunity. *Urban Education, 36*(5), 553–571.

Clark, E. (1930, February). Mr. Jefferson's university. *The American Mercury,* 202.

Creswell, J. W. (1994). *Research design: Qualitative and quantitative approaches.* Thousand Oaks, CA: Sage Publications.

Cuyjet, M. J. (2006). African American college men: Twenty-first century issues and concerns. In M. J. Cuyjet & Associates (Eds.), *African American men in college* (pp. 3–23). San Francisco: Jossey-Bass.

D'Augelli, A. R., & Hershberger, S. L. (1993). African American undergraduates on a predominantly White campus: Academic factors, social networks, and campus climate. *Journal of Negro Education, 62,* 67–81.

Drewry, H. N., & Doermann, H. (2004). *Stand and prosper: Private Black colleges and their students.* Princeton, NJ: Princeton University Press.

Fleming, J. (1984). *Blacks in college: A comparative study of students' success in Black and White institutions.* San Francisco: Jossey-Bass.

Gossett, B. J., Cuyjet, M. J., & Cockriel, I. (1998). African Americans' perception of marginality in the campus culture. *College Student Journal, 32,* 22–32.

Guba, E. G., & Lincoln, Y. S. (1989). *Fourth generation evaluation.* Newbury Park, CA: Sage.

Guiffrida, D. A. (2003). African American student organizations as agents of social integration. *Journal of College Student Development, 44,* 304–319.

Hefner, D. (2002, February 14). Black cultural centers: Standing on shaky ground? *Black Issues in Higher Education, 18,* 22–29.

Hill, C. E., Thompson, B. J., & Williams, E. N. (1997). A guide to conducting consensual qualitative research. *The Counseling Psychologist, 25,* 517–572.

Hirt, J. B., Strayhorn, T. L., Amelink, C. T., & Bennett, B. R. (2006). The nature of student affairs work at historically Black colleges and universities. *Journal of College Student Development, 47*(6), 661–676.

hooks, b. (1994). *Teaching to transgress.* New York: Routledge.

Kvale, S. (1996). *InterViews: An introduction to qualitative research interviewing.* Thousand Oaks, CA: Sage.

Lincoln, Y. S., & Guba, E. G. (1985). *Naturalistic inquiry.* Newbury Park, CA: Sage.

Manning, K. (1992). The ethnographic interview. In F. K. Stage (Ed.), *Diverse methods for research and assessment of college students* (pp. 91–104). Washington, DC: American College Personnel Association.

Miles, M., & Huberman, A. (1994). *An expanded sourcebook: Qualitative data analysis* (2nd ed.). Thousand Oaks, CA: Sage Publications.

Patton, L. D. (2006a). Black culture centers: Still central to student learning. *About Campus, 11*(2), 2–8.

Patton, L. D. (2006b). The voice of reason: A qualitative examination of Black student perceptions of Black Culture Centers. *Journal of College Student Development, 47*(6), 628–646.

Patton, M. Q. (1990). *Qualitative evaluation and research methods* (2nd ed.). Newbury Park, CA: Sage.

Pittman, E. (1994, October 6). Cultural centers on predominantly White campuses: Campus, cultural, and social comfort equals retention, last word. *Black Issues in Higher Education, 11*, 104.

Roseboro, D. L. (2005). Icons of power and landscape of protest: The student movement for the Sonya Haynes Stone Black Cultural Center at the University of North Carolina at Chapel Hill. *Dissertation Abstracts International, 66*(06A), 2056.

Roseboro, D. L. (2006). Coming out Black: The student movement for the Sonja Haynes Stone Black Cultural Center at UNC-Chapel Hill. *NASAP Journal, 9*(1), 67–82.

Stewart, G., Russell, R. H., & Wright, D. B. (1997). The comprehensive role of student affairs in African American student retention. *Journal of College Admission, 154*, 6–11.

Strauss, A., & Corbin, J. (1998). *Basics of qualitative research: Techniques and procedures for developing grounded theory* (2nd ed.). Thousand Oaks, CA: Sage.

Strayhorn, T. L. (2008). Influences on labor market outcomes of African American college graduates: A national study. *The Journal of Higher Education, 79*(1), 29–57.

Strayhorn, T. L., & Hirt, J. B. (2008). Social justice and student affairs work at minority-serving institutions. In M. B. Gasman, B. Baez, & C. S. V. Turner (Eds.), *Understanding minority-serving institutions* (pp. 203–216). Albany: State University of New York Press.

Sutton, E. M., & Kimbrough, W. M. (2001). Trends in Black student involvement. *NASPA Journal, 39*(1), 30–40.

Tatum, B. D. (1997). *Why are all the Black kids sitting together in the cafeteria? And other conversations about race.* New York: Basic Books.

Thomas, S. L., & Perna, L. W. (2004). The opportunity agenda: A reexamination of postsecondary reward and opportunity. In J. C. Smart (Ed.), *Higher education: Handbook of theory and research* (Vol. 19, pp. 43–84). Dordrecht, Netherlands: Kluwer Academic Publishers.

Tinto, V. (1993). *Leaving college: Rethinking the causes and cures of student attrition* (2nd ed.). Chicago: University of Chicago Press.

University of Missouri renames Black Cultural Center. (2002). *Black Issues in Higher Education, 18*(23), 14.

U.S. Department of Education, National Center for Education Statistics. (2006). *The condition of education 2006* (NCES 2006–071). Washington, DC: U.S. Government Printing Office.

U.S. Department of Education, National Center for Education Statistics. (2007). *The condition of education 2007* (NCES 2007). Washington, DC: U.S. Government Printing Office.

Van Gennep, A. (1960). *The rites of passage* (M. Vizedon & G. Caffee, Trans.). Chicago: University of Chicago Press.

Williamson, J. A. (2003). *Black power on campus: The University of Illinois, 1965–1975.* Urbana, IL: The University of Illinois Press.

Young, L. W., & Hannon, M. D. (2002, February 14). The staying power of Black cultural centers. *Black Issues in Higher Education, 18*, last word.

8

THE UNIQUENESS OF AN HBCU ENVIRONMENT

How a Supportive Campus Climate
Promotes Student Success

Robert T. Palmer and Estelle Young

Abstract: In this chapter, the authors discuss a qualitative study of Black males who entered an HBCU as academically underprepared and persisted to gradua-tion. More specifically, this chapter delineates the impact a supportive HBCU climate had on the Black males' persistence. In particular, the participants noted that individuals in the institutional community exhibited a caring and con-cerned mentality, which was critical to their academic success. Using the students' voices, we focus on this supportive climate and urge other institutions to engender such an environment to facilitate the success of their Black male students.

Historically Black colleges and universities (HBCUs) have played a central role in educating Blacks when other venues excluded their participation. Despite persistent inequalities in infrastructure, resources, and operating budgets (Brown, Bertrand, & Donahoo, 2001; Brown & Davis, 2001; Drewry & Doermann, 2004; Palmer, in press), these institutions continue to provide broad access while retaining their rich legacy of producing charismatic leaders who valiantly advocate for societal change for all and serve as positive role models to many African Americans (Palmer, 2008; Palmer & Gasman, 2008).

While HBCUs represent only 3% of the nation's institutions of higher learning (Allen, 1992), they enroll 16% of African Americans at the under-graduate level and award nearly one-fifth of all bachelor degrees to Blacks

(Allen, Jewell, Griffin, & Wolf, 2007). Black colleges also award 20% of all first professional degrees to Blacks (Hoffman, Liagas, & Snyder, 2003). The cultural and social capital embedded in the fabric of these institutions is a unique aspect of Black colleges that help to foster an empowering educational climate (Brown & Davis, 2001; Palmer & Gasman, 2008). In this chapter, we draw from a qualitative study of African American men attending a Black college to discuss the supportive campus climate and its relationship to fostering academic success.

Review of Literature

HBCUs were established with the assistance of the Freedman's Bureau, Black churches, Northern missionaries, private philanthropists, and governmental initiatives (e.g., Morrill Act of 1890) to provide access to higher education for Blacks. From approximately 1865 until the 1960s, the majority of African Americans attended these universities, which helped to promote their social equality and social mobility. These universities have nurtured strong, courageous leaders who helped to usher in social advancement for all Americans (Drewry & Doermann, 2004; Palmer & Gasman, 2008).

Over the years, there has been a precipitous drop in the number of Blacks attending HBCUs, prompted by several government actions, including *Adams v. Richardson* (1972), *Brown v. Board of Education* (1954), the Civil Rights Act of 1964, and implementation of federal aid and affirmative action programs. Whereas earlier a critical mass of African Americans attended HBCUs, by 1973 three-fourths of Blacks were attending predominantly White institutions (PWIs) (Allen & Jewell, 2002; Brown et al., 2001; Green, 2001; Moore, 2001). In spite of the origin of these institutions, their historic relevance, and their continuing prominence in promoting access to African Americans, particularly students who are educationally disadvantaged, some scholars fear that HBCUs may disappear (Blake, 1991; Day, 1992; Stefkovich & Leas, 1994), as more African Americans choose PWIs over HBCUs. The impact of legal and legislative action to eradicate de jure segregation by promoting student integration and eliminating program duplication has increased the presence of Black students in PWIs at the expense of HBCUs (i.e., *Adams v. Richardson*, 1972; *United States v. Fordice*, 1992).

Despite the declining number of Black students attending HBCUs, researchers consistently argue that HBCUs foster a nurturing, family-like environment and faculty members are supportive of Black students (Hirt, Strayhorn, Amelink, & Bennett, 2006). Research has also shown that Black students on Black campuses exhibit positive psychosocial adjustments, cultural awareness, increased confidence, and higher academic performance (Allen, 1992; Fleming, 1984; Fries-Britt & Turner, 2002; Palmer, 2008; Palmer & Gasman, 2008). HBCUs' mission-driven admissions policies provide access to academically underprepared students. Once admitted, students at HBCUs show disproportionate gains in academic performance and graduate with the skills necessary to compete successfully in society (DeSousa & Kuh, 1996; Fleming, 1976; Kim & Conrad, 2006; Outcalt & Skewes-Cox, 2002). Research also indicates that the HBCU experience propels more African Americans into graduate and professional degree programs than PWIs (Allen, 1991, 1992; Brown & Davis, 2001; Garibaldi, 1997; Palmer & Gasman, 2008; Perna, 2001; Roebuck & Murty, 1993; Wenglinsky, 1996).

According to the United Negro College Fund, of the top 10 colleges that graduate African Americans who go on to earn PhDs or MDs, 9 are HBCUs, as are 8 of the 10 top producers of African American graduates in mathematics and statistics. And the 12 top producers of African American graduates in the physical sciences are all Black colleges, including Xavier University of Louisiana, which is ranked first among the 12 (Gasman et al., 2007). Brown and Davis (2001) report that 75% of all Black army officers, 80% of Black federal judges, and 85% of Black doctors attended HBCUs as undergraduates. Buttressing this information, Strayhorn (2008) found that African Americans who graduate from HBCUs assume more prestigious occupations, compared to their peers who graduate from PWIs.

The experiences of Black students at Black colleges stand in sharp contrast to their experiences at PWIs. Researchers have found that Black students attending PWIs often experience alienation and are not engaged in the campus (Allen & Haniff, 1991; Feagin, Vera, & Imani, 1996; Pascarella & Terenzini, 2005; Rankin & Reason, 2005; Tinto, 1987). Person and Christensen (1996) indicate that Black students attending private PWIs complained of lack of access to student support services, expressed discontentment with their social experiences, and talked about experiencing racism. Researchers (D'Augelli & Scott, 1993; Hall & Rowan, 2001) provide additional evidence of the racism and hostility that many African American students at PWIs experience. Solorzano, Ceja, and Yosso (2000) found that African American students attending three elite PWIs experienced more racial microaggressions, which they defined as unconscious and subtle forms of racism. These experiences triggered participants in their study to seek a "positive collegiate racial climate" (p. 70).

The Purpose of the Study

Numerous researchers (Allen, 1987, 1992; Davis, 1994; Fleming, 1984; Fries-Britt, 1997; Fries-Britt & Turner, 2002) have compared the experiences of African Americans attending PWIs to those attending HBCUs. However, many of these studies do not disaggregate the experiences of African Americans by gender and academic achievement (Kimbrough & Harper, 2006; Strayhorn & Saddler, 2009). Furthermore, there is a lack of current literature (e.g., Harper, 2006; Ross, 1998) documenting the experiences of African American men at Black colleges. Because of the dearth of up-to-date, comprehensive research on Black colleges, Kimbrough and Harper (2006) voiced the need for more research to examine the social conditions at Black colleges and their impact on African Americans, especially Black males.

Consequently, this chapter discusses the supportive campus climate that exists at one Black university located in a Mid-Atlantic state. In our discussion, we draw from a study of 11 academically underprepared African American men who entered a public, urban HBCU and persisted to graduation, to present evidence of the supportive campus climate. This study is meant to illustrate students' perceptions regarding the supportive campus climate and its implications for their persistence.

Methodology

We conducted this study at a public, doctoral-research-intensive HBCU in a Mid-Atlantic state. According to the Office of Institutional Research (OIR) at this university, approximately 6,000 undergraduate and 400 graduate students were enrolled when data were collected. With regard to the freshmen class, the average high school grade point average is a 3.00. Twenty-four percent of the new students scored over 500 on the SAT verbal exam, and 25% scored over 500 on the SAT math exam.

We used a qualitative approach to guide this study because we sought to understand the social experiences of African American men in a particular context. Specifically, we used in-depth interviews complemented by secondary data. As such, our epistemological approach was anchored in the constructivist tradition to construct knowledge, understanding, and meaning through human interactions (Jones, Torres, & Armino, 2006).

Participants

Participants in this study were African American male juniors and seniors who entered a public HBCU through its precollege outreach program and persisted to graduation. The precollege program serves as an intervention for academically unprepared students who do not meet traditional academic standards (e.g. GPA, SAT, and ACT) for admission to the university. Students in this study participated in this six-week intensive summer preparatory program to strengthen their academic skills for college. To complete the program successfully, students must earn at least a grade of C in all precollege courses, complete all assignments, and attend all scheduled events.

Recruitment Procedures

The university's Office of Institutional Research provided us with a list of 111 African American male students who entered the university through its precollege outreach program during the summers of 2000 through 2003. Of the 111 students, 38 had graduated by the time we began the study, leaving 73 potential participants. We e-mailed the 73 students a poster about the study and asked them to contact us if they were interested in participating. We later followed this e-mail with a letter to the students' on-campus address or home residence. As an incentive, we offered potential participants a $20 gift certificate. We also sought the help of staff members (or gatekeepers) at the university whom we believed knew students who matriculated through the precollege outreach program. The staff members identified and contacted students who met the study's criteria. We recruited additional participants through snowball sampling (i.e., asking those who joined the study to recommend others who might meet our criteria).

Although we contacted 73 students, few displayed an interest in participating. With snowball sampling and help from university administrators, we recruited 11 African American men to participate. The average student involved was 21 years old, majored in business, earned 93 credits, and had a 2.7 grade point average (GPA). Participants' fathers' occupations included a teacher, lawyer, police officer, minister, and maintenance worker. Participants' mothers' occupations included a pediatrician, minister, congressional representative, daycare worker, and U.S. Postal Service (USPS) employee. Educational attainment among the participants' fathers ranged from a high school diploma to doctoral and professional degrees. Participants' mothers' educational attainment ranged from high school to professional degree (i.e., medical school). Seven participants were raised in the suburbs, three were raised in a large city, and one was raised in a small city. Many of the participants came from a two-parent household, and most planned to continue beyond their baccalaureate degrees. Specifically, four participants planned to obtain doctoral degrees, six planned to obtain master's degree, and one did not have plans to further his education.

Data Collection

We conducted 90- to 110-minute, face-to-face, in-depth interviews with each participant. We completed all interviews within six weeks. Prior to beginning the interviews, participants signed a consent form and completed a brief demographic form and a short, open-ended questionnaire to understand factors germane to their academic success. With the participants' consent, we also obtained information about their grades and GPAs from the director of the precollege outreach program, who tracked the participants' academic progress since their matriculation into the university. During these interviews, we engaged participants about their academic and social experiences at the university. We placed particular emphasis on understanding their precollege experiences and investigating key factors to their success. Many of the questions were open-ended, which enabled participants to talk in-depth about their experiences. We recorded our observations of how the participants responded to a question and their willingness to engage in the interview. We also conducted follow-up phone interviews to clarify issues that emerged. We audiotaped and transcribed all of the interviews.

Data Analyses

We used constant comparative analysis on field notes, observations, and interview transcripts. Constant comparative analysis engages the researcher in collecting and analyzing the data simultaneously at "all stages of the data collection and interpretation process, and results in the identification of codes" (Jones et al., 2006, p. 44). We used ATLASTi, a qualitative data management software program, to organize, manage, and code the data. We used open coding to identify themes, analyzed the interview data obtained from each participant independently, and included cross-case analysis (Yin, 2006). In discussing the findings, we present excerpts from the participants' responses verbatim to reveal their voices. We used pseudonyms to maintain the anonymity and confidentiality of each participant, and we excluded information that would compromise the confidentiality of any participant, administrator, or faculty or staff member.

Credibility and Trustworthiness

We used several of Merriam's (1998) techniques to ensure credibility of the study. For example, we provided thick description of our site and participants in this chapter so that others interested can draw their own conclusions from the data. Moreover, providing thick description enables the reader to vicariously experience the participants' challenges at the university and the supportive strategies they used to surmount them.

We also returned the transcribed interviews to all participants so they could check for accuracy and clarity in the information we gleaned from open-ended interviews. Last, we used feedback from five peer debriefers who were well versed in qualitative research methods. These debriefers provided their own interpretations of the themes from the data to ensure creditability (Jones et al., 2006).

Limitations

A limitation of qualitative research is that the findings can only be generalized to other cases similar to the case of focus. In other words, these findings may not be applicable to other HBCUs (e.g., public HBCUs, smaller/larger institutions) or even generalizable to this institution. Moreover, interviews may not be an effective way to collect reliable information when the questions deal with matters the participants perceive as personally sensitive; thus, readers should exercise a degree of caution when interpreting these findings. In addition, the accuracy of the findings is contingent on how well we analyzed the data, although this is true for all research studies.

Despite these shortcomings, we proceeded with the qualitative methodology because we wanted to investigate the social experiences of academically unprepared Black men. We specifically focused on Black men at a Black institution because of the scarcity of research on retention and persistence among African American men attending such institutions.

Findings

We group our findings in four categories. First, we present students' perceptions about faculty. Next, we summarize students' assessments of campus administrators. Students also described their relationships with people they regarded as mentors and role models. Finally, we include students' reflections on the overall climate on campus.

Faculty: Personally Concerned and Connected to Student Success

Participants commented on the link between supportive faculty members and academic success. Students described faculty who supported these students by displaying concern, not only for their academic success, but also for their personal welfare. Faculty members displayed empathy for their students and tried to help them maximize their potential. James, a business major, noted the importance of building rapport with faculty by taking initiative to interact with them during their office hours. He emphasized that these relationships enabled his professors to know that he was diligent about his studies and serious about succeeding academically:

> All of my teachers know me on a first-name basis. I'm able to make that relationship with them, and they know if I'm trying or if I'm not, or, you know, they just know me personally, so I've been able to make that relationship with them, so it kind of helps me out.

Chris, an industrial engineering major, indicated how faculty supported his academic success by motivating him and helping him to demonstrate his potential when he doubted it. He emphasized how important it is to listen to your professor. Chris stated:

> [There was a] swimming class I wasn't doing too good in. And my teacher was, "Like . . . you know you have a lot of potential, I've seen you swim before." I'm, like, "Coach, I can't swim." He said, "Stop saying that, you can swim. I'm motivating you to swim. So just try it, get in the water." I said, "No, I'm going to drown." He said, "You're not going to drown. I've been doing this for about 40 years, and no one has ever drowned." He said, "Just get in the water and just relax your body." He's, like, "Get in the deep end and just relax. I relaxed all my muscles and I floated on top of the water." I'm, like, "I'm floating. Yo, Coach, I'm floating on top of the water!" [His words] encouraged me to stay in the water and stay afloat. You have to listen, and once you listen and open up your ears, it will help you achieve success.

Anderson, a theater major, commented on the faculty's care and concern for his welfare and how this extended beyond academic issues. He also explained that faculty members were there for him and took extra time to make certain he understood the information presented in class:

Yeah, faculty has been great, man. I always tell myself [if I had] gone to
another university, would I have gotten this experience? I hear people say
bad things about the [university] to me it . . . doesn't get any better than
this. The faculty really has just cared beyond caring, you know. These are
people with doctoral degrees, "Like, why are you even talking to me? Like,
what can I offer you?" Absolutely nothing! I have no money. I have no
advice to give you. I have nothing to offer you. Yet you sit down for hours
and you just try to help me. I come to your office and you sit there for an
extra hour, and it's just amazing. I never knew people [could] be that
generous. I didn't know that kind of generosity still existed. I thought it
died out in the '60s.

Simmons, a sociology major, also explained how his faculty supported
his success. Specifically, he recalled how his professor caught him cheating
on a test and instead of turning him in to the dean, she was willing to work
with him. She suggested that he come to her office hours to learn the material better. Simmons, of course, was flabbergasted because he could not imagine his professor being so supportive. He thought she would be antagonistic.

I had one teacher. She was like a mom to everybody in the class [and] she
used to always tell us, don't cheat on our test because they're simple. But
being a hard-head, I had a cheat sheet under my sleeve . . . she walked up
to me, and she whispered in my ear, "I know you have a sheet under your
arm. You can either do it the hard way, or the easy way. If you just give it
to me, and we'll talk after class, or you can make a big deal about it." So,
as soon as she said that, I just started sweating, I was, like, "Man, what do
I do?" So I just grabbed it and gave it to her. There were 60 questions on
the test.

He continued to explain:

I gave it to her. . . . I waited to make sure I was the last person, so I
waited and I talked to her, and I explained to her about all the stuff, and I
apologized. She was, like, "Am I apologizing just because I got caught, or
am I apologizing because I know it was wrong. . . . She could have took
that to the dean and got me kicked out of school. But she didn't. . . . She
had office hours for me to come talk to her . . . she offered to help me. [I
am like] you just caught me cheating on the test, and you're still helping
me out?

Samuel, a sociology major, also commented on how his professors made
themselves available and accessible:

Knowing the professors there, [one professor] has really stepped in. . . . You can e-mail [him]. You can call him. You can knock on his door. He'll open and he [is] willing to tell you things that some professors won't tell you. He's willing to tell you things that you just need to know, but somehow do not know. He takes the extra initiative.

Many of the participants reported that faculty members took a genuine interest in getting to know and building relationships with them. They developed an interest in the students' academic and personal lives and made attempts to relate to the students' life situations. This approach strengthened the faculty members' overall rapport with the students. Guiffrida (2005) notes that faculty members who do not limit their professional responsibilities solely to teaching and research, but also work to enhance students' psychosocial and emotional development, are student-centered.

Faculty went beyond their professional duty to form supportive relationships with students, which research has shown to be critical to Black students' success (Palmer & Gasman, 2008; Strayhorn, 2008). They created a close-knit community where students felt a part of the institutional fabric of the campus. They also used empathy to foster a better connection with the students, helping students to identify personally with faculty. Furthermore, students reported that Black professors tried to maximize their potential because they knew the students possessed the capability, desire, and motivation to achieve great feats.

Supportive Administrators: Creating a Warm, Welcoming Environment to Enhance Student Success

Participants commented that administrators are another vital component of their support system. These administrators are helpful, accessible, and demonstrate a caring attitude about student success. Anderson shared:

There's . . . staff and sometimes I forget they work here because they're so kind, and so generous. . . . You become on a first-name basis with people because they just take you under their wing as a freshman and they show you that [there's] more to school than doing well. If you have a bad semester, if you have a bad class, [they say] come talk to us. We'll work these things out for you and we'll try to help you. The whole honors department . . . really care about their students and care about their work, and you begin to really care so much about these people . . . if you do not do well, it will not only hurt you, but it will hurt them. You become more concerned about not hurting them that you try so hard. Those things helped me, having administrators that actually care. . . . Like Dr. Howard, her door is always open. I asked the lady one day, "When do you get any work done because you always help students in here?" She just replied simply, "The students are my life," and I was, like, "Damn."

Lawrence, a sociology major, concurred with Anderson's assertion about the importance of supportive administrators. "You know the administrators and staff—they all got open arms, so they're willing to mentor you without you even knowing you're being mentored."

Samuel echoed this sentiment: "You can look up to them, people that really care, not telling you what you want to hear, more so telling you things that can really impact your life, making it comfortable here." Students commented that some administrators, like faculty members, demonstrated a personal interest in them and were supportive. These administrators adopted an "open door policy" and illustrated caring that extended beyond their academic performance. Some of these administrators also served as role models and mentors to these students, which illustrates the richness of social capital at this institution.

Role Models and Mentors: Illuminate the Pathway Toward Success

Many participants explained how access to role models and mentors emerged as a significant factor to support their academic success. James noted that having access to someone who has been successful certainly affects success. "I think . . . if maybe we can reach out to the freshmen more. If they know that, you know, I was in the same position as [them]. I was in precollege, and now . . . I'm graduating . . . and you know I'm in these organizations." Anderson agreed with James's assertions, but added that having some commonalities (e.g., gender, ethnicity, educational background, socioeconomic status) with the successful person can also foster a sense of self-efficacy. Recalling a visit by Frank, an alumnus and successful lawyer, Anderson explained:

> I think it's . . . a male seeing another male doing something that he wants to do. Frank is [on] the university council, and he came down to my [residence hall] one time. I invited him to come down and speak with some of the guys when I was a RA. A lot of people said, I want to be a lawyer, I want to be a doctor, but you don't see any Black lawyers, you don't see any Black doctors, . . . how feasible [is it] to ever reach that goal if you don't see anyone that looks like you? So when he came down, that

guy is young man. He's a lawyer really, in actuality that's instant inspiration because you're, like, "If he could do it, I could do it; he looks just like me." So I think males on campus, African American males in general, on a college level, if you see someone doing something that you want to do, it will inspire you to do it.

Anderson added:

But when you see someone that's not like you, and you want to do it . . . it's already enough stacked up against the Black male, and I'm not saying there's some external force that's trying to keep the Black male down. Personally, I think a lot of what keeps us down is ourselves. But the inspiration you can get when you see another [Black] man do what you want to do, there's nothing like it. That's why I think a lot of students or a lot of [Black] males want to be athletes, because that's all they can see, or they want to be musicians, 'cause that's all they see. But if you saw a whole bunch of Black doctors running around all day, and saving lives, that's what you want to do, because it's feasible.

Walter, an architecture major, talked about how his fraternity brother on campus serves as a positive, supportive influence. Specifically, he stated:

Well, my brother in the fraternity and I have a wonderful relationship. He continues to look out for me. He's always supportive of me, man, and he is a role model for me as well. . . . I look up to him a lot. He was academically successful, and he's here to serve as a motivational tool. Again, it's just a continual process of motivation.

Douglas, a business major, also indicated that access to role models drives success: "I say, have more Black male role models. Because if you have Black male role models, you'll look at them and say, 'This person has been in the same situation I have, and look how successful he is.'"

Participants also identified a relationship between mentoring and persistence. Access to mentors is important because they provide support and guidance. Simmons offered this explanation about mentoring:

Mentoring has played a big part because if mentoring wasn't there, I think I'd probably failed my English class—my freshman year. The teacher . . . how she used to want us to write our papers, was very different from what I was used to. So the first paper I wrote, she failed me. She gave me a 50 something on it. . . . So I let my mentor read it, and . . . [he] thought it was okay, but when I explained to . . . [him] how . . . she wanted me to write it, then he understood it more and then he helped me out a little more with it. So after that, I passed the class with a B.

Omar, a business major, agreed with the impact of mentoring on African American males' academic success. He encouraged young students to form a mentoring relationship with someone older. This mentorship would positively enhance students' success because they would have access to an experienced person to help them navigate the rough terrain of college life and circumvent the pitfalls that lead to poor academic performance. In Omar's words:

> I think that . . . older Black men need to sit down with younger Black men and just rap together, just talk. I mean not about just hip-hop, but about growing up, dealing with women, dealing with living on your own, because when you grow and you move out on your own, it's hard, especially if you're from a different state. It's kind of like, moving to a different country, 'cause you don't know anybody. So you're dealing with all this temptation and it's, like, I remember there is a Bible verse that says, "The old know the way, the young they have strength." The old are wise because they know the way, but the young, they're good because they're strong. I mean it's all about connecting with Black men who know the way already.

And Wilson, a physical therapy major, emphasized the centrality of a mentor to his academic success:

> I know one of the most important things, I've probably said this about a billion times already, is to get a mentor. You must get a mentor. Without a mentor, you're lost. Without anybody to look up to, it's like you don't have a sense of where you could be. One of the first things I got was a mentor around this campus; my grandfather introduced me to Dr. Johnson. And once you start talking with mentors and socializing, you begin to understand where and start setting goals for yourself, and . . . then you can go from there, and whenever you need him, he'll be there. It's like a brotherly relationship, and also like a parental figure above you.

Supportive Campus Climate and Success

Many participants described the overall environment as supportive and caring. Anderson noted that it is hard to identify one factor at this HBCU that has enabled him to succeed. He credited all of the university personnel (i.e., faculty, administration, and staff) for providing a source of support, motivation, and words of encouragement. Specifically, he said:

> It's just the environment that the [university] fosters. When I came here, it's so hard to pinpoint one thing that really got me to this point. 'Cause one without the other, it's like mayonnaise without bread. I mean, like, you know, you've got to have a sandwich in order to get what you want. Everything here at [the university] just came together to get me to this point. . . . The most important thing, I think, was the administration and the faculty and the staff that helped me out. From talking to maintenance staff who tell you to stay in school, from talking to a doctoral student, or someone with a PhD telling you to file your taxes, it all broadens to this point. So, it's hard to pinpoint one thing.

Lawrence agreed that the university offered a family-like environment: "There's really good people on campus that really care about you, and it's all been an uphill ride for me since I've been at the [university]."

While Walter described the university as supportive, he noted that students need to be proactive about seeking assistance:

> It's important for the student to take action. Don't expect teachers to go running after you, . . . if you don't seek help, they will probably assume that you don't need it. They'll [faculty] always be available to you, [but] you have to take the opportunity [to seek support]. Be prepared for the opportunity when it presents itself.

James mentioned that social support systems at the university helped him to raise his GPA: "The social aspect is completely different at Black colleges, which I'm very thankful for. I probably wouldn't have the grades I have [if I had gone elsewhere]." James also offered that a PWI seemed to be less personal (based on his visits to friends at PWIs), whereas an HBCU seems more personal. He indicated that professors are available and demonstrate a willingness to build relationships with students:

> At a predominantly White university, it's easy for you to just feel like a dot or just [a] number. But here, it's more . . . personal, its more relationship-building . . . it's very easy for you to go to your teacher and be, like, "Listen I'm not understanding," and half the time they will take time out to help you. So, I think that's what it is—it's the smallness of the classes and the close feeling—you can really get to kind of know your teachers, so you don't get lost in the whole college setting. So I try to think of it . . . it's

the classroom sizes, which are good 'cause initially my whole vision of college was, you know, I want to be in a classroom with 400 people. I wanted that, but now that I'm here. I'm really glad that I didn't because I'm so thankful that I'm in these small classes, and my teachers know me on a first- and last-name basis. That I can easily call them up and [say], "Hey, I need a recommendation," or I need help with this and that [and], they have the time to devote to me to do this.

Anderson, Omar, and Lawrence described the positive effect of the university's racial homogeneity. Specifically, they explained that having access to a cadre of Black students who are motivated and focused on attaining their baccalaureate degrees is linked to success. Simmons articulated, "It's like most of the African American males here are, like, we're striving for one thing—to be successful, and that makes me want to be successful." Omar commented:

Seeing other Black people [makes] us want to succeed, too. Like so much of society, they show us as scavengers . . . they show us as not intelligent. Corporate America shows us what they want us to see, and they show people what they want us to be thought [of as], and I don't like that. But when I came to the [university] . . . I saw Black people. I saw Trinidadian people. I saw people from all shades of Black . . . who [are] motivated [and] driven for success.

Lawrence added:

It makes you want to do better, 'cause you're at an institution with a majority of your race, and you don't want to be a failure. You want to succeed and you already know that some people will look at a[n] HBCU as being on a smaller level, so you want to try to get the most out of it that you can.

Anderson, Omar, and Lawrence offered comments that are of interest because this HBCU environment seems to trigger a sense of cognitive dissonance for the participants regarding the phenomenon of acting White (see Fordham & Ogbu, 1986; Lundy, 2003; McWhorter, 2001). In other words, the participants' predilection for education was enhanced by their ability to observe and interact with other Blacks (African Americans and Africans of various nationalities), thus weakening the socially constructed perception that displaying an affinity for education is equated with Whiteness. Because the participants were immersed in a community where Black students embraced education, they were challenged to view education as a necessary component for empowerment, social mobility, and academic success.

Samuel stated that the environment at the university positively shaped his professional preparedness for the world:

> [The university] has groomed me and made me a contender for the world. Many times, like, I said, when you [graduate from an] HBCU, people look at you . . . a little strange, but it's not where you come from, it's what you learned from where you come from. . . . When someone sees my application, sees my resume or something like that, they'll see the knowledge that I possess, that I can write and speak. I am marketable . . . [the university] has made me a marketable, Black, young man.

Discussion

Findings from this study on Black males are consistent with previous studies on HBCUs and their impact on Black students (Allen, 1987, 1991, 1992; Berger & Milem, 2000; Fleming, 1984; Fries-Britt & Turner, 2002; Hirt et al., 2006; Palmer, 2008; Palmer & Gasman, 2008). Participants indicated that professors and administrators were accessible and displayed a willingness to form supportive relationships with students. These relationships encouraged persistence because students realized that professors and administrators cared about them and their success. Faculty members and administrators mentored and served as role models to many of the students. They also directed and encouraged student participation in student support services, campus organizations, internships, and scholarship programs. In many ways, the interactions and experiences created a climate that the participants perceived as supportive and nurturing.

Research has shown that positive student-faculty interactions are linked to academic achievement and success for all students (Astin, 1993, 1999; Davis, 1999; Eimers & Pike, 1997; Pascarella & Terenzini, 2005). While research supports the relationship between faculty interaction and success, some researchers (Allen & Haniff, 1991; Feagin et al., 1996; Pascarella & Terenzini, 2005; Rankin & Reason, 2005; Tatum, 1997; Tinto, 1987; Watson et al., 2002) posit that African Americans generally lack close contact with faculty at PWIs. However, other researchers (Allen, 1987, 1991, 1992; Berger & Milem, 2000; Fleming, 1984; Fries-Britt & Turner, 2002) argue that students have close, supportive relationships with faculty at HBCUs. In fact, Davis (2006) indicates that, "at HBCUs, it takes the entire institutional family to produce competent graduates. The administration, faculty, staff, alumni, and community people who take a personal interest in the . . . student" act as an extended family (p. 44).

The perceptions of the Black males in this study mirror Allen's (1992) assessment of HBCUs. He asserts, "Black universities provide positive social and psychological environments for African American students that compare to those experienced by White students who attend [a] White university" (p. 40). Allen explains that the social aspects encompass networks of peers, social outlets, and supportive relationships. The psychological component, on the other hand, includes a heightened level of self-confidence, self-esteem, a sense of belonging, and ownership of the campus. Green (2002) explains, "[T]he collegiate experience for African Americans at HBCUs is a cathartic one, in that it is a nurturing environment; faculty members at HBCUs discern student's difficulties and offer to them the social, cultural, and psychological support" to achieve and thrive academically (p. 16).

Lavant, Anderson, and Tiggs (1997) found that when universities implement mentoring programs, African American men are more successful academically. They highlight six mentoring models at various institutions: (a) the Black Man's Think Tank, (b) the Student African American Brotherhood, (c) the Black Male Initiative, (d) the Meyerhoff Program, (e) the Bridge, and (f) the Faculty Mentor Program, all of which have been instrumental in reducing attrition for African American males. Although there are some differences among these programs, they provide a safe place for African American men and help them to cultivate leadership skills and develop positive mentoring relationships with the university's constituencies. Institutions such as City University of New York and University of West Georgia have implemented programs to enhance African American male retention. This list is not exhaustive, as there are similar programs at many institutions across the country. Craig (2006) and Green (2002) also indicate a relationship between mentoring and academic success for African Americans. These groups provide guidance, nurturing, social networks, support, encouragement, and, as Tinto (1987) indicates, help socially integrate students into the university's community.

Recommendations

Supportive campus climates continue to be a critical factor underlying the achievement, attainment, and overall well-being of Black students at higher education institutions. This environment enables HBCUs to outperform

PWIs despite persistent inequalities in institutional resources and disparities in the academic preparation and financial resources of some incoming students. Their informal and formal efforts to foster a supportive campus climate ensure the efficacy of HBCUs in fulfilling their mission.

The faculty, staff, and administrators described in this chapter are present at all universities. They are identified by their above-and-beyond actions rather than by their positions. Students and staff alike generally know them well, but they often work in isolation. Identifying ways to enable these caring and committed individuals to collaborate will unleash their capacity to contribute to the creation of a supportive campus climate. For example, at this university, we created an informal committee to create and implement activities that foster positive interactions among students, staff, faculty, and administrators. Because of the committee's informal and all-volunteer nature, the strategy cost little to nothing. For example, we created a laminated "Helping Hands" decal that could be taped to staff and faculty's doors or desks to indicate to passing students that that they are willing to help. The photos of the Helping Hands are displayed in the lobby of the university's student services building.

Universities can also build the capacity of existing formal initiatives to create a supportive campus climate by actively encouraging collaboration. For example, on our campus we are forging a formal collaboration between two extracurricular initiatives with explicit goals of student development, achievement, and retention. The first program focuses on leadership development, which is reflected in its mantra: "We grow together, we lead together, we graduate together." The second project is a service-learning initiative whereby students build the capacity of campus-based, community service organizations by performing administrative tasks such as marketing and evaluation. The efficacy of the leadership development program will be increased by the participation of its students in structured service learning. The leadership skills developed by students engaged in service learning will be reinforced by participation in the leadership development program.

The academic, social, and financial needs of students attending HBCUs, coupled with the limited resources of these institutions, demands that we return to our most precious and most powerful commodity: our capacity to care. Caring is a powerful resource. It does not require money, it is infinite and enduring, and it is immediately credible. With relatively minor interventions on the part of institutions, this capacity to care can make our institutions as resilient as our students.

References

Adams v. Richardson, 351 f.2d 636 (D.C. Cir. 1972).

Allen, W. R. (1987, May/June). Black colleges vs. White colleges: The fork in the road for Black students. *Change, 28–34.*

Allen, W. R. (1991). Introduction. In W. R., Allen, E. G. Epps, & N. Z. Haniff (Eds.), *College in Black and White: African American students in predominantly White and in historically Black public universities* (pp. 1–14). Albany: New York: State University of New York Press.

Allen, W. R. (1992). The color of success: African American college students outcomes at predominantly White and historically Black public colleges and universities. *Harvard Educational Review, 62*(1), 26–44.

Allen, W. R., & Haniff, N. Z. (1991). Race, gender, and academic performance in U.S. higher education. In W. R. Allen, E. G. Epps, & N. Z. Haniff (Eds.), *College in Black and White: African American students in predominantly White and in historically Black public universities* (pp. 95–109). Albany: New York: State University of New York Press.

Allen, W. R., & Jewel, J. O. (2002). A backward glance forward: Past, present, and future perspectives on historically Black colleges and universities. *Review of Higher Education, 25*(3), 241–261.

Allen, W. R., Jewell, J. O., Griffin, K. A., & Wolf, D. S. (2007). Historically black colleges and universities: Honoring the past, engaging the present, touching the future. *Journal of Negro Education, 76*(3), 263–280.

Astin, A. W. (1993). *What matters in college: Four critical years revisited.* San Francisco: Jossey-Bass.

Astin, A. W. (1999). Involvement in learning revisited: Lessons we have learned. *Journal of College Student Personnel, 40*(5), 587–598.

Berger, J. B., & Milem, J. F. (2000). Exploring the impact of historically Black colleges in promoting the development of undergraduates' self-concept. *Journal of College Student Development, 41*(4), 381–394.

Blake, E., Jr. (1991). Is higher education desegregation a remedy for segregation but not educational inequality? A study of the *Ayers v. Mabus* desegregation case. *Journal of Negro Education, 60,* 538–565.

Brown v. Board of Education, 347 U.S. 483 (1954).

Brown, C. M., II., & Davis, E. J. (2001). The historically Black college as social contract, social capital, and social equalizer. *Peabody Journal of Education, 76*(1), 31–49.

Brown, M. C., Bertrand, R. D., & Donahoo, S. (2001). The black college and the quest for educational opportunity. *Urban Education, 36,* 553–573.

Civil Rights Act of 1964 (Title VII), 42 U.S.C. 2000 *et seq.* 29 C.F.R. 1600–1610.

Craig. K. (2006). Factors that influence success for African American students. In F. W. Hale (Ed.), *How Black colleges empower Black students: Lessons for higher education* (pp. 101–108). Sterling, VA: Stylus.

D'Augelli, A. R., & Scott, H. (1993). African American undergraduates on a predominantly White campus: Academic factors, social networks, and campus climate. *Journal of Negro Education, 62*(1), 67–81.

Davis, J. E. (1994). College in Black and White: Campus environment and academic achievement of African American males. *Journal of Negro Education, 63*(4), 620–633.

Davis, J. E. (1999). What does gender have to do with the experience of African American college men? In V. C. Polite & J. E. Davis (Eds.), *African American males in school and society: Practices and policies for effective education* (pp. 134–148). New York: Teacher College Press.

Davis, L. A. (2006). Success against the odds: The HBCU experience. In F. W. Hale (Ed.), *How Black colleges empower Black students: Lessons for higher education* (pp. 43–50). Sterling, VA: Stylus.

Day, D. S. (1992). Brown blues: Rethinking the integrative ideal. *William and Mary Law Review, 34,* 53–74.

DeSousa, D. J., & Kuh, G. D. (1996). Does institutional racial composition make a difference in what Black students gain in college? *The Journal of College Student Development, 37*(3), 257–267.

Drewry, H. N., & Doermann, H. (2004). *Stand and prosper: Private black colleges and their students.* Princeton, NJ: Princeton University Press.

Eimers, M., & Pike, G. (1997). Minority and non-minority adjustment to college: Differences or similarities. *Research in Higher Education, 38*(1), 77–97.

Feagin, J. R., Vera, H., & Imani, N. (1996). *Agony of education.* New York: Routledge.

Fleming, J. (1976). *The lengthening shadow of slavery: A historical justification for affirmative action for Blacks in higher education.* Washington, DC: Howard University Press.

Fleming, J. (1984). *Blacks in college: A comparative study of student success in Black and White institutions.* San Francisco: Jossey-Bass.

Fordham, S., & Ogbu, J. (1986). Black students' school success: Coping with the burden of acting White. *Urban Review, 18*(3), 176–206.

Fries-Britt, S. (1997). Identifying and supporting gifted African American men. In M. J. Cuyjet (Ed.), *Helping African American men succeed in college* (pp. 5–16). San Francisco: Jossey-Bass.

Fries-Britt, S., & Turner, B. (2002). Uneven stories: Successful Black collegians at a Black and a White campus. *Review of Higher Education, 25*(3), 315–330.

Garibaldi, A. M. (1997). Four decades of progress . . . and decline: An assessment of African American educational attainment. *Journal of Negro Education, 66*(2), 105–120.

Gasman, M., Baez, B., Drezner, N. D., Sedgwick, K., Tudico, C., & Schmid, J. M. (2007). Historically Black colleges and universities: Recent trends. *Academe, 93*(1), 69–78.

Green, P. (2001). The policies and politics of retention and access of African American students in public White Institutions. In L. Jones (Ed.), *Retaining African Americans in higher education: Challenging paradigms for retaining students, faculty and administrators* (pp. 45–58). Sterling, VA: Stylus.

Green, P. (2002). African American men and the academy. In L. Jones (Ed.), *Brothers of the academy: Up and coming Black scholars earning our way in higher education* (pp. 2–20). Sterling, VA: Stylus.

Guiffrida, D. (2005). Othermothering as framework for understanding African American students' definitions of student-centered faculty. *Journal of Higher Education, 76*(5), 701–723.

Hall, R. E., & Rowan, G. T. (2001). African American males in higher education: A descriptive qualitative analysis. *Journal of African American Men, 5*(3) 3–12.

Harper, S. R. (2006). Peer support for African American male college achievement: Beyond internalized racism and the burden of acting White. *Journal of Men's Studies, 14*(3), 337–358.

Hirt, J. B., Strayhorn, T. L., Amelink, C. A., & Bennett, B. R. (2006). The nature of student affairs work at historically Black colleges and universities. *Journal of College Student Development, 47*(6), 661–676.

Hoffman, K., Liagas, C., & Snyder, T. D. (2003). *National Center for Education Statistics. Status and trends in the education of Blacks.* Washington, DC: U.S. Department of Education. Retrieved from http://nces.ed.gov/pub2003/2003034.pdf

Jones, R. S., Torres, V., & Arminio, J. (2006). *Negotiating the complexities of qualitative research in higher education: Fundamental elements and issues.* New York: Taylor and Francis.

Kim, M., & Conrad, C. F. (2006). The impact of historically Black colleges and universities on the academic success of African American students. *Research in Higher Education, 47*, 399–427.

Kimbrough, W. M., & Harper, S. R. (2006). African American men at historically Black colleges and universities: Different environments, similar challenges. In M. J. Cuyjet (Ed.), *African American men in college* (pp. 189–209). San Francisco: Jossey-Bass.

Lavant, B. D., Anderson, J., & Tiggs, J. W. (1997). Retaining African American men through mentoring initiatives. *New Directions for Student Services, 80*, 43–53.

Lundy, G. F. (2003). School resistance in American high schools: The role of race and gender in oppositional culture theory. *Evaluation and Research in Education, 17*(1), 6–27.

McWhorter, J. (2001). *Losing the race: Self-sabotage in Black America.* New York: Harper Collins

Merriam, S. B. (1998*). Qualitative research and case study applications in education.* San Francisco: Jossey-Bass.

Moore, J. L., III. (2001). Developing academic warriors: Things that parents, administrators, and faculty should know. In L. Jones, (Ed.), *In retaining African Americans in higher education: Challenging paradigms for retaining students, faculty, and administrators* (pp. 77–90). Sterling, VA: Stylus.

Morrill Act of 1890, Ch. 841, 26 stat. 417.

Outcalt, C. L., & Skewes-Cox, T. E. (2002). Involvement, interaction and satisfaction: The human environment at HBCUs. *Review of Higher Education, 25*(3), 331–347.

Palmer, R. T. (2008). Promoting HBCUs: Black colleges provide a superior education; they just need to toot their horns a little louder. *Diverse Issues of Higher Education, 24*(26), 29.

Palmer, R. T. (in press). The perceived elimination of affirmative action and the strengthening of historically Black colleges and universities. *Journal of Black Studies.*

Palmer, R. T., & Gasman, M. (2008). It takes a village to raise a child: The role of social capital in promoting academic success for Black men at a Black college. *Journal of College Student Development, 49*(1), 52–67.

Pascarella, E. T., & Terenzini, P. T. (2005). *How college affects students: A third decade of research* (3rd ed.). San Francisco: Jossey-Bass.

Perna, L. W. (2001). The contribution of historically Black colleges and universities and preparation of African American faculty careers. *Research in Higher Education, 42*(3), 267–292.

Person, D. R., & Christensen, C. M. (1996). Understanding Black student culture and Black student retention. *NASPA Journal, 34*(1), 47–56.

Rankin, S. R., & Reason, R. D. (2005). Differing perceptions: How students of color and White students perceive campus climate for underrepresented groups. *Journal of College Student Development, 46*(1), 43–61.

Roebuck, J. B., & Murty, K. S. (1993). *Historically Black colleges and universities: Their place in American higher education.* Westport, CT: Praeger.

Ross, M. (1998). *Success factors of young African American males at a historically Black college.* Westport, CT: Bergin and Garvey.

Solorzano, D., Ceja, M., & Yosso, T. (2000). Critical race theory, racial microaggressions, and campus racial climate: The experience of African American college students. *The Journal of Negro Education, 69*, 60–73.

Stefkovich, J. A., & Leas, T. (1994). A legal history of desegregation in higher education. *The Journal of Negro Education, 63*(3), 406–420.

Strayhorn, T. (2008). The role of supportive relationships in supporting African American males' success in college. *NASPA Journal, 45*(1), 26–48.

Strayhorn, T. L., & Saddler, T. N. (2009). Gender differences in the influence of faculty-student mentoring relationships on satisfaction with college among African Americans. *Journal of African American Studies, 13*(4), 476–493.

Tatum, B. D. (1997). *Why are all the Black kids sitting together in the cafeteria? And other conversations about race.* New York: Basic Books.

Tinto, V. (1987). *Leaving college.* Chicago: The University of Chicago Press.

United States v. Fordice, 112 S. Ct. 2727(1992).

Watson, W. L., Terrell, M. C., Wright, D. J., Bonner, F. A., II., Cuyjet, M. J., & Gold, J. A., et al. (2002). *How minority students experience college: Implications for planning and policy.* Sterling, VA: Stylus.

Wenglinsky, H. H. (1996). The educational justification of historically Black colleges and universities: Policy responses to the U.S. Supreme Court. *Educational Evaluation and Policy Analysis, 18,* 91–103.

Yin, R. K. (2006). Case study methods. In J. L. Green, G. Camilli, & P. B. Elmore (Eds.), *Handbook of complementary methods in education research* (pp. 111–122). Mahwah, NJ: Lawrence Erlbaum.

9

COLLEGE-BOUND SONS

Exploring Parental Influences on the Pre-Entry Attributes of African American Males

Darryl B. Holloman and Terrell L. Strayhorn

Abstract: This study explores parental influences on the pre-entry attributes of college-bound African American males. It uses life histories to reveal the educational experiences, including challenges and supports, of senior-level African American male faculty members of higher education who reflect on their K–12 experiences as Black male youth. The study finds that, as college-bound students, these men were exposed to three parental influences: (a) parent polarity, (b) parental occupation, and (c) parental involvement.

A college degree is a critical component in obtaining success and mobility in contemporary society (Freeman, 2005; Smith & Fleming, 2006). In the fall of 2005, approximately 17.5 million undergraduates were enrolled in American colleges and universities, and by 2015, it is anticipated that college enrollments will increase by at least 13 percent (U.S. Department of Education, 2006). In addition, the Department of Education reports that approximately 1.5 million bachelor's degrees, 584,000 master's degrees, and 49,500 doctor's degrees were conferred during the 2005–2006 school year. Researchers suggest that, because of the increased market-rate competition associated with a postsecondary degree, it is important for institutions of higher education to understand the various influences that affect the growth and development of prospective students (Goff, Patino, & Jackson, 2004; Kern-Kelpe, 2000). An investigation of factors that influence college-bound students may be of particular importance in supporting underrepresented groups as they matriculate to postsecondary settings.

Research shows that African American males, irrespective of institutional type, represent a small proportion of conferred degrees in the United States (Cuyjet, 1997; Davis, 1999; Fleming, 1984; Harper, 2006; Jones, 2001; McClure, 2006). Only 7.5% of African American men between the ages of 18 and 25 in the United States received bachelor degrees in 2005, compared to 75% of White men, 72% of White women, and 11% of Black women in the same age group (U.S. Department of Education, 2006). These data regarding African American males also follow a very similar pattern for both master's and doctoral degree attainment in the United States, with African American men receiving less than 7% and 4% of those degrees, respectively, compared to 63% and 52% for their White male counterparts (U.S. Department of Education, 2006).

Such low numbers pose interesting questions to researchers and practitioners in the field of education. For example, how are African American male college-bound students influenced as they prepare to enroll in higher education. Although there is a growing body of literature that examines the experiences of African American male students once they have arrived on their college campuses (e.g., Cuyjet, 1997; Davis, 1999; Feagin, Vera, & Imani, 1996; Fleming, 1984; Harper, 2006; Jones, 2000, 2001; Pascarella & Terenzini, 2005; Strayhorn, 2008), few studies focus on the influences that shape college-bound African American males before their initial entry into postsecondary settings. This chapter explores parental influences on the pre-entry attributes of college-bound African American males. Drawing on data from a qualitative study, we present empirical evidence that is likely to inform existing and new initiatives to support African American male college students. Such insights are important in the advancement of educational policies and practices because they provide a cultural context from the perspective of Black men who have successfully navigated the educational pipeline.

The Influence of Pre-Entry Attributes on the College Choice Process

Researchers agree that, once a student decides to attend college, he or she makes substantial transitions throughout his or her K–12 experience (Freeman, 2005; Hossler & Gallagher, 1987; Pitre, 2006). Letawsky, Schneider, Pedersen, & Palmer (2003) suggest that choosing a college or university is a critical step in the development of high school students, and for many students it initiates their ascent into adult decision-making processes. Somers,

Haines, and Keene (2006) further indicate that these decision-making processes are complex and involve several influential factors for college-bound
students. Current studies that examine the factors that influence college-
bound students have largely focused on the experiences of students post-
enrollment, and many of these studies address how those factors affect the
retention rates of students within the postsecondary setting (e.g., Watson &
Kuh, 1996). When studies have focused on the pre-entry attributes of students, these studies have been concerned primarily with the effects of pre-
entry attributes on the college choice process.

The literature on college choice suggests that the decisions of college-
bound students are influenced by such pre-entry attributes as socioeconomic
status, academic ability, aspirations, parents, race, gender, availability of
financial aid, proximity, and high school involvement (Freeman, 2005; Pitre,
2006; Smith & Fleming, 2006; St. John, Paulsen, & Carter, 2005; Strayhorn,
2010; Tienda & Niu, 2006; Zimbroff, 2005).

In conducting a quantitative study of college choice, Pitre (2006) found
that the pre-entry aspirations of college-bound African American students
are similar to those of their White peers, even though African American
students have lower levels of academic achievement. Additionally, in a qualitative study Freeman (2005) reports that family and community influence
African Americans who aspire to attend an institution of higher education.
Somers, Haines, and Keene (2006) conclude that college-bound students
who opt to attend community colleges are influenced by their aspirations
and encouragement, institutional characteristics, and finances, most of
which are pre-entry factors.

Tienda and Niu (2006) determined that high school seniors are just as
inclined to select an out-of-state college when their choices and decisions are
based on admission requirements, affordability, and opportunity to attend
such a school. Thomas (2004) reports that in Texas, Black and Hispanic
high school students are more likely to choose selective schools outside their
home state. According to Letawsky, Schneider, Pedersen, and Palmer (2003),
college-bound student athletes are just as influenced in their college choice
decisions by the academic environment of their prospective schools as they
are by the institutions' athletic environments. Zimbroff (2005) suggests that
the choices and decisions of college-bound, economically disadvantaged students are influenced by their individual and collective group decision-making
processes. Again, all of these stress the important role pre-entry attributes
play in the college choice process.

Although important to advancing an understanding of the college choice process, these studies of college choice have failed to reveal the complexity that surrounds the influence of pre-entry attributes on how college-bound students are taught to face challenges and seek support in collegiate settings. For example, although college choice studies indicate the presence of pre-entry attributes, few of these studies closely examine the variance found among pre-entry attributes or how these compounded attributes influence college-bound students after they have matriculated to college. In addition, even fewer studies have attempted to disaggregate either the pre-entry attributes of college-bound students or the variant effects of these attributes on individual college-bound student groups (Schwitzer, Griffin, Ancis, & Thomas, 1999), such as African American males. Consequently, the pre-entry attributes of college-bound students are often reported in a homogenous fashion, which suggests that all college-bound students are influenced similarly by their pre-entry attributes. Treating these attributes homogenously implies that each pre-entry attribute has equal influence on the growth and development of all college-bound students, although we have some data to suggest this is probably not true.

Parental Influences on Minority College Students

We identified four studies that address the direct influence of parents on the experiences of minority college students. Bank, Slavings, and Biddle (1990) examine the social influences on the decisions of undergraduates to remain at an institution of higher education. They surveyed 715 students at a large Midwestern state university where they investigated the effects of peer, faculty, and parental influences on students' persistence. The authors concluded that parental influences gradually become insignificant as students move through their college experience. Fisher and Padmawidjaja (1999) investigated parental influences on the career development of African American and Mexican American college students. Guided by social learning theory, they concluded that the parents of their study participants overwhelmingly want their children to surpass their own educational and occupational levels. When they examined the relationship between parental involvement as social capital with regard to minority college enrollment, Perna and Titus (2005) found such parental involvement is positively related to college enrollment regardless of institutional type and individual resources.

Finally, Smith and Fleming (2006) investigated parental influence on the college choice processes of urban African American undergraduate students. Using responses from 11 African American parents (9 mothers, 1 grandmother, and 1 father) who reported on their involvement in the college choices of their daughters or sons, the authors found that parents of college-bound African American students are more supportive of their daughters attending 4-year institutions while they encourage their sons to attend 2-year institutions. Smith and Fleming (2006) state, "Likewise, they encourage their sons to fly, but on a route noticeably lower in attitude and closer in proximity to home than [that of] their African American sisters" (p. 41). Results indicate that African American parents are actively involved in the college experiences of their children beyond the college choice process, but that there were differences in the level of involvement with respect to the gender of the student.

Significance of the Study

Goff et al. (2004) argue that institutions of higher education should seek to develop different marketing strategies and support networks that speak to the individual needs of the various student groups they attract to their campuses. Exploring parental influences on the pre-entry attributes of college-bound African American males reveals that these efforts are met for this subset of the student population. Studies of this kind take a proactive approach in preparing African American males, as well as their campuses, for these students' arrival at postsecondary settings. This not only assists in the recruitment efforts aimed at these students, but it also helps individuals who seek to understand how these prospective students are influenced even before they matriculate to postsecondary settings. In addition, as more higher education institutions eliminate such things as race-based criteria from their admissions policies, focusing on the parental influences of college-bound students helps to provide a more holistic composite of students who come from more racially diverse backgrounds.

Conceptual Framework: The Affects of Pre-Entry Attributes on the College Experience

Tinto (1993) argues that "individual departure from institutions can be viewed as arising out of a longitudinal process of interactions between an individual with given attributes, skills, financial resources, prior educational experiences, and dispositions (intentions and commitments)" (p. 113). Tinto postulates that the attrition and retention of college students is closely associated with their abilities to connect with the social and academic systems of their institutions. He further believes that a student's integration into postsecondary settings involves the extent to which that student shares the normative values and attitudes of his or her college or university. Thus, a student's ability to integrate within postsecondary settings is largely influenced by the pre-entry attributes that a student brings to the college setting. He posits:

> Individuals enter institutions of higher education with a range of differing family and community backgrounds (e.g., as measured by social status, parental education and size of community), a variety of personal attributes (e.g., sex, race, and physical handicaps), skills (e.g., intellectual and social), financial resources, dispositions (e.g., motivations; intellectual, social, and political preferences), and varying types of precollege educational experiences and achievements (e.g., high school grade-point average). (1993, p. 115)

Regarding the college experiences of African American students specifically, Tinto (1993) suggests that, like their White peers, these students integration into institutions of higher education involves their ability to develop substantive relationships, which means connecting socially and academically to their college environments. However, African Americans have more difficulty integrating academically than they do socially into higher education institutions because they "are more likely to come from disadvantaged backgrounds and to have experienced inferior schooling prior to college" (Tinto, p. 73). As a result, African American college students find it difficult to integrate into institutions of higher education because of their inability to find other students who mirror their previous experiences.

Tinto's theory has been criticized by scholars who refute the validity of his work on the college experiences of minority students (Braxton, Milem, & Sullivan, 2000; Dennis, Phinney, & Chuateco, 2005; Guiffrida, 2005, 2006; Kuh & Love, 2000; McClure, 2006; Nora, 2001). According to Guiffrida (2006), "One significant cultural limitation of the theory that is well established in higher education literature relates to Tinto's assertion that students need to 'break away' from past associations and traditions to become integrated into the college's social and academic realms" (p. 451). Critics explain that Tinto's theory ignores bicultural integration or the ability of minority students to navigate multiple cultural worlds—that of their own and mainstream environments. Several adaptations to Tinto's work have been proposed.

Guiffrida (2006) advances one alternative by suggesting that three primary value systems influence the growth and development of minority college students: home social systems, cultural connections, and motivational orientation. Home social systems include family, friends, and members of the minority students' extended communities who assist them as they matriculate to higher education institutions. Second, cultural connections (language, dress, religion, etc.) that are transmitted to minority students through these home social systems help minority students deal with racism, cultural isolation, and other adversities in postsecondary settings. Finally, motivational orientation and intrinsic/extrinsic cultural norms of college-bound minority students help them to become autonomous learners who are academically competent and socially adept.

In this chapter, we use Guiffrida's (2006) conceptual framework to explore parental influences on the pre-entry attributes of college-bound African American males. The chapter focuses primarily on the home social systems of these men to explore how their parents influenced them even before their matriculation to an institution of higher education. Findings indicate that, prior to their matriculation to postsecondary settings, respondents were most influenced by their parent's polarity, occupational examples, and involvement.

Research Design and Method

This chapter is based on data from a larger qualitative study of the experiences of senior-level African American male faculty members who worked in predominantly White institutions (PWIs) located in the Northeast. Life histories were used to reveal the experiences of the men in this study. These histories are useful to researchers when examining contemporary events from the living memory of individuals in an effort to place those memories within their larger social and cultural context. By their very nature, life histories are important tools in conveying the lives of individuals to better understand how those lives are shaped by social and institutional settings (Tierney, 2000). Life histories provide a snapshot of the lives of individuals as they perceive and interpret the world from their own perspectives and experiences. Such an intense analysis of a human life is often missed in quantitative studies or, for that matter, in large qualitative studies that fail to reveal the complexity of the individual self.

Procedures

To collect data, we conducted 12 in-depth, face-to-face interviews with 4 senior-level African American male faculty members over the course of a year. We selected participants using purposeful sampling and recruited them from two national education conferences (Merriam, 1998). Participants were located in New Jersey, Illinois, and Pennsylvania, and they taught and worked at both public and private American research institutions, holding ranks that ranged from associate to full professor.

At the beginning of each interview, we gave participants a brief overview of the purpose of the study, the topics that would be covered, and the probable length of time the interview would require. To allow respondents an opportunity to explore their ideas and areas of personal significance, each interview concluded with a short open-ended discussion.

Data Analysis

As we collected the data, we compared, coded, categorized, and analyzed common themes and salient issues according to methods used by Dey (1993) and Seidman (1998). Recognizing that dependability, transferability, credibility, and conformability are important criteria for trustworthiness in qualitative research, we used the process of verification to interpret the data. Each person was given a copy of his original transcript for review and to check its content. Each study participant provided comments on both the written transcriptions and the final written account of the study. Peer examination was sought by consistent review from an outside reader as well as colleagues who were familiar with the study. Further, realizing that triangulation of the data is an important component in establishing internal validity, we used multiple methods as a means of "confirming emerging findings" (Merriam, 1998). Consequently, we achieved triangulation through a combination of interviews, observations, and document analysis. Document analysis and persistent observation were achieved by reviewing each man's curriculum vita, his school's web pages, his work setting and environment, and, when possible, his home life.

The next section presents key findings from the study, along with a discussion of relevant implications for future research and policy.

Findings and Discussion

Parental Polarity

The following quotation reflects the sentiment of many participants. Most of the men discussed how their pre-entry attributes were influenced by parents who sometimes viewed life from different ideological polarities. Several men reported that their parents' viewpoints were harmonious, but others said there were times when they were keenly aware of their parents' ideological differences:

> My father is still alive and my mother isn't. And there is this thing around how he orders the world in such a way that it fits in this nice box for him in a linear, orderly fashion, which I still don't accept entirely. I am much more open to complexity and believe that things are fuzzy, and so you can't always order or plan for them. And sometimes as a child there was a prevailing element that all of us still remark about, having a home, where you have both this need to fit into a certain place, and others, where there is this flexibility to kind of be anything. (Drew, December 2, 2004)

> I was born to a teenage mother, so her parents, my maternal grandparents, were responsible for raising me because my natural mother was still a high school student. She was 17 when I was born, so she was 16 when she became pregnant with me. So we all coexisted together. But my maternal grandmother was responsible for most of the childrearing duties; she was the typical mother age, at the time, so she took on most of those responsibilities. We were later, my brother and I, actually adopted by my maternal grandparents (Marion, December 19, 2004).

It was notable that the men discussed varying family structures, which often contributed to a sense of polarity between their parents. For example, some explained how their parents' regional location, backgrounds, educational level, and physical separations helped to shape their growth and development before the study participants enrolled in college. Participants indicated that there were often differences in opinions between their parents about such things as the most appropriate childrearing practices or what constituted a sound education for their sons. For example, turning again to the quotation that began this section, Marion discussed how, even though his family "coexisted," his biological mother and his maternal grandmother had differing opinions about how to raise him and his brother. Whereas his biological mother often bowed to the wisdom and experience of her mother, Marion Drew discussed how he witnessed his parents' having fundamentally different ideological perspectives. However, his parents worked through their differences in an effort to reach some level of consensus. Witnessing two parents with divergent opinions come together in agreement taught him how to disagree while remaining respectful of others' opinions as he faced challenges in college.

Amilcar revealed that his parents' divorce and the natural separation as the result of the divorce contributed to his parents' being at different ends of an ideological spectrum. Despite their polarized opinions, they agreed on issues of race and ethnicity in American culture. Amilcar's parents were of Caribbean descent, and he often discussed how they agreed on such things as the lack of militancy among native-born African Americans or on their reminiscences about life in Jamaica:

> My mother talked a lot about politics; my father did as well. You know race politics, the plight of Black people, there was always commentary about where Black people were at that moment, where they needed to go, why don't we do things like other minorities, that kind of discussion was always common in the house between both my mother and father (Amilcar, January 7, 2005).

Amilcar indicated that seeing his parents facilitate their polarity on such matters as race helped him to be aware of and sensitive to racial issues once he entered college. Like most of the other men in the study, Marion and Amilcar said that witnessing parents who had differing opinions but who sought some level of commonality regarding their differences helped the men to adjust to their postsecondary settings after leaving home. For example, Marion spoke of how he was able to adjust to the socioeconomic differences at his predominantly Black college. Marion indicated that it was a shock to go to college and realize that there were such things as affluent African Americans, which represented a major culture shock to him. Amilcar said that he felt better equipped to address and handle racial matters that arose at his predominantly White college and added that he felt being exposed to racial conversations as a child, particularly with immigrant parents, helped him to place race in a historical context in his American college experiences.

Participants agreed that having parents who resolved their ideological differences helped them to adjust to the social and academic support systems of their respective college settings. Understanding how to navigate the differences of other individuals helped them to connect to peers who were different because of their socioeconomic status, race, or ethnicity. In addition, they were able to communicate with faculty members who sometimes had different opinions from their own. Seeing parents disagree taught these men that the world is complex, and that everyone has an opinion that should be valued. Being aware of such things before attending college helped them to be active participants both in and outside classroom settings. For example, participants felt prepared to discuss sensitive issues such as race or social class when such topics arose in their academic and social settings. Adam states:

> My educational experiences were awesome! What is good about my development through [college] is that I wasn't dependent upon other people and how they treated me. I was only dependent upon myself and my immediate family and what was expected. So I never had to look externally to feel validated. Being at a White school was just another way that I looked around and saw all these positive people. And you knew you were where you were supposed to be (Adam, December 28, 2004).

Even when their parents were not physically available to help them navigate a difficult situation that arose while in college, participants said that being able to draw on the examples provided by their parents was helpful in their transition to postsecondary settings.

Parental Occupation

All participants reported being members of families that were financially better off than most of the others in their communities, but they also said that many families were doing better financially than their own. Drew reported:

> I would describe my family as lower, middle or working class, particularly before my mother got her job. But we lived in a very multi-class neighborhood. So the folks who lived next door to us had no running water, and we played with their kids. They had a pump outside for water, which was actually better than running water because it was colder and you didn't have to come inside, so you could stay outside playing and you wouldn't have to take a break. It was kind of better for us. But looking back, it was [a] different life condition for our friends. Now they eventually moved out of that, too, but even going back into the woods there were folks even poorer than our neighbors. So there was a range of poverty. We were doing better than some [of] those folks, and others in the neighborhood might be doing better than us (Drew, December 2, 2004).

The professions or career patterns of the men's parents were vastly different, but also similar in that each man described his parent(s) as having "good" jobs. Three out of four had parents who were involved in what would be considered professional careers. And even Marion's parents, who, he said held more menial jobs, remained in those jobs for a considerable period. All of the men discussed how their parents were well-respected members of their communities and how neighbors viewed their parents as doing "okay." Adam discussed how his family was the first on his street to own a television, and Drew said his family periodically opened their home to disadvantaged relatives.

Generally speaking, parents were very active in their sons' careers and modeled career patterns that sons could emulate in the college setting. Adam stated, "It was always something from my dad's point of view that you got an education, but at the same time my dad said to be self-supportive, because an education alone isn't going to bring you the independence of living your life the way you need." Participants described parents as hard-working and noted how their parents insisted that they also exhibit a strong work ethic. Marion, who attended a prestigious historically Black college, attributed his success in that environment to his parents because they had taught him to work harder than his peers even before he went to college.

Drew's mother advanced through college to obtain a master's degree, but most of the parents took correspondence courses or risked starting their own business in an effort to improve or advance in their careers. Such efforts by their parents taught the men the importance of longevity in making a decision in college but also the feasibility of making adjustments when that decision did not work. For example, one respondent discussed changing his major from photography to mathematics once he understood that mathematics was a better fit for his talents and abilities. The occupational experiences of his parents and their ability to change careers helped him to have the confidence to change his major course of study.

Parental influences stretched beyond mere job attainment to encouraging their sons to seek fulfillment in their college aspirations. And whether or not one's parents had acquired a great deal of formal education themselves, each participant reported that his parents stressed the importance of their son's advancing his formal education as a means of providing flexibility in career choices after college. Parents viewed postsecondary education as a means to increase revenue, and they often saw a postsecondary degree as a way of "leveling the playing field" or promoting a sense of liberation as Black men in American society.

Parental Involvement

Parental involvement was also important. Parents encouraged the study participants to be responsible in the community and to do well in school. Additionally, parents reinforced these beliefs by being actively involved in their sons' educational endeavors before and after their matriculation to college. This case held true for each of the men regardless of family structure, background, geographical location, or social class. It is perhaps surprising that all participants reported having fathers who were extremely involved in their education, including Amilcar, whose parents divorced while he was in middle school. He explained that his father was very active in his educational endeavors and was the one to whom "I had to go to if I did not do well on a report card." The other men also recounted similar experiences regarding their fathers' influences on developing their sons' pre-entry attributes:

> I think early on my parents knew I was different, sort of, intellectually and how I positioned myself in the world. So it was kind of natural and my father would always say . . . he always thought I was peculiar and thought that it was very important for me to do well in school because he thought I might not be able to do other things [he laughs]. My parents created this environment, where I was protected and encouraged to do the best possible, and to do the best in school (Marion, December 19, 2004).

All participants reported having very close relationships with their fathers, who instilled in them a strong sense of self-worth, determination, direction, and guidance. Dads also served as role models and provided their sons with strong examples of manhood within the African American community. The men spoke about the importance of having these examples to draw on as they matriculated to college and how these values enabled them to connect to their campus's infrastructure as they faced challenges or sought academic and social support.

Both fathers and mothers, however, expected their sons to thrive in college. This held true even when parents disagreed on the value of a formal education:

> My mother was really the person who pushed us around education, to do well, and think outside of Delaware . . . to see the world as being much more broadly. So she constantly had us exposed to city life, reading lots of stuff about the world outside of Delaware—like music, jazz, gospel, all kinds of music, classical as well. . . . My father was supportive in a lot of ways but mostly supportive about what we really wanted to do. He was in a lot of ways also stuck around southern Delaware . . . so his sort of saying was, you know, it's one thing to have good sense but if you don't have common sense then you don't have sense at all (Drew, December 2, 2004).

Parents were involved in other ways, too, for example, either by supporting their sons or challenging the education system in which their sons were enrolled. Some parents were not satisfied with their sons' receiving just an adequate education. They encouraged them to do well in the educational system, and they ensured that the educational system did well by their sons.

Parents tended to value education, but they also wanted their sons to learn the importance of living life on their own terms. Consequently, parents taught their sons to be responsible and to question their place in society, even in educational arenas. Participants agreed that having involved parents as they prepared to enter college helped them to learn how to navigate the various collegiate systems. Being able to rely on their parents' involvement helped them to integrate socially and academically into their respective campuses. Some of the respondents indicated that their parents' involvement even helped them to decide on a major, select a fraternity, or relate to peers or faculty members.

Most of the participants admitted that, as they advanced to college, having parents who were involved throughout their educational experience helped to make them feel more secure on campus. For example, regardless of their institutional type, men felt a sense of belonging to their respective colleges. They attribute this sense of belonging to parents who were encouraging when difficult matters arose or who supported their decisions throughout their matriculation experience. Respondents who attended PWIs described having a strong sense of self-worth and -respect as a result of parents who insisted that, even in college, these men understand their role in that setting. Even Marion, who attended a historically Black college, said he felt connected to campus even though it was one of the most affluent Black environments he had ever seen. Each of the participants reported that having parents who were involved in explaining racial differences helped him to negotiate a collegiate environment that was at times foreign to him, and this was true whether their campus environment was predominantly Black or White.

Implications and Conclusions

Although the results come from a limited sample of African American men, they provide important implications for those concerned with supporting African American males on contemporary college campuses. First, African American parents, regardless of their educational level, may be involved in the college decisions of their sons. Second, the belief that all, or even most,

African American males come from economically disadvantaged back-grounds is erroneous. Some of them do arrive on college campuses academi-cally and socially equipped to handle the rigors of college life, but they may face challenges post-matriculation that hamper their success in college settings. Thus, college educators would do well to establish and implement programs and services (e.g., Student African American Brotherhood [SAAB], support groups, advising sessions) that provide the necessary support for Black men to adjust comfortably. Third, African American males may need supportive networks when they arrive at college (Strayhorn, 2008). For example, higher education institutions should try to promote and facilitate better relationships with African American parents as a means of supporting African American male students after they have matriculated to college set-tings. Fourth, higher education institutions should reflect the various per-sonal and cultural experiences that African American males bring to the college environment and ensure that those experiences are infused into all aspects of college life, including curriculum, programs, services, and outreach activities. Last, higher education institutions must become aware of the cul-tural biases and prejudices that this subset of their student population may face and devise solutions that enable Black men to succeed both academically and socially.

References

Bank, B., Slavings, R., & Biddle, B. (1990). Effects of peer, faculty, and parental influences on students' persistence. *Sociology of Education, 63*, 208–225.

Braxton, J. M., Milem, J. F., & Sullivan, A. S. (2000). The influence of active learning on the college student departure process: Toward a revision of Tinto's theory. *Journal of Higher Education, 71*, 5.

Cuyjet, M. (1997). *Helping African American men succeed in college.* San Francisco: Jossey-Bass.

Davis, J. E. (1999). What does gender have to do with the experiences of African American college men? In V. C. Polite & J. E. Davis (Eds.), African American males in school and society: Practice and policies for effective education (pp. 134–148). New York: Teachers College Press.

Dennis, J. M., Phinney, J. S., & Chuateco, L. I. (2005). The role of motivation, parental support and peer support in the academic success of ethnic minority first-generation college students. *Journal of College Student Development, 46*, 3.

Dey, I. (1993). *Qualitative data analysis: A user-friendly guide for social scientists.* Lon-don & New York: Routledge.

Feagin, J. R., Vera, H., & Imani, N. (1996). *The agony of education: Black students at white colleges and universities.* New York: Routledge.

Fisher, T., & Padmawidjaja, I. (1999). Parental influences on career development perceived by African American and Mexican American college students. *Journal of Multicultural Counseling and Development, 27,* 3.

Fleming, J. (1984). *Blacks in college: A comparative study of students' success in Black and White institutions.* San Francisco: Jossey-Bass.

Freeman, K. (2005). *African Americans and college choice.* Albany: State University of New York Press.

Goff, B., Patino, V., & Jackson, G. (2004). Preferred information sources of high school students for community colleges and universities. *Community College Journal of Research and Practice, 28,* 795–803.

Guiffrida, D. A. (2005). To break away or strengthen ties to home: A complex question for African American students attending a predominately White institution. *Equity and Excellence in Education, 38,* 1.

Guiffrida, D. A. (2006). Toward a cultural advancement of Tinto's theory. *The Review of Higher Education, 29*(4), 451–472.

Harper, S. R. (2006). Peer support for African American male college achievement: Beyond internalized racism and the burden of "acting White." *The Journal of Men's Studies, 14,* 3.

Hossler, D., & Gallagher K. S. (1987). Studying college choice: A three-phase model and the implication for policy makers. *College and University, 62,* 3.

Jones, L. (2000). *Brothers of the academy: Up and coming black scholars earning our way in higher education.* Sterling, VA: Stylus.

Jones, L. (2001). *Retaining African Americans in higher education.* Sterling, VA: Stylus.

Kern-Kelpe, C. W. (2000). College choice influences: Urban high school students respond. *Community College Journal of Research and Practice, 24,* 487–494.

Kuh, G. D., & Love, P. G. (2000). A cultural perspective on student departure. In J. M. Braxton (Ed.), *Reworking the student departure puzzle.* Nashville, TN: Vanderbilt University Press.

Letawsky, N. E., Schneider, R., Pedersen, P. M., & Palmer, C. J. (2003). Factors influencing the college selection process of student-athletes: Are their factors similar to non-athletes? *College Student Journal, 37*(4), 604–610.

McClure, S. (2006). Voluntary association membership: Black Greek men on a predominately White campus. *The Journal of Higher Education, 77,* 6.

Merriam, S. B. (1998). *Qualitative research and case study applications in education* (2nd ed.). San Francisco: Jossey-Bass.

Nora, A. (2001). The depiction of significant others in Tinto's "rites of passage": A reconceptualization of the influence of family and community in the persistence process. *Journal of College Student Retention, 3,* 1.

Pascarella, E. T., & Terenzini, P. T. (2005). *How college affects students, Vol. 5*. San Francisco: Jossey-Bass.

Perna, L. W., & Titus, M. A. (2005). The relationship between parental involvement as social capital and college enrollment: An examination of racial/ethnic group differences. *The Journal of Higher Education, 76*, 5.

Pitre, P. E. (2006). College choice: A study of African American and White student aspirations and perceptions related to college attendance. *College Student Journal, 40*(3), 562–574.

Schwitzer, A. M., Griffin, O., Ancis, J., & Thomas, C. (1999). Social adjustment experiences of African American college students. *Journal of Counseling and Development, 77*, 189.

Seidman, I. (1998). *Interviewing as qualitative research: A guide for researchers in education and the social sciences* (2nd ed.). New York & London: Teachers College Press.

Smith, M. J., & Fleming, M. K. (2006). African American parents in the search stage of college choice: Unintentional contributions to the female and male enrollment gap. *Urban Education, 41*, 1.

Somers, P., Haines, K., & Keene, B. (2006). Towards a theory of choice for community college students. *Community College Journal of Research and Practice, 30*, 53–67.

St. John, E. P., Paulsen, M. B., & Carter, D. F. (2005). Diversity, college costs, and postsecondary opportunity: An examination of the financial nexus between college choice and persistence for African Americans and Whites. *The Journal of Higher Education, 76*, 5.

Strayhorn, T. L. (2008). The role of supportive relationships in facilitating African American males' success in college. *The NASPA Journal, 45*(1), 26–48.

Strayhorn, T. L. (2010). When race and gender collide: The impact of social and cultural capital on the academic achievement of African American and Latino males. *The Review of Higher Education, 33*(3), 307–332.

Thomas, M. K. (2004). Where college-bound students send their SAT scores: Does race matter? *Social Science Quarterly, 85*, 5.

Tienda, M., & Niu, S. X. (2006). Flagships, feeders, and the Texas top 10% law: A test of the "brain drain" hypothesis. *The Journal of Higher Education, 77*, 4.

Tierney, W. G. (2000). *Undaunted courage: Life history and the postmodern challenge*. In N. Denzin & Y. Lincoln, *The handbook of qualitative research* (2nd ed., pp. 537–553). San Francisco: Sage.

Tinto, V. (1993). *Leaving college: Rethinking the causes and cures of student attrition*. Chicago: The University of Chicago press.

U.S. Department of Education, National Center for Education Statistics. (2006). *The condition of education 2006* (NCES 2006–071). Washington, DC: U.S. Government Printing Office.

Watson, L. W., & Kuh, G. D. (1996). The influence of dominant race environments on student involvement, perceptions, and educational gains: A look at historically Black and predominantly White liberal arts institutions. *Journal of College Student Development, 37,* 4, 422

Zimbroff, J. A. (2005). Policy implications of culturally based perceptions in college choice. *Review of Policy Research,* 22, 6.

10

MENTORING AND AFRICAN AMERICAN UNDERGRADUATES' PERCEPTIONS OF ACADEMIC SUCCESS

Tonya N. Saddler

Abstract: Unlike graduate students who report having faculty mentors, undergraduate students are less likely to have had a faculty mentor, and African American undergraduates are even less likely to be mentored by faculty members. Mentoring undergraduate students, however, can be rewarding for students and can contribute significantly to their development and overall success in college. Mentoring has the potential to be rewarding for faculty members as well. This chapter explores the research-collaborative experiences that undergraduate students in summer research programs have with their faculty mentors to better understand the nature of these relationships and what participants perceive as benefits of engaging in these relationships. Qualitative interviews with 9 undergraduate students and 10 faculty mentors at a predominantly White institution (PWI) reveal that research-collaborative mentoring relationships are not collaborative in nature as anticipated. Rather, participants identified gaining a holistic view of the research process, increased research skills and experience, and future opportunities as benefits of the summer research experience, and personal and university support systems also affected participants' success in college.

D espite the steady increase in enrollment of traditional college-age students in American colleges and universities over the past few decades, access to postsecondary education for African Americans remains inequitable. African Americans continue to lag behind their White peers in degree completion (Harvey & Anderson, 2005; Perna, Milem, Gerald, Baum, Rowan, Hutchens, 2006). In 2000, African Americans ages 18 to 24 accounted for 11% of four-year college and university enrollment. African American female students accounted for nearly two-thirds (63%) of the African American enrollment, outnumbering their African American male counterparts (37%) (U.S. Department of Education, 2003).

Once enrolled in college, African American students often find themselves struggling to adjust socially and academically due to institutional factors that isolate them from the institutional culture. Other factors, such as being the first in their families to attend college, for example, also present challenges for some African American collegians, pressuring them to achieve academically in higher education when others in their families may not have (Freeman, 1999). Dilemmas of adjusting and achieving academically and socially, in many cases, require support systems to make this transition successful.

Support systems like mentoring programs have become successful in raising college retention rates (Allard, Dodd, & Peralez, 1987) and exposing undergraduates to graduate education with research experience (Merkel & Baker, 2002). Recent research has found that exposure to research at the undergraduate level positively influences the outcome of the college experience and undergraduate students' decision to pursue graduate study (Russell, Hancock, & McCullough, 2007). Based on these findings, I suggest that support mechanisms such as mentoring and exposing undergraduate students to research opportunities will yield positive outcomes for undergraduates engaged in research with faculty mentors.

In this chapter, I briefly review the literature on mentoring in higher education and its role in socializing undergraduate students to the research culture of higher education and to their respective scientific disciplines. Next, I present key findings from a study I conducted of undergraduate collegians and faculty members participating in summer research programs at a PWI to understand the nature of their research collaborative relationships, what they perceived as benefits of engaging in those relationships, and student participants' perceptions of factors contributing to their academic success in college. I conclude by discussing implications of this research for practice, research, and theory in higher education.

Literature Review

Mentoring in Higher Education

Mentoring, and its functions and ultimate goals, has several definitions. A mentor is often described as one who offers advice and counsel, and helps in the overall personal, professional, and social development of the individual being mentored. Mentoring relationships generally involve an experienced member of an organization providing information, support, and guidance to a less-experienced, usually new, member of an organization (Blackwell, 1989; Campbell & Campbell, 1997; Kram, 1985; Tierney & Rhoads, 1994). Mentoring functions include protection, coaching, information sharing, modeling, sponsorship, and counseling (Blackwell, 1989; Kram, 1985; Luna & Cullen, 1995). Mentors have also been known to challenge their mentees (i.e., encourage critical thinking and stepping out of one's comfort zone), which has the potential to result in identity transformation for the mentee (Johnson, 2007). Still other authors suggest that mentors are also spiritual in nature because they guide individuals along some carefully crafted journey (Lyons, Scroggins, & Rule, 1990).

Despite these varying definitions, most scholars agree that mentoring involves a senior person (Blackwell, 1989; Kram, 1985). This definition of mentoring, however, situates mentoring as a function the mentor provides to the mentee and not as a relationship that involves both the mentor and the mentee. If performed correctly, however, mentoring is an intentional and reciprocal relationship (Johnson, 2007; Mertz, 2004; Zey, 1991).

Empirical support for the link between mentoring and academic support is unclear. Several studies suggest indirect links between mentoring and academic success (Jacobi, 1991), career choice, development of research skills (Merkel & Baker, 2002), and retention and satisfaction with college (Strayhorn & Terrell, 2007). Quality interactions between faculty members and students have also been proven to be strong predictors of student success and whether a mentoring relationship will even form (Johnson, 2007). For example, Merkel and Baker (2002) suggest that mentoring provides intellectual stimulation for the protégé (mentee). They further state that working closely on research with a faculty member helps to identify the student as a colleague, giving that student the ability to learn, ask questions, and offer ideas. Similar results were found in an undergraduate study of African American students. Strayhorn and Terrell (2007) found that establishing a mentoring relationship with a faculty member had a positive impact on African American students' satisfaction with college. In particular, researchers found that establishing meaningful research-focused mentoring relationships seemed to offer the maximum benefit to the student (Strayhorn & Terrell, 2007). These characteristics (providing intellectual stimulation, developing research skills, developing career focus, and providing a source of satisfaction) suggest important benefits of mentoring undergraduate students.

Undergraduates and Research Missions

Academic leaders at public universities, particularly research universities (RUs), are beginning to integrate undergraduate students into the research missions of their institutions (Elgren & Hensel, 2006; Gonzalez, 2001). The mission of RUs is to engage in the discovery of new knowledge, accomplished by conducting government- or privately funded research that benefits society. Most of this research is conducted by faculty and graduate students (Bowen & Rudenstine, 1992). Recently, faculty members involved in funded research projects have introduced undergraduate students to research (Elgren & Hensel, 2006; Merkel & Baker, 2002). These findings suggest an emergence of undergraduate students' involvement in university research and an important role this population will assume: advancing the research missions of colleges and universities.

Mentoring as a Socializing Agent in Higher Education

Several scholars have contributed to our understanding of how individuals are socialized into organizations. For example, organizational socialization (Tierney, 1988), undergraduate student socialization (Weidman, 1989), graduate and professional student socialization (Weidman, Twale, & Stein, 2001), and social exchange theory (Chadwick-Jones, 1976; Homans, 1974, Molm, 2003) have been helpful particularly in understanding how students and faculty members in higher education come to learn about an organization's norms and customs.

Organizational socialization (Tierney, 1988), undergraduate socialization (Weidman, 1989), and graduate and professional student socialization (Weidman et al., 2001) all suggest that individuals go through a stage-like process, both informal and formal, during which they acquire knowledge, skills, and belief sets needed to successfully navigate the higher education culture (Tierney & Rhoads, 1994) and their respective fields (Weidman et al., 2001). The socialization process involves interaction with faculty and student colleagues that results in individuals' adapting the norms and culture of the higher education organization (Saddler, 2008; Tierney & Rhoads, 1994; Weidman et al., 2001).

Social exchange theories, not tested in higher education settings on students, assume that individuals in organizations enter into relationships because of some anticipated benefit or reward (Chadwick-Jones, 1976; Homans, 1974; Zey, 1991). Applied to mentoring relationships, Zey posits that the mentor, mentee, and organization all benefit from the social exchange relationship. The mentor is assumed to gain benefits that include career enhancement, new knowledge or information, and psychological rewards, such as personal fulfillment and pride from helping the mentee or organization. The mentee is said to gain benefits that include knowledge or information, personal support, protection, and career advancement from the mentor. Last, the organization gains as well. For example, organizations that support mentoring are said to gain managerial succession and development, less turnover, and greater productivity (Zey). Figure 10.1 displays the mutual benefits model of social exchange.

The present study uses Zey's (1991) Mutual Benefits model of social exchange theory to understand the nature of the research-collaborative mentoring relationships between undergraduates and faculty mentors participating in summer research programs. This framework assumes that both the undergraduate students and faculty members are gaining some type of benefit from these relationships. Benefits gained by the organization (in this case, summer research programs and higher education institutions) were not examined.

The Study

Since I was interested in examining the experiences of undergraduate students and faculty members involved in research mentoring relationships, I conducted a study to address this issue. The purpose of the qualitative study on which this chapter is based was to explore the research-collaborative experiences of undergraduate students and faculty members participating in summer research programs to better understand the nature of the relationships and what the participants perceived as benefits of engaging in these relationships (Saddler, 2008). Additionally, this study sought to identify factors that undergraduates perceived as necessary to their academic success in college. The study uses social exchange theory, specifically, the Mutual Benefits model of mentoring developed by Zey (1991), to understand these relationships. For purposes of this study, I define faculty mentor as the individual who collaborated with the undergraduate student on a research project. Research collaboration refers to engaging in research-related activities (e.g., conducting research, writing a research paper or report, presenting research, etc.). Thus, the main research question was: How do undergraduate students and faculty members participating in summer research-collaborative mentoring relationships describe their experiences, and what do they say are the

FIGURE 10.1
The Mutual Benefits Model, Zey (1991)

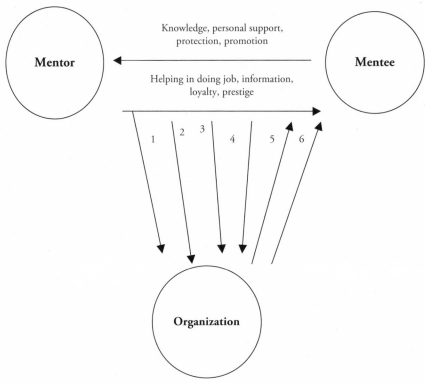

1. Managerial succession
2. Managerial development
3. Less turnover
4. Greater productivity
5. Advancement of mentor, mentee
6. Increased power, perks

Note. The term *protégée*, originally used in Zey's (1991) model, was changed to mentee in this study.

benefits of being in the mentoring relationships? The following sub-questions guided the overall analysis:

1. How do undergraduate students and faculty mentors participating in summer research programs describe the nature of their mentoring relationships?

2. What are the perceived benefits of the research collaborative mentoring relationships for faculty mentors and their student mentees?
3. What factors do undergraduate students participating in summer research programs identify as contributing to their success in college?

Sample

The sample consisted of nine undergraduates at a large, predominantly White research institution (PWRI) in the southeastern region of the United States. Additionally, I sampled 10 faculty members who served as mentors to undergraduates participating in summer research programs, but data from the faculty interviews are not discussed.

The majority of the student participants (78%) were female. Most participants were African American (89%) and comprised mostly seniors (78%), majoring in the physical and hard sciences ($n = 4$) and the social sciences ($n = 5$). Ages ranged from 15 to 26, with 56% of participants between the ages of 15 and 20. Table 10.1 displays a summary of demographics of the sample participants.

Data Collection

Data from undergraduate student participants were collected via in-depth, one-on-one interviews, each of which lasted an average of about 40 minutes. The interview protocol sought to elicit data that directly related to the study's research questions: (a) nature of the research collaborative mentoring relationship, (b) perceived benefits of the mentoring relationship, and (c) factors contributing to the mentee's college success. Interview questions were purposely designed to elicit data related to elements of the mutual benefits (Zey, 1991) model.

Data Analysis Procedures

I approached the analysis process by first reading the interview transcripts several times. I then used the constant comparative method (Glaser & Strauss, 1967), a method for code building that develops patterns, themes, and, ultimately, overarching conclusions related to the participants' experiences. I also referred to the Anfara, Brown, and Mangione (2002) iterative data analysis process as a guide to develop relationships among the data, codes, categories, and themes that are formed to make meaning of the data. This analytical process seeks to make analysis transparent for the outside reader. The first iteration involved the use of both deductive and inductive coding. Deductive codes were first established from themes (or key terms)

TABLE 10.1
Summary of Demographics of Student Participants (*n* = 9)

Characteristic	n
Classification	
Senior	7
Junior	2
Sophomore	0
Freshman	0
Total	9
Major	
Physical and Hard Sciences	4
Social Sciences	5
Total	9
Gender	
Male	2
Female	7
Total	9
Ethnicity	
Asian/Pacific Islander	0
Black/African American	8
Caucasian/European American	1
Hispanic/Latino/a	0
Total	9
Age	
15–20	5
21–26	4
Total	9
Mentor's Characteristics	
Professional Status	
Full	3
Associate	3
Assistant	0
Research	1
Don't know	2
Total	9
Ethnicity	
Black/African American	1
Caucasian/European American	8
Total	9
Research Activities	
Conducting research	9
Writing papers/reports	6
Publishing research	2
Presenting research	2

identified in the literature. These included terms related to mentoring undergraduate students of color and the overall experiences of undergraduates in college. Inductive codes were also developed for unanticipated new issues. Axial coding was used to group the data into categories to analyze meanings and relationships among categories (Charmaz, 2006). The next iteration of data analysis involved developing focused categories from initial codes, followed by the development of themes (coding dictionary is shown in Appendix B at the end of this chapter). The last stage of data analysis involved developing overarching themes or conclusions. I took several steps to ensure the validity of this study's findings. The next section elaborates on these steps.

Trustworthiness

Trustworthiness (and validity) in qualitative research refers to the quality and rigor of the investigation, including the study's findings. To establish trustworthiness of my interpretations and to bracket my biases throughout the analysis process, I used several steps outlined by Guba and Lincoln (1994) to achieve credibility, transferability, dependability, and confirmability. For instance, credibility is concerned with how trustworthy a study's conclusions are and how these conclusions match with reality. To achieve credibility, I used member checking (Creswell, 2003) during and after the interview process to ensure that I was accurately restating and interpreting participants' experiences. I also used multiple data sources (e.g., field notes, interview transcripts, and demographic forms) to ensure the credibility of findings (Creswell, 2003). As a third strategy, I set aside two transcripts that were used as negative cases for analysis later. These data represented perspectives that ran counter to a majority of the perspectives (or themes) in the study and were considered negative cases (Creswell, 2003).

Findings from this study are most directly transferable or generalizable to populations similar to the one I used in this study (Schwandt, 2001). To aid readers in making judgments about the transferability of findings, I provide thick description of participants, the program site, and elements of the program, where possible. Last, I achieved dependability and confirmability by developing and maintaining an audit trail (Anfara et al., 2002); preparing a coding matrix of findings; and using an independent reviewer (external auditor) to review the research design, analysis, and interpretations (Creswell, 2003; Schwandt, 2001). As a result, I believe these findings are credible and trustworthy. The next section presents key themes and findings.

Key Themes

Three themes emerged from the data regarding the nature of research-collaborative mentoring relationships between undergraduates and faculty members participating in summer research programs and the elements contributing to college student success. First, research-collaborative mentoring relationships undergraduates have with faculty mentors were not as collaborative as anticipated. Second, participants identified gaining a holistic view of the research process, increased research skills and experience, and future opportunities as benefits of the summer research experience. Third, participants identified personal and university support systems as positive and negative contributors to their success in college. The next section highlights key themes with supporting quotes from participants. I have used pseudonyms in place of participants' real names or any other identifying information.

Research-Collaborative Mentoring Relationships— Not So Collaborative

Relationships between faculty members serving as mentors and undergraduate student researchers participating in summer research programs are not necessarily collaborative in terms of working together one-on-one on research or meeting daily to conduct and discuss research. Six respondents indicated that the nature of the research mentoring relationship involved their working mostly independently on research projects. Participants discussed receiving direction from their mentors on what to do with their projects, but they performed very little work (e.g., conducting experiments, writing, or presenting research) collaboratively as anticipated. Consider a response from Mary, an African American senior and biological sciences major:

> When it comes to my mentor, I don't work directly with her, instead, I receive direction from her, but I follow her instruction every day—what I should do every day, how my timeline should look. Every now and then she checks in on me, but I work directly with her lab technician who knows what I will be doing, who is familiar with the material.

Mary's comment suggests that she is receiving guidance from her faculty mentor, but that she works primarily with the lab technician in her area. Similarly, Lorien, an African American senior majoring in physics and mathematics, also discussed having little interaction with his mentor on his research because of the stage of his project, but he was checking in with his mentor on occasion. He stated:

> I meet with my mentor, usually by e-mail. Generally, it's meeting with a graduate student or working by myself. Typically, I come in in the mornings around 6 a.m., and my professor's not there yet. I'll go into the lab and sit in front of the computer and work on my program that I am doing and I'll occasionally check in with her. I did so more in the beginning, but at the point where I was, I just have to work on the programs, so I have not really been in contact with her. Like today, I did not see her at all. She was in a meeting, but I'll probably have to start meeting with her again soon, since I am at the point where I need to discuss things with her.

Lorien explained that his limited contact with his mentor was due to where he was in the research process, working on computer programming. He anticipates more interaction with his mentor in the future.

Even though a majority of the participants were working independently on their research projects, they did expect the relationships with their faculty mentors to continue after they completed their projects. Those participants who did not expect the relationship to last generally were unable to make the connection needed to sustain a long-term mentoring relationship. Most participants ($n = 6$) expected to use their mentors as future references, for networking opportunities, and for assistance with graduate school admittance, as the next section discusses in more detail.

Three Benefits of Research Mentoring Relationships

Undergraduate researchers participating in summer research programs got involved in research projects with faculty mentors for the research experience and, in most cases, expect their relationships with their mentors to last beyond the summer. Participants said they gained a holistic view of the research process, which included better research skills, more experience, and learning about the realities of the research process (e.g., research does not go as planned or takes time). A holistic view of the research process involved learning about research protocol, research design, analysis, writing research proposals, reviewing relevant literature, and, in the analysis stage of the research process, learning that unexpected findings can be useful. In terms of gaining future resources, references, and opportunities, participants referred to recommendation letters from faculty mentors, opportunities to get into graduate school, access to a network of colleagues in their respective disciplines, gaining new perspectives on research, and new friendships. Overall, eight ($n = 8$) participants commented that they had gained a holistic view of the research process and were exposed to future reference possibilities, resources, and opportunities during their participation in summer research with a faculty mentor. For example, Nadia, a Caucasian/European American junior majoring in sociology, said: "I feel I'm gaining experience with research, especially with—we've had a lot of issues getting IRB [Institutional Review Board] approval. I've gained a lot of technical experience learning how to do that, how to format documents technically and concisely." Nadia's comment is consistent with the other participants who expressed learning about the research process and gaining increased research skills and an "insider view" of the process. Consider the statement by Shana, an African American senior and psychology major, who knows more about the research process than she ever imagined:

> I've learned a lot. I never knew the behind the scenes of the research, like the coding and transcribing, I'm thinking—the research I have done on my own was, send out a survey, you get the results back from the survey, and I had already some kind of coding scheme. So, once we put it into SPSS [Statistical Package for the Social Sciences], it generated the analyses and everything and we took that and did our own work. I didn't think much of it. And I start working with her, and there is coding that you have to change letters for, and I'm thinking—I never knew it was this complex. I thought it was something simple. She's [my mentor] has opened up my eyes to a lot. Like transcribing, how you have to write word for word, you know, does "Uh hm" mean one word or two words. The counting, I've learned a lot.

When asked what she had gained from her research experience, Shana replied:

> I have gained a lot of knowledge concerning, like I said, the background work [involved with research], all of the parts that make up the whole. Like, we only see the finished product when we see articles and stuff like that, but to actually see how everything is put together, I am blown [away]. I did not understand. . . . At one point, all I would see are the articles. I am thinking, this is how it is, okay, these are their results, but I've learned that things can go wrong and you have to go back and change things before things can be published or before you can continue with your study.

Shana, who said she had gained research skills, now has a clearer picture of the entire research process, the result of her summer research experience.

Participants also noted future opportunities as gains of their research experience. More than half of the participants (*n* = 5) reported having more access to resources and a network of professionals because of their experience. Respondents plan to use their faculty mentors for references for graduate school or to assist them in the future with their careers. Consider the statement by Jack, a biochemistry major: "She will be able to give me a good letter of recommendation for graduate school. So, yeah, definitely; it's not just one summer thing." Jack's comment is consistent with those of other participants who plan to remain in contact with their faculty mentors for future references for graduate school.

Positive and Negative Contributors of College Success—Personal and University Support Systems

Undergraduate students participating in summer research programs identify personal and university support systems, such as family, friends, financial, and the university culture, as contributing to their overall success in college. In some cases, they also considered these same support systems as challenges to their success in college. Overall, six participants identified personal attributes (e.g., personal determination/motivation to succeed) as positive factors contributing to their success in college. Five participants identified support systems (e.g., family members, campus community, finances, and friends) as contributors to their academic success. Identifying factors that played little or no role in their college success was a bit more challenging for participants. Support systems also played a significant role in participants' academic success in college. Consider the statement of Bianca, an African American, political science and international studies major:

> The fact that I have a full ride at my university, just because I don't have to worry about money as much and through the fellowship that I have, I have a lot of resources. I have a lot of staff support, who watch[es] after you, funding to go to different conferences. So, I just have a lot of background support so I don't have to worry about it. Second, even though I have a full scholarship, I work. My family doesn't give me money to go to school, but that's because I have a full scholarship and I really don't ask for money. I work because I think it looks better for me as a person, like on my resume, that I have a scholarship, but I still have two jobs. I think it helps me be busier because if I am really busy, I can get my work done, that constant pressure—that works for me. You also have new networks of people that you haven't met before. So I think working definitely helps me with time management. I get things done quickly, efficiently, and working

hard. Third, I think what helped me is being very involved on campus. I am in a lot of clubs, [on] a lot of boards, like the YWCA board, the Black Cultural Center board, the Women's Center board, and I am on a whole lot of different committees and things like that. It gives you new networks of people who will recommend you for things or people you can talk to. It helps you gain more prestige in the community.

Bianca has many personal attributes that keep her involved on campus and developing networks of people who will help in her future. Perhaps most important, she has a full scholarship that allows her to focus on other aspects of her college experience. Shkiya, a psychology major with very little previous research experience prior to her summer research opportunity, also talked about personal attributes contributing to her college success:

My family, especially my grandmother; that's my inspiration, because if I don't come with good grades, that's a problem. As well, I see the struggle. I am first generation, so I want to leave that print down, where you know, "We can do it, we overcome." I don't know how to put it into words, it's just great. It's something to prove as well as being a stepping-stone for future generations in my family. They can see that we did, [and] they can do it too. I think adversity, too, because I have doubters in my family that thought I was not going to amount to anything, where, like I said, I am first generation, my mother didn't attend school. She got her GED rather than graduating with a high school diploma and going on to college. So, they [my family] thought that me, my brother, and my sister would not amount to anything and we are the ones that are succeeding. So adversity as well as issues at home.

Family support was a motivating factor for Shkiya. She was able to turn the "lack of support" from some of her family members into positive energy to perform well in college. Personal attributes like self-motivation and a personal desire to prove herself also contributed significantly to her success in college. Unlike Bianca, finances were not significant in contributing to Shkiya's success in college, but at several points during her college tenure, they were challenges. Consider her statement about challenges to her success in college:

Finances—there are a lot of things financially that try to deter me from my success. Like I said, God is amazing. In many ways, I don't know how I am going to pay for school. It's last minute that I am able to go back [to school].

Financial distractions were challenges to participants who, unlike Bianca, did not have a full scholarship. See Appendix A for a list of findings by participant, focusing on the steps I took to reach conclusions.

Discussion and Recommendations for Educational Practice

The purpose of this qualitative study was to examine the research-collaborative experiences of undergraduates and faculty members participating in summer research programs to understand the nature and perceived benefits of these relationships for both the student and the faculty mentor. Data from this study revealed three themes: (a) research-collaborative mentoring relationships are not as collaborative in nature as anticipated; (b) participants identified gaining a holistic view of the research process, increased research skills and experience, and future opportunities as benefits of the summer research experience; and (c) personal and university support systems served as both supports for and challenges to participants' success in college.

Findings from this research relate most directly to faculty members who supervise undergraduate research and serve as mentors to undergraduates engaged in research. Considering the finding that the research-collaborative relationships between undergraduate participants and faculty mentors were not as collaborative as one might imagine, faculty members who work with undergraduates on research projects might reconsider their engagement and investment levels in the relationship. As primary socializing agents for students, a mentor should maintain a more intentional engagement with the undergraduate student and provide explicit research opportunities that will prepare the student for graduate study. More important, "being present" with the undergraduate researcher throughout the research process is a critical element in helping the student learn about the research process.

University administrators in charge of research programs seeking to expose undergraduate students to research may also benefit from this study. Apparently, research programs are effective ways to foster closer relationships between students and faculty members and expose undergraduate collegians, particularly African American collegians, to graduate school opportunities.

This study found that the research mentoring relationships between undergraduate participants and faculty members was not always collaborative in that the student and the faculty member did not always work one-on-one on research projects. Several participants received direction from their mentors, but they worked on their projects independently. Participants did, however, report learning a lot about research and gaining from the experience despite working independently. These findings suggest that, while undergraduate students may be learning about research, they may not be benefiting from their mentoring relationships with faculty members as much as we think they are. Findings may suggest that faculty members who are mentoring undergraduates are not fully invested in the research mentoring relationship. For undergraduate students to get the most from the research mentoring experience, mentoring requires time and investment by both mentor and mentee (Merkel & Baker, 2002; Weidman et al., 2001). These findings stress the importance of "intentionality" in creating and maintaining research mentoring relationships. Program administrators would do well to stress faculty members' responsibilities as mentors.

Research programs for undergraduate students are extremely important, but simply having such programs is not enough. University administrators in charge of research programs for undergraduates might use this information to reexamine their programs to see what measures they might take to make sure program participants (e.g., undergraduate students) are being challenged when learning about research design and methods under the careful tutelage of faculty mentors. Administrators also might evaluate the effectiveness of their programs' faculty mentors throughout the program, not just at the end. Strategies such as these would provide continuous feedback about the mentoring relationships and would allow for necessary interventions.

Faculty members who serve as mentors to undergraduate students might use this information to reexamine how much time and effort they are investing in mentoring relationships, particularly those involving African American college students or other underrepresented groups. Considering the finding that undergraduates in this study learned about the research process—in particular, the holistic picture of research (e.g., research design, analysis, writing research papers, unexpected nature of research)—faculty mentors might do more to tap into these acquired skills and push students to develop important critical thinking and problem-solving skills that are also characteristic of conducting research (Merkel & Baker, 2002). Faculty members who are research mentors to undergraduate collegians also might consider the importance of making time for their mentees. Even a few minutes a day spent talking about the research project and their mentees' future plans may be helpful to students.

Consistent with earlier studies, this study found no direct link between mentoring undergraduates and college success (Jacobi, 1991). Instead, participants attributed much of their academic success to personal and university support systems. Personal support systems included members of participants' family, their peers, and personal motivation and determination to succeed. University support systems included faculty and staff and extracurricular involvement, which made campus life easier to navigate. This finding suggests that participants' personal attributes would have made them successful in college with or without a faculty mentor. In addition, the consistent family support system reported by several participants is consistent with previous research highlighting the importance of family influence in African American collegians' academic success (Herndon & Hirt, 2004). In a few cases, family support (or the lack of it), in addition to a lack of financial support, also challenged participants' success in college. This finding suggests that the institution can do more to support the financial needs and concerns of students who have them. This financial support might extend beyond the financial perks often associated with participating in summer or year-long research programs that include a monthly stipend, room and board for the duration of the research, or resources needed to assist with research project (e.g., supplies, travel to research conferences, etc.). Full or partial scholarships for undergraduate collegians in research programs who show exemplary promise of entering graduate study and consistent academic success (e.g., above average grade point average) should be offered as incentives and rewards.

Considering the finding that family support was also a challenge for some participants in achieving academic success, it is important for other support systems at the university level to encourage undergraduate collegians to continue their education and adhere to high academic standards when such support from the family may not be present. Weekly mentoring activities for program participants can focus more on the developmental needs of the student and not only on the research needs. Graduate students, postdoctoral research fellows, new and junior faculty members, or upper-level administrators can be effective mentors for undergraduate collegians who desire (and look to) role models for encouragement and support. Such support would complement the faculty mentoring offered through the program.

This study has implications for future research using larger African American undergraduate samples at similar research universities. It is likely that a larger sample will yield similar results or confirm existing ones. In addition, this study focused on the experiences of African American undergraduates. Future research might examine the research experiences and perceptions of college success of other ethnic minorities (e.g., Hispanic, Native Americans) or perceptions of other underrepresented groups' exposure to research opportunities in higher education (e.g., female undergraduates). Researchers should use quantitative approaches in the future to test the extent to which these findings are common across larger groups of students from various campus types.

Indeed, directions for future research are plentiful. Still, this exploratory study offers compelling information about the challenges and supports that influence African American collegians' success in college. By participating in summer research programs with faculty mentors, students, despite challenges, learn a lot about the research process, gain valuable research skills, and establish supportive relationships that may serve them well in the future when applying to graduate school or entering the workforce.

References

Allard, W. G., Dodd, J. M., & Peralez, E. (1987). Keeping LD students in college. *Academic Therapy, 22,* 359–365.

Anfara, V. A., Brown, K. M., & Mangione, T. L. (2002). Qualitative analysis on stage: Making the research process more public. *Educational Researcher, 31*(7), 28–36.

Blackwell, J. E. (1989). Mentoring: An action strategy for increasing minority faculty. *Academe, 75,* 8–14.

Bowen, W. G., & Rudenstine, N. L. (1992). *In pursuit of the Ph.D.* Princeton, NJ: Princeton University Press.

Campbell, T. A., & Campbell, D. E. (1997). Faculty/student mentor program: Effects on academic performance and retention. *Research in Higher Education, 38*(6), 727–742.

Chadwick-Jones, J. K. (1976). *Social exchange theory: Its structure and influence in social psychology.* New York: Academic Press.

Charmaz, K. (2006). *Constructing grounded theory: A practical guide through qualitative analysis.* Thousand Oaks, CA: Sage.

Creswell, J. W. (2003). *Research design: Qualitative, quantitative, and mixed methods approaches* (2nd ed.). Thousand Oaks, CA: Sage.

Elgren, T., & Hensel, N. (2006). Undergraduate research experiences: Synergies between scholarship and teaching. *Peer Review, 8*(1), 4–7.

Freeman, K. (1999). No services needed?: The case for mentoring high-achieving African American students. *Peabody Journal of Education, 74*(2), 15–26.

Glaser, B. G., & Strauss, A. (1967). *The discovery of grounded theory: Strategies for qualitative research.* Chicago: Aldine.

Gonzalez, C. (2001). Undergraduate research, graduate mentoring, and the university's mission. *Science, New Series, 239*(5535), 1624–1626.

Guba, E. G., & Lincoln, Y. S. (1994). Competing paradigms in qualitative research. In N. K. Denzin & Y. S. Lincoln (Eds.), *Handbook of qualitative research* (pp. 105–117). Thousand Oaks, CA: Sage.

Harvey, W. B., & Anderson, E. L. (2005). *Minorities in higher education 2003–2004: Twenty-first annual status report.* Washington, DC: American Council on Education.

Herndon, M. K., & Hirt, J. B. (2004). Black students and their families: What leads to success in college. *Journal of Black Studies, 34*(4), 489–513.

Homans, G. C. (1974). *Social behavior: Its elementary forms* (Rev. ed.). New York: Harcourt-Brace.

Jacobi, M. (1991). Mentoring and undergraduate academic success: A literature review. *Review of Educational Research, 61*(4), 505–532.

Johnson, W. B. (2007). *On being a mentor: A guide for higher education faculty.* Mahwah, NJ: Lawrence Erlbaum.

Kram, K. E. (1985). *Mentoring at work: Developmental relationships in organizational life.* Glenview, IL: Scott, Foresman.

Luna, G., & Cullen, D. L. (1995). *Empowering the faculty: Mentoring redirected and renewed* (ASHE-ERIC Higher Education Report No. 3). Washington, DC: The George Washington University, School of Education and Human Development.

Lyons, W., Scroggins, D., & Rule, P. B. (1990). The mentor in graduate education. *Studies in Higher Education, 15*(3), 277–285.

Merkel, C. A., & Baker, S. M. (2002). *How to mentor undergraduate researchers.* Washington, DC: Council on Undergraduate Research.

Mertz, N. T. (2004). What's a mentor anyway? *Educational Administration Quarterly, 40*(4), 541–560.

Molm, L. D. (2003). Theoretical comparisons of forms of exchange. *Sociological Theory, 21*(1), 1–17.

Perna, L. W., Milem, J., Gerald, D., Baum, E., Rowan, H., Hutchens, N. (2006). The status of equity for Black undergraduates in public higher education in the south: Still separate and unequal. *Research in Higher Education, 47*(2), 197–228.

Russell, S. H., Hancock, M. P., & McCullough, J. (2007). Benefits of undergraduate research experiences. *Science, 316,* 548–549.

Saddler, T. N. (2008). *Socialization to research: A qualitative exploration of the role of collaborative research experiences in preparing doctoral students for faculty careers in education and engineering.* Unpublished doctoral dissertation, Virginia Polytechnic Institute and State University, Blacksburg.

Schwandt, T. A. (2001). *Dictionary of qualitative inquiry* (2nd ed.). Thousand Oaks, CA: Sage.

Strayhorn, T. L., & Terrell, M. C. (2007). Mentoring and satisfaction with college for Black students. *The Negro Educational Review, 58*(1–2), 69–83.

Tierney, W. G. (1988). Organizational culture in higher education. *Journal of Higher Education, 59*(1), 2–21.

Tierney, W. G., & Rhoads, A. R. (1994). *Faculty socialization as cultural process: A mirror of institutional commitment* (ASHE-ERIC Higher Education Report No. 93–6). Washington, DC: The George Washington University, School of Education and Human Development.

U.S. Department of Education, National Center for Education Statistics. (2003). *Status and trends in the education of Blacks* (NCES 2003–034). Washington, DC: Author.

Weidman, J. C. (1989). Undergraduate socialization: A conceptual approach. In J. C. Smart (Ed.), *Higher education: Handbook of theory and research* (Vol. 5, pp. 289–322). New York: Agathon.

Weidman, J. C., Twale, D. J., & Stein, E. L. (2001). *Socialization of graduate and professional students in higher education: A perilous passage?* (ASHE-ERIC Higher Education Report No. 28, no. 3). Washington, DC: Association for the Study of Higher Education.

Zey, M. G. (1991). *The mentor connection: Strategic alliances in corporate life.* New Brunswick, NJ: Transaction.

APPENDIX A
Matrix of Findings for Themes and Sources ($n = 9$)

Themes	Jack	Mary	Bianca	Nadia	Lorien	Shkiya	Amy	Shana	Ashley
1. Relationships not collaborative	X	X	X		X		X		X
2. Benefits: Holistic view of research process, skills & experience, future opportunities	X	X	X	X	X	X		X	X
3. Support systems as positive & negative contributors of academic success	X+		X+	X+	X+	X+ –	X+ –	X+	X+ –

Note. Plus and minus symbols indicate positive (+) and negative (-) statement/theme as contributors of college success for participant.

APPENDIX B
Coding Dictionary—Complete List of Codes, Categories, and Definitions

Code Name	*Code Description*
Conducting research	The act of analyzing data, interviewing participants, conducting literature searches, running experiments
Realities of research	Involves the ability to be flexible, research process/analysis is unexpected; involves problem solving
Research process	Content knowledge, methods, how to carry out a project
Future resources, references, & opportunities	Recommendations from faculty mentor, opportunities to get into graduate school, network of colleagues, new perspectives on research, and friendship
Holistic research process	Involves research protocol, research design, analysis, writing research proposals, reviewing literature, and, in the analysis stage of the research process, understanding that unexpected findings are useful
Research skills and experience	How to conduct research, develop problem solving skills, how to apply research to "real world" applications, content knowledge
Support systems	Includes financial, family, friends, university community that aid in success of college student; also could not aid in success of college student

Note. Coding dictionary includes definitions for initial codes and categories developed during analysis.

11

NEW DIRECTIONS FOR FUTURE RESEARCH ON AFRICAN AMERICAN COLLEGIANS

Terrell L. Strayhorn

In her book, *Blacks in College*, Jacqueline Fleming (1984) presented historical data, national trends, and statistics to illustrate the challenges Black college students faced at historically Black colleges and universities (HBCUs) and predominantly White institutions (PWIs). Additionally, she noted how "educators, including student affairs professionals, are in a position not only to encourage . . . but also to help Black students . . . cope with social and psychological forces that stifle their confidence and growth [in college]" (p. xii). The groundbreaking study ended with a series of poignant questions that lingered, despite the comprehensiveness of Fleming's cross-sectional analysis. And she maintained that "all of the remaining questions [could] still be answered" through "future volumes looking at college life from vastly different perspectives" (p. 193). In many ways, *The Evolving Challenges of Black College Students: New Insights for Policy, Practice, and Research* responds to Fleming's prescient, even prophetic, pronouncement.

This volume seeks to understand the *challenges* that Black students face in college using new empirical evidence and "different perspectives," thereby identifying ways to *support* African American students in higher education. Chapter 1 examines the role of spirituality in the lives of African American college students and calls attention to how some Black students use spirituality to adapt to, manage, and navigate the college environment. Stewart presents persuasive evidence that Black college students use spiritual resources to resist isolation, overcome negative experiences, and craft meaningful, productive responses to often overwhelming race-related stress. In chapter 2, Winkle-Wagner investigates the ways in which 28 first-generation African American women reflect on their college decisions. Describing college choice as a matter of "life or death," the women with whom Winkle-Wagner spoke indicated that "going to college" can have a deleterious effect on one's stress level, emotional state, and everyday life.

A multivariate study of resiliency and self-efficacy, reported in chapter 3, reveals that academic self-efficacy and college grade point average (GPA) are positively correlated, indicating that higher levels of confidence in one's academic abilities tend to be associated with higher GPAs. Additionally, academic self-efficacy and resilience are associated with first-year GPA over and above high school grades. Strategies for increasing students' academic self-efficacy are outlined in the chapter. Casting a critical gaze on today's college student population, chapter 4 addresses college choice, academic and social integration, institutional climate, identity development, and mentoring for African American collegians. Bonner balances his analysis of Black college students' challenges with a smooth blend of practical recommendations for the support necessary for African American student success.

While several chapters focus on the experiences of African American college students in general, others zero in on the *challenges* and necessary *supports* of particular subgroups, including Black gay male undergraduates (chapter 5) and student leaders (chapter 6). As one of the first contemporary empirical studies of African American male undergraduates who identify as gay or bisexual, the investigation conducted by Strayhorn, Blakewood, and DeVita breaks new ground on the ways in which multiple identities converge and shape the collegiate experiences of this group of men. Similarly, McFeeters draws on social influence network theory to explain how student-to-student interaction affects change in opinion; then, she masterfully links this larger work to the experiences of African American college students.

In consonance with ecological systems theory (Bronfenbrenner, 1976), the experiences of African American college students are shaped, even determined, at least in part, by individuals, roles, norms, and rules in various contexts or "systems." Consequently, issues of setting, environment, and location come to the fore when studying individual behaviors. Adopting this ecological perspective, Strayhorn, Terrell, Redmond, and Walton (chapter 7) present findings from a cultural excavation of a Black cultural center, thereby highlighting essential elements of its supportive environment. In chapter 8,

Palmer and Young contribute to the existing body of evidence that suggests the uniqueness of historically Black college environments. Highlighting the role that parents play in the lives of African American college students is the focus of chapter 9 by Holloman and Strayhorn. Finally, Saddler (chapter 10) draws on qualitative interviews with 9 undergraduates and 10 faculty members to investigate the research mentoring experiences of African American undergraduates as well as the perceived benefits that accrue from such engagement. Taken together, these chapters tackle many of the *enduring challenges* and *necessary supports* for African American college students. It is to these two major themes that we now turn.

Challenges

The needs of Black college students are many, as outlined in this volume, and they often differ from those of White and non-Black minority students. For instance, college enrollment rates have increased over the last decade among African American students by an impressive 42% since 1995. However, a number of disparities persist. Black enrollment gains vary by state, with some of the largest gains reported in Arizona, Nevada, and South Dakota (see figure 11.1). Comparatively small gains were reported in Louisiana and New York as well as Alaska, where there was an actual decline in Black enrollment. Black college enrollment rates also vary by sex, socioeconomic status, and ethnicity, although very few studies attempt to measure differences among groups whose ancestral origins lie in any of the individual Black racial groups of Africa (e.g., African American compared to Haitian and West Indian). Indeed, future work should address this gap in our knowledge about Black students' experiences.

There also is clear and compelling evidence that challenges differ *among* Black student populations—the within-group heterogeneity referenced by Harper and Nichols (2008); see chapters 3 and 5 for examples. Thus, college student educators are well situated to provide not only traditional student services such as leadership development programs and intramural sports but also support to specific sub-populations such as culturally relevant counseling and/or safe zones to Black gay male undergraduates (see chapter 5) and precollege outreach interventions to Black women (see chapter 2). The time is ripe for college student educators to take the lead in providing the support African American collegians view as critical to their success.

Several authors present empirical research findings that underscore the role student involvement plays as a necessary, but not sufficient, condition

FIGURE 11.1
Percent Gain in Black Student Enrollment, 1995–2005

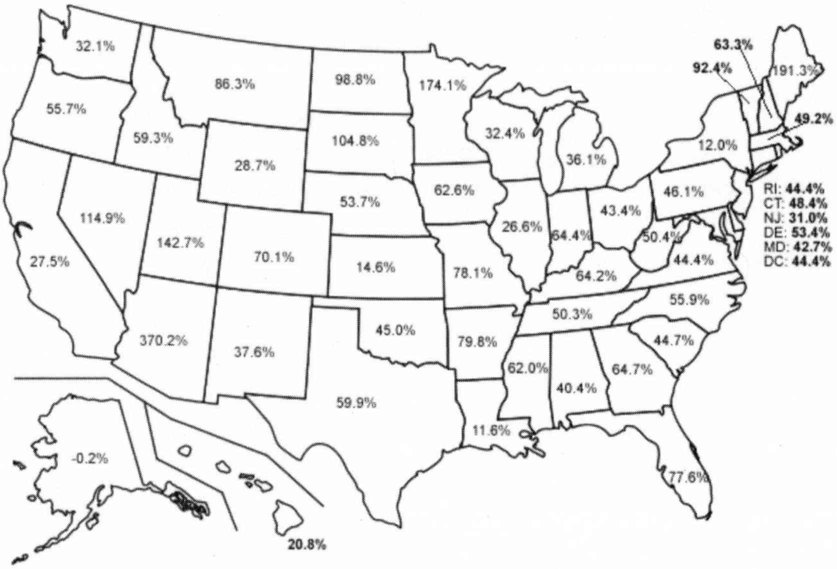

Note. Public domain image with statistics created by author.

for student success. Just like majority students, African American college students tend to achieve at higher rates, earn higher grades, and report more robust learning gains when they are actively and deeply engaged in educationally purposeful activities, such as resilience-building exercises, faculty-student mentoring, peer interactions, and undergraduate research. Despite the important role that involvement plays, the weight of empirical evidence suggests that African American students are less likely than are Whites and Asians to be involved in campus clubs and organizations (e.g., DeSousa & King, 1992; McKay & Kuh, 1994) due to myriad challenges (see chapter 5, for example). This is particularly true for African Americans attending PWIs (e.g., Fleming, 1984; DeSousa & Kuh, 1996) and subpopulations such as Black men or Black gay male undergraduates.

Supports

According to ecological systems theory (e.g., Bronfenbrenner, 1976) and the interactionist paradigm (Sanford, 1962), the greatest opportunities for growth and development occur when student experiences are complemented by supportive and inclusive environments. Designing such conditions requires using extant research and theory to assist students with their issues. College student educators have many opportunities to help Black college students overcome or manage the challenges they face in campus environments. The authors here offer the following suggestions to administrators looking to help students successfully navigate their academic lives.

First, student affairs practitioners should implement programs that encourage African American students to engage "big questions" about life's purpose, vocation, and identity. Having direct conversations with students about spirituality and religious practices may also be helpful. Participation is often predicated on information; in other words, students cannot access what they do not know is available. To this end, educators should make visible and easily accessible any information about opportunities through which Black students can explore their faith (e.g., gospel choir).

Second, college student educators can encourage Black students' participation in Federal TRIO Programs (e.g., Talent Search, McNair Program) or other precollege outreach programs that serve a compensatory purpose—that is, programs that supplement instruction or academic preparation for low-performing schools or students deemed to be at risk for failure (Tierney, Corwin, & Colyar, 2005). Furthermore, professionals in specific functional areas, like academic advisors, can provide detailed information to students, so they will have a better idea of their options. A number of authors explained the influence of precollege experiences and achievement on postsecondary success (see chapter 4, for example); these findings point to the role teachers and guidance counselors can play in preparing Black students for college.

As one of relatively few empirical studies on Black cultural centers (BCCs), chapter 7 presents findings from a mixed-methods analysis that go beyond providing evidence of the role BCCs play in African American students' success in higher education. Findings also illuminate experiences Black students identify as critical to their academic and social success. Having the BCC as a "home away from home," gaining practical skills through BCC work experiences, and receiving both verbal and emotional support (e.g., hugs) from BCC staff, all seem to nurture an optimism that enables students to stay motivated in college. Student affairs professionals, especially BCC directors, might consider these findings when working with students and staff in the future.

Practitioners are also challenged to continue, enhance, or expand their role in engaging African American college students in educationally purposeful activities both inside and outside the classroom. For example, Strayhorn (chapter 3) suggests that faculty members offer students multiple opportunities at incremental success on academic tasks such as homework, quizzes, and papers. Indeed, engaging students in high-impact activities, such as first-year seminars, learning communities, study-abroad experiences, writing-intensive courses, or faculty-student research experiences, can have a profound influence on their academic achievement and persistence (Kinzie & Kuh, 2004), and several chapters in this volume illuminate the importance of these activities for Black students. Institutional conditions, such as campus climate, can also foster student engagement in meaningful activities.

Developing and maintaining a supportive campus climate for African American students is important. And as Harvey (2007) points out, several campus constituencies can play a role in making the campus environment welcoming for all students. Student affairs professionals can foster Black students' sense of belonging (Strayhorn, 2008b), validate their experiences, and nurture confidence in their ability to succeed in college. Faculty and academic administrators (e.g., deans, department heads, provosts) also have major opportunities to foster positive student behaviors among African Americans by providing a stimulating learning environment that is free from oppression and prejudice, welcomes intense debate and dialogue among faculty and students, and engages students in faculty members' research, for example.

Supportive interpersonal relationships are necessary for academic and social development during the college years (Loevinger, 1976; Strayhorn, 2008b). In several chapters, authors describe various ways in which African American collegians benefit from relationships with "instrumental others" (Ceja, 2006) on whom they rely for tremendous academic and social support. Informal relationships with peers, role models, and faculty members, to name a few, are important sources of support to Black students generally (chapters 1 and 4), Black women (chapter 2), Black gay male undergraduates (chapter 5), student leaders (chapter 6), users of the BCC (chapter 7), HBCU students (chapter 8), and undergraduate researchers (chapter 10).

Several authors present a list of resources or potentially effective strategies from which administrators can select one or two to try on their campus. For instance, chapter authors recommend establishing new, or improving existing, programs that help Black men to adjust to college (e.g., Student African American Brotherhood [SAAB]), building meaningful partnerships between campus administrators and parents, infusing the curriculum with intercultural perspectives, and implementing or improving campus-wide undergraduate research experience programs. Leveraging resources in this way is likely to lead to higher academic achievement, increased student engagement in high-impact activities, enhanced self-efficacy, and higher retention rates among African American college students.

Attempting to serve this population in new and different ways opens us up to myriad opportunities for collaboration across units (e.g., student and academic affairs); functional areas (e.g., housing, career services, multicultural affairs); campus types (e.g., historically Black and predominantly White institutions); and/or institutional classifications (e.g., liberal arts colleges, research universities). Indeed, the possibilities are endless and are limited only by our creativity, professional imagination, and, perhaps most important, our will to match Black students' challenges with appropriate levels of support.

It goes without saying that some strategies mentioned here can be difficult to mount or far too expensive to implement in times of financial exigency. For example, broadening participation in study-abroad opportunities among African Americans requires significant financial resources to support—even subsidize—the students' travel. Similarly, establishing new first-year seminar or undergraduate research programs requires money to pay instructors, meet overhead or administrative costs, and offer stipends to encourage participation. Still, educators are encouraged to launch or continue such initiatives as the benefits that accrue to our students far outweigh the costs in time, effort, and money. Supporting African American college students, however, need not be cost prohibitive or resource draining.

Although most earlier research on Black college students provides general information about their needs and challenges, this text differs by identifying specific challenges and supports that hold promise for helping African American students succeed in higher education. This information can be used to guide future policy in ways that best meet the needs of students. One example is that admission counselors might change application requirements to elicit additional information. Specifically, counselors might pay attention to evidence in an applicant's file that he or she overcame adversity, which may reflect the resilience necessary for success in college. Several other chapters identify multiple policy levers (e.g., admissions, college choice, achievement) to improve the condition of higher education for African Americans.

Mentoring has been linked with academic achievement and fostering a sense of belonging on campus (see chapter 4, for example). Thus, policies that emphasize mentoring programs and other means to reduce isolation among Black college students are likely to improve academic success. Policymakers and educators are encouraged to consider the role students (e.g., peer mentoring) and professionals (e.g., faculty-student mentoring) might play in formal mentoring programs. Educational policies that emphasize the role of peer mentors would support the conclusions presented in this volume that students learn best when they teach, when they are engaged with peers in educationally purposeful activities, and when they perceive their classmates as supportive.

A number of chapters demonstrate the importance of parents and family members to Black students' success in college, and these findings have implications for policymakers. Educational policy should increase attention to parental involvement in the learning experiences of Black youth. For instance, information presented here reinforces the need for college access programs such as Gaining Early Awareness and Readiness for Undergraduate Program (GEAR UP) and Upward Bound. Funding policies might require program directors to devote a certain proportion of funds to activities for parents. The findings in this volume support funding for fatherhood (see chapter 9) and parent cooperation programs (see chapters 2, 5, and 9).

Last, much more research is needed on Black students in college, specifically studies that disaggregate findings by ethnicity (e.g., African American versus Haitian); sex/gender; sexual orientation; urbanicity (e.g., urban, suburban, or rural); campus racial composition (e.g., historically Black versus predominantly White institution); socioeconomic status; and a host of other background traits (e.g., first-generation status, age, spirituality). Educational policies, then, should also address these dimensions of identity and institutional settings. Policymakers should encourage research to better understand the challenges that subpopulations face and to identify supports for their success.

Future Research

Reexamining how academic and student affairs engages African American college students means that existing programs may be modified or terminated, or new programs may be created.

Although recent research, some of which is my own (e.g., Strayhorn, 2008a, 2009), shifts scholarly attention to the experiences of high-achieving

African American collegians (e.g., Harper, 2004), continuing the line of inquiry developed by Bonner (2001) and Fries-Britt (1997, 1998): "[A]ny thorough and critical examination of the educational pipeline [experiences] for African American students must shed light on the relative underachievement of African American students in comparison to other groups" (Howard, 2007, p. 21). That comparison, however, need not use White students as the standard or rule by which all other groups are measured. As mentioned in the previous sections, future researchers might carefully examine differences between Black students and non-Black minorities such as Latinos (e.g., Strayhorn, 2010) or unpack the within-group heterogeneity that exists among Black student populations.

Future research on African American college students might follow a number of promising directions. Scholars should conduct studies using the vast array of methods and techniques available to study the diverse pathways African American students follow to earn their college degrees. For example, one can use hierarchical linear modeling (HLM) techniques to analyze National Survey of Student Engagement (NSSE) data from multiple institutions on the influence of institution-level characteristics (e.g., expenditures on academic support) on student-level behaviors (e.g., perceived learning gains, engagement, persistence).

Using advanced statistical methods and multilevel modeling techniques, future researchers might examine the experiences of African American collegians in science, technology, engineering, and mathematics (STEM); the role faculty members play in Black students' research self-efficacy; and the extent to which academic and social interactions affect Black gay male undergraduates' satisfaction with college, to name but a few. Not only should future researchers contemplate the use of quantitative methods, but they also should bring to bear the most rigorous qualitative techniques. Conducting one-on-one interviews with Black gay men in college, facilitating multiple focus groups with Black student athletes, and sorting and analyzing historical documents and even images about the Civil Rights Movement are just a few ways to use qualitative methods in research on African American collegians.

Research has shown consistently that the college years are a period during which students make critical choices about their future. Several chapter authors address aspects of the college choice process for African American college students. Recall chapter 2 by Rachelle Winkle-Wagner and chapter 5 by Strayhorn, Blakewood, and DeVita, which allude to college choice decisions among Black women and Black gay male undergraduates, respectively.

Where African American students go to college probably will remain a matter of individual choice, determined at least in part by family, financial, and academic factors, as posited by Hossler and Gallagher (1987) and Freeman (1999). Still, future research might examine the college choice process of other Black student subpopulations (e.g., low-income Black students, student athletes), juxtapose existing theories against new and emerging ones (e.g., multiple identities theory), or clarify the widely cited stages of college choice: predisposition, search, and choice.

This volume has given research in this area a new impetus: some old problems are examined with new and different perspectives. With these advancements we can better understand the experiences of African American college students—their *evolving challenges* and *necessary supports*.

References

Bonner, F. A., II. (2001). *Gifted African American male college students: A phenomenological study*. Storrs, CT: National Research Center on the Gifted and Talented.

Bronfenbrenner, U. (1976). The experimental ecology of education. *Educational Researcher, 5*(9), 5–15.

Ceja, M. (2006). Understanding the role of parents and siblings as information sources in the college choice process of Chicana students. *Journal of College Student Development, 47*(1), 87–104.

DeSousa, D. J., & King, P. M. (1992). Are White students really more involved in collegiate experiences than Black students? *Journal of College Student Development, 33*, 363–369.

DeSousa, D. J., & Kuh, G. D. (1996). Does institutional racial composition make a difference in what Black students gain from college? *Journal of College Student Development, 37*, 257–267.

Fleming, J. (1984). *Blacks in college: A comparative study of students' success in Black and White institutions*. San Francisco: Jossey-Bass.

Freeman, K. (1999). The race factor in African Americans' college choice. *Urban Education, 34*, 4–25.

Fries-Britt, S. L. (1997). Identifying and supporting gifted African American men. In M. J. Cuyjet (Ed.), *Helping African American men succeed in college* (pp. 65–78). San Francisco: Jossey-Bass.

Fries-Britt, S. L. (1998). Moving beyond Black achiever isolation: Experiences of Black collegians. *The Journal of Higher Education, 69*(5), 556–576.

Harper, S. R. (2004). The measure of a man: Conceptualizations of masculinity among high-achieving African American male college students. *Berkeley Journal of Sociology, 48*(1), 89–107.

Harper, S. R., & Nichols, A. H. (2008). Are they not all the same? Racial heterogeneity among Black male undergraduates. *Journal of College Student Development, 49*(3), 199–214.

Harvey, W. B. (2007). Maximizing higher education attainment: The critical factor to improving African American communities [preface]. In J. F. L. Jackson (Ed.), *Strengthening the African American educational pipeline: Informing research, policy, and practice* (pp. xiii–xvii). Albany: State University of New York Press.

Hossler, D., & Gallagher, K. S. (1987). Studying student college choice: A three-phase model and the implications for policymakers. *College and University, 62,* 207–221.

Howard, T. C. (2007). The forgotten link: The salience of Pre-K–12 education and culturally responsive pedagogy in creating access to higher education for African American students. In J. F. L. Jackson (Ed.), *Strengthening the African American educational pipeline: Informing research, policy, and practice* (pp. 17–36). Albany: State University of New York Press.

Kinzie, J. L., & Kuh, G. D. (2004). Going DEEP: Learning from campuses that share responsibility for student success. *About Campus, 9*(5), 2–8.

Loevinger, J. (1976). *Ego development: Conceptions and theories.* San Francisco: Jossey-Bass.

McKay, K. A., & Kuh, G. D. (1994). A comparison of student effort and educational gains of Caucasian and African American students at predominantly White colleges and universities. *Journal of College Student Development, 35,* 217–223.

Sanford, N. (1962). Developmental status of the entering freshman. In N. Sanford (Ed.), *The American college* (pp. 253–282). New York: Wiley.

Strayhorn, T. L. (2008a). Academic advising needs of high-achieving Black collegians at predominantly White institutions: A mixed methods investigation [Electronic Version]. *The Mentor: An Academic Advising Journal.* Retrieved from http://www.psu.edu/dus/mentor/080507ts.htm.

Strayhorn, T. L. (2008b). The role of supportive relationships in facilitating African American males' success in college. *NASPA Journal, 45*(1), 26–48.

Strayhorn, T. L. (2009). The burden of proof: A quantitative study of high-achieving Black collegians. *Journal of African American Studies, 13*(4), 375–387.

Strayhorn, T. L. (2010). When race and gender collide: The impact of social and cultural capital on the academic achievement of African American and Latino males. *The Review of Higher Education, 33*(3), 307–332.

Tierney, W. G., Corwin, Z. B., & Colyar, J. E. (Eds.). (2005). *Preparing for college: Nine elements of effective outreach.* Albany: State University of New York Press.

Terrell L. Strayhorn is associate professor of higher education and sociology at The Ohio State University, where he is also director of the Center for Higher Education Research and Policy (CHERP) and research fellow in the Kirwan Institute for the Study of Race and Ethnicity. His research centers on the experiences of historically underrepresented racial/ethnic minorities in higher education, particularly how socioeconomic and racialized disparities cascade over time, yielding persistent inequities in labor market outcomes and unequal access, retention, achievement, and persistence outcomes. Strayhorn has authored more than 70 publications and over 125 international or national conference presentations. Strayhorn's work appears in prestigious journals in his field and has been recognized with awards from the American College Student Personnel Association, National Association of Student Affairs Professionals, and Council on Ethnic Participation within the Association for the Study of Higher Education. More than $700,000 in grants from the National Science Foundation, U.S. Department of Education, Tennessee Higher Education Commission, and National Association of Student Financial Aid Administrators support his research program. He earned a BA in music (piano/vocal performance) and religious studies from the University of Virginia, an MEd in education policy from the Curry School of Education at UVA, and a PhD in higher education from Virginia Tech.

Melvin C. Terrell is vice president emeritus at Northeastern Illinois University in Chicago. From 1988 to 2008, he served as vice president for student affairs (and he continues his role as professor of counselor education) at Northeastern. Formerly, he served as director of minority affairs and adjunct assistant professor of educational leadership at the University of Toledo. He is past president of the National Association of Student Affairs Professionals and served as editor of the *NASPA Journal*, one of the premier student affairs journals in print today, for 11 years. Terrell has authored more than 30 publications and co-edited the book, *Creating and Maintaining Safe College Campuses: A Sourcebook for Evaluating and Enhancing Safety Programs* (2007). He has received several awards, including the NASPA Outstanding Contribution to Literature or Research Award and the Scott Goodnight Award for

Outstanding Performance as a Student Personnel Administrator, NASPA Region IV East. He earned his MEd in college student personnel with an emphasis on counseling from Loyola University (Chicago) and his PhD in higher education administration and Black studies from Southern Illinois University at Carbondale. Northeastern recently named an award in his honor, The Melvin Cleveland Terrell Award for Outstanding Contribution to Research and Literature.

ABOUT THE CONTRIBUTORS

Amanda M. Blakewood is a PhD candidate in higher education administration, and research associate for the Center for Higher Education Research and Policy at the University of Tennessee, Knoxville. She received her BA in psychology at the University of Central Florida and her MS in college student personnel from the University of Tennessee, Knoxville. She has presented at several national and international conferences, including the annual meetings of the American College Personnel Association and the National Association of Student Personnel Administrators. She has collaborated on several research publications and grant projects, most recently publishing "Factors Affecting the College Choice of African American Gay Male Undergraduates: Implications for Retention" in the *NASAP Journal*. Additionally, she attended the Association for the Study of Higher Education Graduate Student Seminar on Higher Education Policy in 2008. Her research interests include intersections of multiple identities, issues of work-life balance for female faculty members in STEM fields, and student retention and persistence.

Fred A. Bonner II is professor of higher education administration in the Educational Administration and Human Resource Development department at Texas A&M University–College Station. He received a BA in chemistry from the University of North Texas, an MSEd in curriculum and instruction from Baylor University, and an EdD in higher education administration and college teaching from the University of Arkansas-Fayetteville. Bonner has received the American Association for Higher Education Black Caucus Dissertation Award and the Educational Leadership, Counseling, and Foundation Dissertation of the Year Award from the University of Arkansas College of Education. He has also published articles and book chapters on academically gifted African American male college students, teaching in the multicultural college classroom, diversity issues in student affairs, and success factors influencing the retention of students of color in higher education. He currently serves as an associate editor of the *NASAP Journal* and has completed three summers as a research fellow with the Yale

University Psychology Department (PACE Center), focusing on issues affecting academically gifted African American male college students. He is also completing a book that highlights the experiences of postsecondary gifted African American male undergraduates in predominantly White and historically Black college contexts. Bonner spent the 2005–2006 year as an American Council on Education Fellow in the Office of the President at Old Dominion University in Norfolk, Virginia. Additionally, he recently received a National Science Foundation grant to focus on factors influencing the success of high-achieving African American students in STEM disciplines in HBCUs.

James M. DeVita is a visiting assistant professor at Iowa State University in the Department of Educational Leadership and Policy Studies. He received his PhD in higher education administration at the University of Tennessee, Knoxville where he also served as a research associate at the Center for Higher Education Research and Policy. He received BA degrees in history and sociology-anthropology from Colgate University and an MS in college student personnel from the University of Tennessee, Knoxville. He has presented at several national and international conferences, including the American College Personnel Association Annual Convention and the National Association of Student Personnel Administrators Conference on Retention and Assessment. DeVita has collaborated on several research publications and grant projects, most recently publishing in the *NASAP Journal*. Additionally, he was selected for the Association for the Study of Higher Education Graduate Student Seminar on Higher Education Policy in 2007 and the Association for Institutional Research Summer Data Policy Forum in 2008. His research interests include issues of multiple identity development, student achievement in STEM, exploring perceptions of gender identity and sexual orientation, and differences in learning styles among college students.

Darryl B. Holloman is assistant vice president for student life and an assistant professor at Columbus State University in Columbus, Georgia. Dr. Holloman has also served in the Department of Educational Leadership at the University of Arkansas-Little Rock (UALR) as an assistant professor of higher education and the program coordinator for the master in student affairs and the student affairs concentration in the UALR Higher Education Doctoral program. His professional positions include associate dean/director of the Paul Robeson Campus Center at Rutgers University in Newark, New Jersey. He has also served as assistant dean of student affairs in the College of Arts and Sciences on the Newark campus. He has presented research papers at conferences of the Association for the Study of Higher Education, American Educational Research Association Division F and J, the Association of College Unions International, the National Academic Advising Association, College Student Educators International, and the Coalition of Urban and Metropolitan Universities and has several articles and book chapters to his credit. His most recent work involves an analysis of the effects of geographic location on college choice. Holloman's research topics include examining how race, social class, motivating factors (parents, community, and culture), and economic cultural capital influence the entry, persistence, and exit of underrepresented populations in postsecondary settings.

Belinda B. McFeeters is educational leadership research & evaluation consultant, with faculty affiliations with the evaluation center at the Center for Creative Leadership, the Leadership Studies PhD Program at North Carolina A&T State University, and the Leadership Development group at the N. C. Rural Economic Development Center. She is also a freelance writer for EBSCO Publishing. McFeeters has more than 15 years of professional experience in developing others, from college student leaders and doctoral students in nonprofit organizations, to adults at for-profit organizations. Her primary research and evaluation focus is on global leadership and diversity (college student leaders and beyond) and leadership studies. McFeeters has authored or co-authored several articles, book chapters, and books on leadership education, multicultural education, higher education, K–12 education, and sociological issues, and has co-edited the new leadership casebook, *Leading Across Differences* (Pfeiffer Publishing, 2010), to prepare leaders to lead in situations where multiple identity groups are represented. She earned a BS in business and community services from the University of North Carolina at Greensboro, an MS in adult education from North Carolina A&T State University, and a PhD in educational leadership and policy studies from Virginia Polytechnic Institute and State University.

Robert T. Palmer is assistant professor of student affairs administration at the State University of New York, Binghamton. His research examines the experiences of minority students, primarily in the context of minority-serving institutions. He is also interested in racial/ethnic minority college students in STEM fields. His work has been published or accepted for publication in a variety of journals, including *Journal of College Student Development*; *Equity and Excellence in Education*; *Journal of College Student Retention:*

Research, Theory; & Practice; Journal of Black Studies; and the *National Association of Student Affairs Professionals Journal.* In addition, he serves on the editorial boards of two journals. He received his undergraduate degree in history with an emphasis on education from Shippensburg University of Pennsylvania, a master's in counseling with an emphasis on higher education from West Chester University of Pennsylvania, and a PhD in higher education administration from Morgan State University.

Jane S. Redmond is assistant vice chancellor for student affairs and founder of the Black Cultural Center at the University of Tennessee, Knoxville, where she also serves as an adjunct faculty member in higher education administration. She received her undergraduate degree from Knoxville College and a PhD in higher education administration from The Ohio State University.

Tonya N. Saddler is assistant professor and director of the Higher Education Administration program at Marywood University in Scranton, Pennsylvania. Her research centers on faculty work-life issues, including tenure, promotion, and effective strategies for recruiting and retaining faculty members of color. Her special research interests include the socialization of doctoral students to faculty careers in education and STEM fields and undergraduate students to research, particularly undergraduates of color. Saddler is an active member of the American College Personnel Association, American Educational Research Association, American Society of Engineering Education, and Association for the Study of Higher Education, serving as conference presenter, proposal reviewer, and session chair during annual meetings. She has presented several papers at national and regional conferences. She earned a BS in elementary education and an MS in counselor education from North Carolina A & T State University and a PhD in higher education administration from Virginia Polytechnic Institute and State University.

Dafina Lazarus Stewart is associate professor of higher education and student affairs at Bowling Green State University. Her research focuses on issues of identity and environmental support for members of targeted groups in colleges and universities. Her published work appears in such prestigious journals as the *Journal of Higher Education* and the *Journal of College Student Development,* as well as *About Campus* and as chapters in books and monographs. Stewart has given more than 50 presentations, workshops, and speeches on such topics as leadership, multicultural competence and diversity, and her own research. She is also a member of the editorial review boards of four journals and occasionally serves as an invited reviewer for the *Journal of Higher Education*. Additionally, Dr. Stewart is the interim chair of ACPA's Commission for Spirituality, Faith, Religion, & Meaning. She has earned a bachelor's degree in sociology with a minor in economics from Kalamazoo College and a master's in higher education and student affairs and a doctorate in higher education and educational administration from The Ohio State University.

Chutney N. Walton is a PhD candidate in higher education administration and a graduate research assistant in the Tennessee Teaching and Learning Center at the University of Tennessee, Knoxville. Her research interests include college ranking systems, historically Black colleges and universities, and institutional quality issues. She earned her undergraduate degree in marketing from Fort Valley State University and a master's in business administration from Tennessee State University.

Rachelle Winkle-Wagner is assistant professor of higher education administration at the University Nebraska, Lincoln. In her research, Winkle-Wagner takes a sociological approach to the issue of race, gender and identity in higher education. She is the author of the book, *The Unchosen Me: Race, Gender and Identity Among Black Women in College* (The Johns Hopkins University Press, 2009); the lead editor of an edited volume, *Bridging the Gap Between Theory and Practice in Educational Research: Methods at the Margins* (Palgrave MacMillan, 2009); and one of the editors of *Standing on the Outside Looking In: Underrepresented Students' Experiences in Advanced Degree Programs* (Stylus Press, 2009). Winkle-Wagner earned a BA in music (piano performance) and communication studies and an MA in student affairs from the University of Nebraska, and a PhD from Indiana University.

Estelle Young is the nursing success and retention coordinator at the Community College of Baltimore County (CCBC). She oversees the development, implementation, and evaluation of student development initiatives for the 500-student program, including preparatory activities to guide students in financial and time management planning prior to entry, complete self-assessments and individual educational plans, practice of anxiety-management techniques, and learning brain-based study strategies. After entry, students are offered sustained peer study support through Supplemental Instruction and Peer Facilitated Study Groups. Before joining CCBC, she was an assistant professor in sociology at Morgan and Bowie state universities. While at Morgan State University (MSU), she also coordinated the MSU BEAMS (Building Engagement and Attainment for Minority Students) initiative, a five-year national project to develop evidence-based initiative building at 100 minority-serving institutions. She earned both her BS and MPA from the University of Wisconsin, Madison, and MA and PhD from Johns Hopkins University.

Also available from Stylus

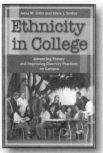

Ethnicity in College
Advancing Theory and Improving Diversity Practices on Campus
Anna M. Ortiz, Silvia J. Santos

"Practitioners will come to find this book a valuable resource for understanding how ethnic identity development is intertwined in all aspects of student life, both inside and outside the classroom. Researchers as well as practitioners will appreciate the deep insight this study provides to our understanding of ethnic relations and the relationship between diversity and development on campus."

With its comparative, multi-ethnic design and its contributions to theory, knowledge, and practice, this book stands out in the higher education literature."—*Anthony Lising Antonio, Associate Director, Stanford Institute for Higher Education Research, and Associate Professor, School of Education, Stanford University*

How Black Colleges Empower Black Students
Lessons for Higher Education
Edited by Frank W. Hale, Jr.
Foreword by Karen A. Holbrook

"How does the Black student experience at HBCUs differ from the experience at traditionally White institutions, and what can be learned? This work should convince any skeptic. Higher education students, faculty, administrators, alumni, and policy makers alike should find interest in and benefit from this book."
—*Journal of College Student Development*

Getting Culture
Incorporating Diversity Across the Curriculum
Edited by Regan A. R. Gurung, Loreto R. Prieto

"Provides a set of 'best practices' for approaching the pedagogical challenges of teaching diversity . . . Recommended."—*Choice*

"This volume's editors have compiled a set of wide-ranging tools for teaching about diversity among diverse student populations. Articles cover an array of topics, including general approaches to diversity education, specific exercises within and across disciplines, and strategies for coping with the stresses of teaching controversial topics. The collection offers guidance that is particularly valuable for those just beginning to incorporate diversity in the classroom – and is pertinent to veteran teachers as well."—*Diversity & Democracy (AAC&U)*

22883 Quicksilver Drive
Sterling, VA 20166-2102

Subscribe to our e-mail alerts: www.Styluspub.com